Marriage

DR JACK DOMINIAN

Also by Jack Dominian

Marital Breakdown
Marital Pathology
Make or Break
Passionate and Compassionate Love
Depression

To my wife, with thanks for nearly forty years of marriage

Contents

Acknowledgements

I want to thank my colleagues at One plus One for their helpful suggestions.

Finally, I wish to acknowledge my debt to my wife and to my daughter, Elise Milne, who, working from my handwritten script, produced several working versions before eventually achieving the final one, dealt with all the corrections and queries, organised the notes and the index and spent many hours in the process.

This book has involved a great deal of research and I am grateful to the following for permission to use material, either quoted or adapted: Academic Press, London, in respect of *Equalities and Inequalities in Family* by R. Chester and J. Peel with reference to chapter on 'Some Variations in Marital Satisfaction' by C. Walker; Basil Blackwell Press in respect of Adultery, an *Analysis of Love and Betrayal* by Annette Lawson; Brooks/Cole Publishing Company in respect of *Liking, Loving and Relating*, second edition by S. S. Hendrick and C. Hendrick; Multi-Media in respect of *I DO: Your Guide to a Happy Marriage* by H. Eysenck; Sage Publications Inc. in respect of *Between Husbands and Wives* by M. A. Fitzpatrick, pp. 20–5, 33; *Romantic Love* by S. S. Hendrick and C. Hendrick; *Courtship* by R. M. Cate and S. A. Lloyd; *Strategies for Maintaining and Repairing Marital Relationships* by K. Dindia and L. A. Baxter, 4:143-158; Virago Press in respect of *You Just Don't Understand* by D. Tannen; Yale University Press in respect of *Psychology of Love* edited by R. J. Sternberg and M. L. Barnes.

Introduction

Almost every man and woman in Western society has had the experience of falling in love. Our personal feelings of this event, unique to ourselves, are constantly reinforced by the media, particularly television. Advertising makes use of the attraction of men and women in order to sell anything from a car to a jar of coffee! A mutual look, a smile, a touch, a kiss, an embrace, all suggest that a couple have an intimate understanding between them which bonds them together.

This initial bonding, extended in films to over an hour or two, is an epic struggle from indifference to intimacy. The process of getting someone to the altar rails or to the registry office, and putting a ring on their finger, has attracted us all. Nowadays, long before the marriage stage is reached, many couples have sex and live together. The journey to cohabitation is as intriguing as that to marriage, but as many as 50 per cent of cohabitees go on to marry.

After the marriage ceremony, the trail is lost. Couples enter a world of several decades in which they are expected to remain married. In theory, the romantic beginning is expected to continue and to see them through to their old age. We know that nowadays this is not the case. In Britain, nearly 40 per cent of marriages end in divorce,[1] and in the United States the figure projected is nearly 66 per cent.[2]

Moreover, in those instances where the couple stay together, we understand very little of the factors that contribute to the maintenance of the relationship. We know much more about what leads to dissolution than about what preserves marital relationships. In an age in which love is considered to be the factor that initiates relationships, love is also expected to maintain them. But what do we know about marital love in the decades that span conjugal survival?

This book tries to answer this question. It must be said that very little is known about the subject, and what is available is not well organised. So this book aims to give a picture of the forces that are loosely called 'love' in the extended period of marriage. It is not a DIY manual for couples who want to stay together, but I hope it will illuminate the numerous processes by which intimacy is maintained. What has emerged is a fascinating study in which the word 'love' is analysed in several ways, illustrated by sociology and psychology.

Unlike several popular books on marriage, this study is based on the clinical experience of the author and the findings of research, which have escalated in the last fifteen years. Most of these studies are American, but they have a wider application and I hope readers will be able to see a reflection in their own marriages as well as gain insights that up to now have been hidden in specialised journals.

It is my hope that this book will fill an urgent need: to give us the beginning of an insight into what maintains marital relationships through love.

CHAPTER 1

From Social to Emotional Aptness

The history of modern marriage can be traced briefly in four phases since the Renaissance. The first stage is a move away from marriage as a family and financial concern, in which the interests of the couple were minimal and the monetary and social power of the family structure were at their maximum. In this phase a young couple had very little say in choosing one another. The decision was left in the hands of the parents of the parties. The parents selected and the young followed. The choice was made on the basis of passing on the land safely to the next generation and safeguarding the interests of the parents when they could no longer work in the fields. The newly married stayed initially with the parents and several generations lived together. The support of society was minimal and the various members of the household helped each other. The notion of love was virtually non-existent. The couple and their relatives served the primary utilitarian service of survival and procreation. In the seventeenth and eighteenth centuries the couple began to withdraw from the immediate influence of their parents and elders in their choice of partner and began to have a choice of their own. They had greater influence but their life was still dependent on their parents, who owned the land. (This phase of marriage is well described in *The Making of the Modern Family,*[1] *The Family, Sex and Marriage in England 1500–1800*[2] and *For Better for Worse, British Marriages 1600 to the Present.*[3]) The independence of the couple from their parents was accelerated during this period in the United States, where the bonds between children and parents were loosened earlier than in Europe.

Until the Industrial Revolution, the couple and their children were still focused on the land from which their living came. In this situation women worked on the farm alongside men but were still subordinate to them. The Industrial Revolution heralded the second major phase of modern marriage. It set in motion a more radical process. Now husbands and wives left the land and worked in different spheres. The man went into the factories or down the mines and most wives were left at home, although some of them worked in factories. During the Victorian period, which covered primarily the second half of the nineteenth century, the upper socioeconomic group of wives stayed at home, whilst the lower group went to work. But at all times those who went to work had to interrupt it for childbearing. Childbearing in those days was a dangerous process, with considerable infant and mother mortality. The separation of the couple into the different domains of work and home was also accompanied by a diminution in the worth of the wife.

The second half of the nineteenth century was accompanied by a subjugation of women, and a reduction in the value of sexuality; marriage was seen primarily as a process of procreation, which with its attendant high mortality was a perilous adventure. It was principally this period that saw the beginnings of the revolution against sexual suppression by Sigmund Freud, and also the emancipation of women, a movement whose fruition is being fully realised in our time. As far as marriage is concerned, the first half of the twentieth century reinforced the separation of husbands and wives, with the former going out to to work and the latter staying at home and being responsible for the children and the care of the home.

This brings us to the third phase of modern marriage, which covers the period up to the 1960s. During this period it was the social aptness of the marriage that mattered. This depended on the husband being the head of the family, the person who went out to work and was the source of the economic viability of the marriage, and the one who took decisions and was the ambassador of the family to the outside world. Thus the husband had the responsibility and was influential in the power, authority and financial maintenance of the family, and the wife was in charge of the children and the home. She was dependent on the husband and this has come to be known as the instrumental pattern of marriage. Emotional nurturing was present in the life of the marriage, but social aptness in the exercise of the respective roles was the key to success. Marriage was a social contract of these respective roles. Thus the husband was expected to be a successful breadwinner and the wife an accomplished homemaker. Such nurturing as occurred was the wife's responsibility and this pattern of marriage is also known as 'traditional'.

In the last thirty years we have witnessed a further revolution in marriage. This revolution is occurring in our midst and is hard to define accurately. It consists of a shift from social to emotional aptness. That is to say, in sociological terms, the contemporary marriage is focused not on instrumentality but on feelings and emotions and it is called the companionate variety. The companionate variety emphasises a male–female egalitarian partnership in which company, communication, support, healing, the exchange of feelings and sexual satisfaction are of paramount importance. It is no longer the discharge of social roles but the quality of the relationship that matters. In a vague and ill-defined way, it is love that matters.

But what is meant by love in these circumstances? It is this which will be examined in detail in this book. However, a word of caution is needed. The nature of love in marriage as examined by sociologists and psychologists reflects qualities such as stability and satisfaction. The measurement of stability is relatively straightforward. People can be classified as married, separated, divorced or never-married. Satisfaction, being a subjective matter, is much more difficult to evaluate.

There are a number of words for marital satisfaction such as happiness, quality, adjustment, lack of distress and integration. These characteristics can be measured by inventories. One inventory is Snyder's Marital Satisfaction Inventory,[4] and I quote representative items from this to give the reader a flavour of the type of areas tapped in such a questionnaire.

The inventory is made up of appropriate positive statements which the participants have to rate.

REPRESENTATIVE ITEMS FROM SNYDER'S MARITAL SATISFACTION INVENTORY

AFFECTIVE COMMUNICATION

'My spouse can usually tell what kind of a day I've had without even asking.'

'My spouse and I frequently sit down and talk about pleasant things that happened during the day.'

PROBLEM-SOLVING COMMUNICATION

'My spouse has no difficulty in accepting criticism.'

'My spouse rarely nags me.'

TIME TOGETHER

'My spouse likes to share his/her leisure time with me.'

'Our daily life is full of interesting things to do together.'

FINANCES

'Serious financial concerns are not likely to destroy our marriage.'

'My spouse and I rarely argue about money.'

SEX

'My spouse rarely refuses intercourse when I desire it.'

'My spouse seems to enjoy sex as much as I do.'

CHILDREN

'Having children has increased the happiness of our marriage.'

'For the most part, our children are well behaved.'

CHILD-REARING

'My spouse and I rarely disagree on when or how to punish the children.'

'My spouse and I decide together what rules to set for our children.'

GLOBAL SATISFACTION

'I have never thought of my spouse or me as needing marital counselling.'

'I am quite happily married.'

CONVENTIONALISATION

'There was never a moment when I did not feel "head over heels" in love with my mate.'

'I have never regretted my marriage, not even for a moment.'

Source: Adapted from Snyder (1981)

Note: The major predictors of marital happiness on this scale are good emotional and problem-solving communication.

In this book, except where love is defined specifically, I relate love to various positive marital characteristics, such as happiness, quality, adjustment, lack of distress and integration, as measured by various studies. This is the first time that an attempt has been made to use the various sociological and psychological studies that measure marital satisfaction, linking them with love or emotional aptness.

PART 1

Love

CHAPTER 2

Love as Attachment

In the previous chapter, marriage was seen to shift from social to emotional aptness, in which love is its basic energy. This love will be considered throughout the book in terms of marital satisfaction, but we begin by examining what social scientists have said about love itself. In this chapter we look at the most basic source of love, which is our childhood experience in terms of attachment.

Childhood is a time in which we move from total dependence to independence. During this period we learn to receive and to give, and become familiar with closeness and distance, acceptance and rejection, nurturing and deprivation, belonging and alienation. All these experiences are intimately connected with love, but is there one basic concept that forms the foundations for all the others?

The English psychoanalyst, John Bowlby, believed that human attachment was the foundation of love. Up to the middle 1950s, it was thought that the bond of love between parent and child was formed in the feeding of the baby by the mother at the breast. In psychoanalytic terms, it was this oral phase that linked mother to child. Later in life, sexuality completed the bond, thus food and sex were considered the basis for attachment. Bowlby denied that this was the case.[1,2,3] He postulated that, in addition to food and sex, there was a basic attachment between the baby and mother that depended on vision, touch, sound and smell. In other words, the baby forms an attachment to its mother that is instinctive and affectionate by recognising her face, the sound of her voice, by holding and being held and through smell. This affective attachment gives the infant comfort when it is afraid, hurt, ill or tired. Under such conditions the baby will cry and as a result be picked up and comforted. As the baby becomes a toddler, its mother or another attachment figure, such as its father, grandparents or any well-recognised figure, acts as a secure base from which the environment can be explored. We see toddlers leaving mother's side, walking or running some distance away, safely exploring the world around them and returning to mother as the secure base when anything frightens them. The relevance of the attachment theory to love is Bowlby's assertion that '"Attachment behaviour" which means attachment, call for help and foundation of a secure base is held to characterise human beings from the cradle to the grave'.[4]

Looking at adult attachment, particularly to our marital partner, this is mediated through looks, sound, touch and smell, which gives us in turn someone to call on for support and comfort when we need it and a basis for security from which to explore other people and situations. Bowlby's attachment theory is the prototype of love for human beings.

Shaver et al. went on to spell out the relationship of attachment between infant and caretaker as the model for later bonds between lovers and spouses.[5] In the table below there is a comparison between the behaviour in infancy and romantic love.

'ATTACHMENT	*ROMANTIC LOVE*
Formation and quality of the attachment bond depends on the attachment object's (AO) sensitivity and responsiveness	The love feelings are related to an intense desire for the love object's (LO) real or imaged interest and reciprocation
AO provides a secure	LO's real or imaged reciprocation causes person to

base and infant feels competent and safe to explore	feel confident, secure, safe, etc.
When AO is present infant is happier, has a higher threshold for distress, is less afraid of strangers, etc.	When LO is viewed as reciprocating, the lover is happier, more positive about life in general, more outgoing and kinder to others
When AO is not available, not sensitive, etc., infant is anxious, preoccupied, unable to explore fully	When LO acts uninterested or rejecting, person is anxious, preoccupied, unable to concentrate, etc.
Attachment behaviour includes proximity and contact-seeking, holding, touching, caressing, kissing, smiling, following	Romantic love is manifest in wanting to spend time with LO, holding, touching, caressing, kissing and making love with LO, smiling and laughing; crying, clinging; fearing separation etc.
When afraid, distressed, sick, threatened, etc., infant seeks physical contact with AO	When afraid, distressed, sick, threatened, lovers would like to be held and comforted by LO
Distress at separation or loss: crying, calling for AO, trying to find AO, becoming sad and listless if reunion seems impossible	Distress at separation or loss: crying, calling for LO, trying to find LO, becoming sad and listless if reunion seems impossible
Upon reunion with AO, infant smiles, greets AO with positive vocalisation or cry, bounces and jiggles, approaches need-	Upon reunion with LO or when LO reciprocates after reciprocatior was in doubt, the lover feels ecstatic, hugs LO

ing to be picked up, etc.	
Infant shares toys, discoveries etc. with AO	Lovers like to share experiences, give gifts, etc., and imagine how LO would react to interesting sights etc
Infant and AO frequently engage in prolonged eye contact; infant seems fascinated with AO's personal features, and enjoys touching nose, ears, hair etc	Lovers frequently engage in prolonged eye contact and seem fascinated with each other's personal features and like to explore noses, ears and hair etc.
Although the infant can be attached to more than one person at a time there is usually one key relationship	Although many adults feel they can and do love more than one person, intense love occurs with one partner at a time
Infant coos, 'sings', talks baby-talk, etc. Mother talks a combination of baby-talk. Much non-verbal communication	Lovers coo, sing, talk baby-talk, use soft maternal tones, etc. and much of their communication is non-verbal
The responsive mother senses the infant's needs, 'reads' the infant's mind. Powerful empathy	The lovers feel almost magically understood and sympathised with. Powerful empathy
The infant appears to get tremendous pleasure from AO's approval, applause, attention, etc.	At least early in the relationship, the lovers' greatest happiness comes from LO's approval, attention, etc.'

From 'Love as Attachment', Shaver, Hazan and Bradshaw in *The Psychology of Love* ed. R.J. Sternberg and M.L. Barnes[5]

It can be seen from the work of Shaver and Hazan that attachment theory as developed by them forms one of the best illustrations of how lovers relate, and that applies also to marital love. The lover stands for mother and offers contact, support, reassurance, security, affection and relief from distress. Throughout marriage the partner offers these possibilities and when he or she dies there is grief, distress and mourning.

The description so far shows the similarity between infants and their attachment figures, lovers and marital partners. But are all these attachments the same? Do all infants and partners form the same attachment to their key figures? The work of Ainsworth and her colleagues showed that there are three types of attachment in infants.[6] The first is called secure attachment (60 per cent of the infants tested); these infants appear to perceive their caretakers as reliable and trustworthy sources of protection. They can rely on them. These infants actively seek contact with their caretakers when distressed and are readily soothed and reassured by the contact.

The second group have been labelled as anxious–resistant or ambivalent (19 per cent); these infants intersperse contact-seeking with angry resistant behaviour and are not easily comforted.

The third group are called avoidant (21 per cent); these infants actively avoid contact with their caretaker when distressed. A great deal of research has opened up in the last fifteen years to find out whether these patterns persist in childhood and, most important of all, in adulthood. The reason why this continuity is important is derived from Bowlby's notion that the emerging person develops persistent internal representations of themselves and others. Their attachment type informs the type of person they are and the relationships they make. As far as the identity of self is concerned, the individual judges himself or herself to be the sort of person towards whom anyone, and the attachment figure in particular, is likely to respond in a positive way. In other words attachment theory gives us the clue to the basis on which we feel lovable and acceptable. As far as the 'other' is concerned, they are considered from the point of view whether they are likely to be responsive to us. Thus attachment theory gives all of us a working model that guides our expectations about relationships – whether we can trust others and whether we feel acceptable and lovable ourselves. The capacity to form loving relationships and to sustain them depends ultimately on whether we trust ourselves and others. Is there a link between self-acceptance and the types of attachment just described? In particular, are secure attachments linked with positive, self-accepting images? The work of Cassidy on six-year-olds showed a positive association.[7] Those children securely attached had positive conceptions of themselves, whilst anxious–ambivalent children revealed more overtly negative descriptions of themselves.

But what about adults? 'Although there are important differences between childhood and adult attachment relationships,[8, 9] the underlying dynamics may be surprisingly similar'.[10] The secure adult is characterised by ease of trusting and getting close to others; the anxious–ambivalent by a desire to merge with a partner, coupled with the fear of not being loved sufficiently and needing constant reassurance; and the avoidant, by discomfort in trusting and becoming close to others. As expected, individuals who chose a secure self-description reported more favourable descriptions of their childhood relationships with their parents than did insecure individuals. Ambivalent–anxious people reported especially high levels of obsessive preoccupation, desire for union and the tendency to fall in love easily. Avoidant individuals reported the lowest trust and the most cynical beliefs about love. This work has been conducted by Hazan and Shaver,[11] and replicated by Collins and Read[12] and Feeney and Noller.[13] In particular, avoidant individuals not only mistrust others and are cynical about love but hold a negative view of themselves with feelings of unacceptability by others. The avoidant variety are in psychological terms cut off from themselves and from others, have difficulty in marrying, and when they do marry, like the anxious–ambivalent, tend to have a difficult time in their relationships because they feel unlovable and unwanted.

To summarise, Bowlby's attachment theory gives us one of the most basic models of love relationships. The infant's attachment to the caretaker is the source of comfort and security from which to explore the world. It bears enormous similarity to the relationship between lovers and spouses. The three types of attachment – secure, anxious–ambivalent, and avoidant – give a basic pattern of relating to ourselves and others, which in all probability follows us for the whole of our lives. Secure attachment is linked with positive self-image and therefore self-acceptance and the acceptance of others. The anxious and avoidant attachments are linked with doubts about ourselves and fears in relating to others. Any couple can assess the type of spouse they are and are married to on this typology, and their type of love as secure or fragile can be glimpsed from the categories to which they belong.

CHAPTER 3

Kinds of Love

The work of Bowlby has shown us that affective attachment is the basis for forming a loving relationship. Further work has indicated the range of love that can be expressed. In this chapter we look at three descriptions of love that have emerged from the study of loving amongst men and women. They have been formulated from descriptions derived from questionnaires.

LOVE STYLES

A Canadian sociologist read much of the historical and philosophical literature on love and then developed an interview questionnaire called the Love Study Card Sort. People selected statements that reflected their own personal love relationship. This approach allowed people to tell the story of how their relationship began and how it continued. John Alan Lee,[1] the sociologist concerned, described primary and secondary love styles. What follows is based on the account of Lee's love styles given by Hendrick and Hendrick.[2]

Eros is often described as 'passionate love', but it is much more than physical passion. It is an intense attraction to the partner, a desire to become sexually intimate, to be in very close touch and to disclose oneself fully. There is a mutual development with exclusive focus on the partner but without possessiveness or jealousy.

Storge is a love that is a feeling of natural affection such as you might have for a brother or a sister. It is an unexciting and often uneventful variety; its underlying strength is friendship – a companionable, secure, trusting relationship with someone who is similar in terms of attitudes and values.

Ludus is 'a type of love that is played as a game, for mutual enjoyment, without any serious intent'. This lover enjoys multiple relationships at a time and enjoys sex as good fun, rather than as a deep involvement. Ludus wants to enjoy life without commitment.

Pragma suggests practical and pragmatic, and here, for instance, the lover goes out shopping for a partner and knows what they want. Pragmatic lovers are not looking for great excitement, but for someone suitable with whom a mutually satisfying experience can be had.

Mania has many qualities of traditional romantic love. It is full of highs and lows. It is jealous, possessive, full of doubts about the partner's commitment and experiences acute excitement with depressive phases. It is an all-or-nothing type of love.

Agape stands for saintly love. It is the rarest type of love. 'It is selfless and giving, concerned about the partner's welfare and undemanding for the self.'

These types of love have a relationship with Hazan and Shaver[3] in that Eros, Agape and Storge would be related to secure attachment, Manic to anxious–ambivalent, and Ludic to the avoidant type of attachment.

The Lee types have been a source of considerable research, described in some detail in Hendrick and Hendrick's work.[2] Amongst the many findings, there is a tendency for women to be more Storgic, Pragmatic and Manic and men to be more Ludic. 'Our interpretation of these findings is that women have been socialised (at least historically) to marry a love partner and an economic provider and, thus they may take a sensible, practical approach to relationships.'[2]

When these types of love are examined in dating relationships, they show that passionate erotic love, combined with a low level of game-playing, is the basis for the satisfactory development of dating relationships, and passionate love is a powerful predictor of married couples' satisfaction.[4]

Further work on satisfaction shows that women's scores on Eros and Agape are highly related to the male partner's satisfaction, but men's scores on Eros and Agape were unrelated to their partner's satisfaction. Thus men are more satisfied when their partners are more passionate and altruistic, but this was not important for women. 'Our explanation of these differences is based on observation as well as existing literature, and it appears that women generally take more responsibility than do men for nurturing and maintaining a relationship'.[2]

Summing up all the research information that has emerged so far in connection with love types, the following portraits can be made.

EROS

Higher self-esteem, more disclosure, related to relationship satisfaction important to both men and women.

LUDUS

Less disclosure, more sensation-seeking, less relationship satisfaction, more pursued by men than by women.

STORGE

Much endorsed by women, involves greater contentment.

PRAGMA

Much in common with Storge, but less quietly contented.

Mexican-American couples more pragmatic than Anglo couples.

MANIA

More endorsed by women, related to less relationship satisfaction for women, lower self-esteem, greater relationship communication, greater relationship turbulence.

AGAPE

More characteristic of persons who are religious and/or who are in long-term love relationships, more agapic women have more satisfied relationship partners, related to greater relationship stability and contentment.

FEHR'S PROTOTYPES OF LOVE

Lee asked lay people to describe types of love; Fehr on the other hand asked for a list of features of love.[5] Fehr's emphasis on features rather than types has been called a prototype of love and is the nearest understanding of what men and women think of love.

Fehr's findings will be described in two stages. First, university students generated sixty-eight features of the concept of love. The most frequently listed ones were caring, happiness, wanting to be with the other, friendship and feeling free to talk about anything. However, the concept was not described in uniformly positive terms: the features of uncertainty and fear were also included. Behaviourally, the features of love included smiling, gazing at each other and laughing, along with altruistic acts such as helping, doing things for each other, sacrifice, and putting the other first. Cognitively, the thinking part of love contained features such as admiration and respect, and also rumination, thinking about the other all the time. Physiological features included heart-rate increase, butterflies in the stomach, and sexual passion. There was also social support such as sharing, empathy and comforting the other. Finally some of the characteristics such as committed, secure and long-lasting implied expectations that the relationship would last.

In a second study, these sixty-eight features were assessed for their prototypicality or the most obvious and typical interpretation of what love is. Those receiving the highest ratings were trust, caring, honesty, respect and friendship. The lowest ratings were assigned to euphoria, gazing at each other, seeing only the other's good qualities, butterflies in the stomach, uncertainty, dependency and fear. Fehr noted that the features receiving the highest typicality ratings ally them only to descriptions of companionate love, whereas the features receiving the lowest ratings portray passionate love.[6] These results reveal that companionate or friendship features are central to the lay person's conception of love. Passionate, romantic features are seen as part of the concept but as much more peripheral. Indeed in our present situation, the passionate, romantic features are the ones associated with falling in love and the companionate ones with the ongoing relationship, usually seen in marriage. A study by Fitness and Fletcher showed that the above prototypes would express themselves in a special way in marriage.[7] Typical love experiences were elicited by events, such as the partner giving time and support, sharing happy times, and thinking about the spouse. Everyone mentioned the urge to be physically close and included hugging and kissing. Other behaviour consisted of verbally expressing one's love and giving presents (Fehr).[5]

LIMERENCE

Dorothy Tennov employs the term 'Limerence' to describe a state of falling in love.[8] It is perhaps the nearest description to infatuation or 'getting a crush' on someone. It is characterised by excitement, idealisation of the beloved, non-stop thinking of them, inability to get them out of one's mind, with mood swings, and feeling wanted and then rejected.

In contrast to Limerence, Beach and Tesser focused on married couples and proposed four components of married love.[9] These are commitment, intimacy, cohesion (sharing and closeness) and sexual interaction.

To sum up this chapter: we have seen a variety of descriptions from Lee's types to Fehr's features. Together they encompass a perspective from passionate to companionate love. Passionate love is exciting, engages the mind and the body, and has a powerful physical quality about it. It is present when we fall in love, when we are involved in an affair and when we are obsessed with the person in our mind. It is the type of love that engages most powerfully the whole of our being and it is something that is reinforced by the media with its emphasis on visual excitement. For most people, however, in the married state, it is the deeper, penetrating, constant evidence of love that engages the couple, which has been identified as companionate love. It is this that will receive our major attention. In the next chapter we examine a particular description of love that is concerned with an interaction of passionate and companionate love.

CHAPTER 4

A Triangular Theory of Love

The triangular theory of love holds that love can be understood in terms of three components, which are intimacy, passion and a decision/commitment (see Figure I).[1]

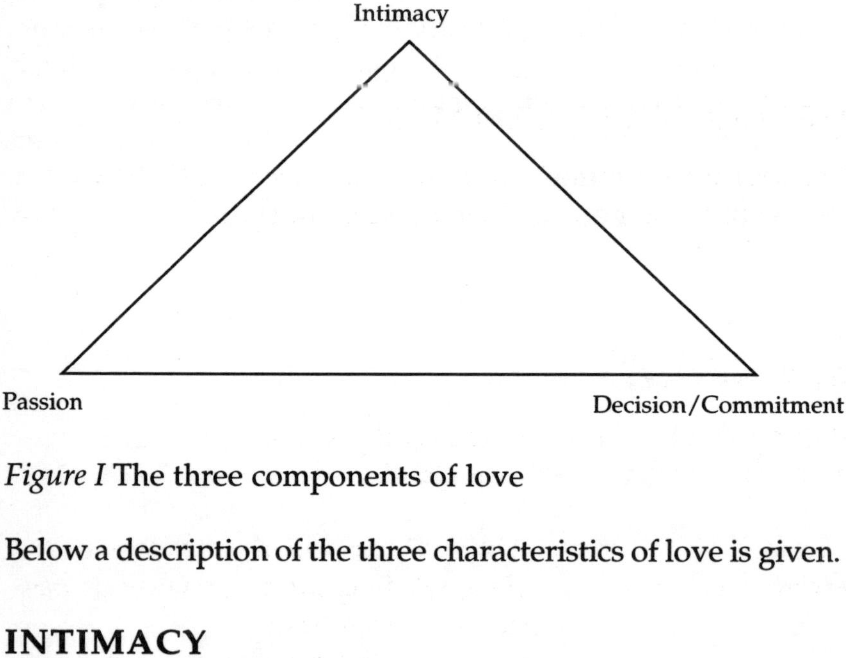

Figure I The three components of love

Below a description of the three characteristics of love is given.

INTIMACY

Intimacy includes feelings that create the experience of warmth in a loving relationship. Sternberg and Grajck identified ten signs of intimacy in a close relationship:[2]

1. The desire to promote the welfare of the loved one.
2. Experience happiness with them.

3. Have a high regard for them.
4. Being able to count on the loved one in times of need.
5. Mutual understanding with the loved one.
6. Sharing one's self and one's possessions with the loved one.
7. Receiving emotional support from them.
8. Giving emotional support to the loved one.
9. Having intimate communication with the loved one.
10. Valuing the loved one in one's life.

PASSION

The passion component consists of those elements associated with sexual attraction, sexual play and sexual intercourse, all consummated in a loving relationship.

DECISION/COMMITMENT

The decision/commitment implies the decision that one is in love with someone and the commitment is the desire to stay in that love.

RESULTING LOVES

Putting together these various components it was found that eight different types of love could be described.

Non love	All three components are absent.
Liking	Here we find intimacy without passion or commitment.
Infatuation	Passion without intimacy or commitment.
Empty love	Commitment without intimacy or passion.
Romantic love	Intimacy and passion but no commitment.

Companionate love	Intimacy and commitment but not passion.
Fatuous love	Passion and commitment with no intimacy.
Consummate love	All three components are present.

Clearly this is a classification with illustrates effectively the kinds of love couples go through. We all start with a number of romantic moments in which there is intimacy and passion and people can return to them in affairs.

We move on to consummate love in which all three components are present and, as the relationship extends over the decades, it can move into companionate love in which there is intimacy and commitment, but no sexual involvement. In the later years of marriage companionate love is common, but nowadays sexual activity extends over many decades

CHAPTER 5

The Evolutionary Basis of Love

So far, the descriptions of love given are based primarily on the presence of feelings and emotions. Another writer, D.M. Buss, stresses an evolutionary understanding of love.[1] He brings out the importance of *action* as against the subjective dimensions of love.

'Love acts are hypothesised to have evolved to serve functions, accomplish tasks or achieve goals that are linked with reproductive success.' The whole point of love here is its link with reproduction. Buss describes seven steps in this theory, which all lead to the maintenance of the race. These are resource display, exclusivity (fidelity and guarding), commitment and marriage, sexual intimacy, reproduction, resource-sharing and parental investment. Their function is to attract a mate, retain their presence, reproduce with them, and invest parentally in the resulting offspring.

RESOURCE DISPLAY

Men think normally of resource display as the attractiveness of women. In women the two strongest cues are age and health, expressed through physical appearance. Thus the woman's sexual attraction is linked with her reproductive ability.

As far as women are concerned, they need to choose men who indicate their capacity to earn well and put their material resources in the children. Thus, traditionally, men may marry when they are older and have made their way in the world, so that they can support their wives, and they marry younger women who can reproduce successfully. The cues are then female physical attractiveness and male possession of money, status and the presence of features such as ambition and hard work.

One can see that these resources have played and still play a crucial part in courting and traditional matching in many parts of the world.

EXCLUSIVITY

We have seen that exclusivity is the psychological expression of attachment theory, in that we are primed to a one-to-one relationship from our infancy. In the present theory, exclusivity is a social phenomenon guaranteeing confidence in paternity and ensuring the mutual commitment of the reproducing pair. There are two essential features of exclusivity, namely fidelity and mate-guarding. Female infidelity threatens the husband's confidence that he is the father of the child. Male infidelity carries the danger of resources being redirected to another woman and her child.

As sexual relations are moving away from creation to the personal level, fidelity becomes a much greater measure of mutual trust and love, and becomes very important to both sexes.

MARRIAGE

In addition to mate-guarding, societies have created social institutions with the same purpose, which they have called marriage. 'Marriage serves to enforce exclusivity, to ensure commitment of resources and to provide a context for the bearing and raising of children.'

SEXUAL INTIMACY

The fourth major goal of love acts is sexual intimacy, which is closely related to love and reproduction. As sexual intercourse is freed from direct involvement with reproduction, it assumes a personal character in which sexual attraction, pleasure and fulfilment become important in their own right, and of equal significance to men and women.

REPRODUCTION

It can easily be seen that the four preceding acts lead naturally to reproduction and this represents a fifth goal of love acts. During the nine months of pregnancy, love acts are now understood in terms of protection by the man of the pregnant woman, and for the woman of avoiding catching diseases that would harm the foetus and also the avoidance of smoking and other acts threatening to the infant.

RESOURCE-SHARING

Sexual intercourse and pregnancy are the woman's part of the reproductive bargain, financial support and protection are the man's responsibility. The man's contribution is intimately concerned with the health and well-being of the wife and children.

This model is again currently being modified by the fact that women can have children but also work, so that they are not entirely dependent on their partner for survival.

PARENTAL INVESTMENT

Once children arrive, a great deal of the energy of the parents is directed to their survival and their upbringing.

This model of love is very persuasive. There is much truth in it but we are in the midst of a psycho-social evolution which is changing it dramatically. The amount of time and energy invested in reproduction, and the rate of reproduction, is increasingly falling. Sexual love is becoming less preoccupied with reproduction and a great deal more with personal love. In this personal love, fidelity is no longer primarily concerned with paternity, but with mutual trust. Sexual intimacy is no longer primarily an issue of reproduction but of mutual support and comfort and sexual intercourse has extended itself before marriage and long after the reproductive years are over. All this demands a new way of looking at love as not only acts which engender reproduction but which sustain a loving relationship.

CHAPTER 6

Passionate and Companionate Love

Summing up the various theories of love we have described so far, psychologists have tended to reach the conclusion that love can be broadly described in two terms: passionate and companionate. Elaine Hatfield, in her chapter on passionate and companionate love,[1] quotes Hatfield and Walster's[2] definitions of these two types of love. Passionate love is described as 'A state of intense longing for union with another. Reciprocate love (union with the other) is associated with fulfilment and ecstasy. Unrequited love (separation) with emptiness, anxiety or despair. A state of profound physiological arousal'. Companionate love is defined as the 'affection we feel for those with whom our lives are deeply entwined'.

PASSIONATE LOVE

What does passionate love consist of? We are much more aware of its presence when it occurs, and find it difficult to describe, but it contains cognitive (thinking), emotional and behavioural components. The cognitive components include intrusive thinking about the loved one and idealisation of them. Despite what others may think, we think that we have found the most wonderful body, mind and heart. There is the desire to know the loved one and to be known.

The emotional items consist of sexual attraction, positive feelings when things go well, and negative feelings when there is rejection. There is a longing for reciprocity. Passionate lovers not only love, but want to be loved back in return. They desire complete and permanent union and there is physiological arousal such as the heart beating fast, sweaty palms, tingling, and butterflies in the stomach.

Finally there is a behavioural component to passionate love. This includes searching for the beloved, taking pleasure in studying their face and movements, enjoying doing things for the other and also maintaining physical closeness with the loved one.

The cognitive (thinking) aspect of passionate love is a mixture of euphoria, happiness, calm, tranquillity, vulnerability, anxiety, panic and despair.

Liebowitz provided a description of the mixed nature of passionate love:[3]

> Love and romance seem to be one, if not the most powerful, activator of our pleasure centres ... Both tend to be very exciting emotionally, being with the person or even thinking of him or her is highly stimulating ... Love is, by definition, the strongest positive feeling we can have. Other things – stimulant drugs, passionate causes, manic states – can induce powerful changes in our brains, but none so reliably, so enduringly or so delightful as that 'right' other person ... If the relationship is not established or is uncertain, anxiety or other displeasure centres may become active as well, producing a situation of great emotional turmoil as the lover swings between hope and torment.

BIOLOGY

We saw in the last chapter that love is directed towards the bonding of a couple for the purposes of reproduction. This bonding would come under the aegis of passionate love and would be expected to have biological components, an anatomical site and physiological associations.

According to Kaplan,[4] the anatomy of passionate love is well understood. The brain's sex centre consists of a network of neurological foci and circuits. These are situated within the limbic system with nuclei in the hypothalamus and in the preoptic regions. It is here that the most powerful emotions are generated. The sexual system is connected by both neural and chemical transmitters to the brain's pleasure and pain centres. All behaviour is shaped by the seeking of pleasure and the avoidance of pain. Brain cells produce a chemical that has been called 'endorphin', which resembles morphine clinically and causes euphoria and alleviates pain. It may be speculated that eating, having sex and being in love, all of which are experienced as pleasurable, produce their sensations by stimulation of the pleasurable centres electrically or by the release of endorphins. The part of the brain that evaluates sensations and thoughts has extensive connections with the limbic system and the pain and pleasure centres coordinating passionate arousal and its abatement.

When passionate arousal takes place, it has been speculated that a giddy feeling compared to an amphetamine high is produced. It is suggested that it is phenylethylamine (PEA) that produces the mood-lifting and energising effects of passionate love. It is reasonable to assume that 'love addicts' and drug addicts have a lot in common; both crave a high. It is possible that men who are so called 'womanisers' have a need for repeated highs, which are obtained from affairs or from breaking up their marriages and starting a new romantic relationship. The crash that follows a break-up in a romantic relationship is very similar to amphetamine withdrawal. Separation anxiety, panic attacks or depression may follow the withdrawal of chemicals that produce highs.

The chemistry of sexual desire is well known. In both men and women testosterone is the libido hormone.

> When in love, libido is high. Every contact is sensuous. Thoughts turn to Eros and the sexual reflexes work rapidly and well. The presence of the loved one acts as an aphrodisiac. The smell, sight, sound and touch of the lover, especially when he/she is excited, are powerful stimuli to sexual desire. In physiological terms, this may exert a

> direct physical effect on the neurophysiological system in the brain which regulates sexual desire.... But again there is no sexual stimulant so powerful, even love, that it cannot be inhibited by fear or pain.[4]

We can sum up what we know of emotional and sexual arousal by saying that cognitive factors – the way we perceive our lover – stimulate us and this in turn excites anatomical and physiological centres in the brain. Arousal is not only a matter of biology, it is an interaction between perception and biology.

COMPANIONATE LOVE

Companionate love is defined as the 'affection we feel for those with whom our lives are deeply entwined'. In other words, it is the feeling we have for those with whom we are intimate. To be intimate means to be close to another. Hatfield defined intimacy as 'a process in which people attempt to get close to another, to explore similarities and differences in the way they think, and behave'.[5]

As far as thought is concerned, intimates are willing to reveal themselves to one another. 'They disclose information about themselves and listen to their partner's confidences. In deeply intimate relationships lovers feel free to reveal most facets of themselves in all their complexities and contradictions. As a result, intimates share profound information about one another's histories, strengths, weaknesses, idiosyncrasies, hopes and fears.'[6, 7, 8] This revelation of one to the other implies trust and expects a high degree of confidentiality. That is why, if the relationship breaks up, the revelation of the disclosed information is experienced as a great betrayal. This sense of betrayal may also take place when the relationship continues but the partners talk about each other to third parties.

In terms of feelings, intimates care deeply about one another. They gaze at one another,[9] lean on one another,[10] stand close to each other,[11] and perhaps touch. 'Yet exactly because intimates care so much about one another, they have the power to elicit intense pain. The dark side of love is jealousy, depression and anger.'

It would seem that passionate love or the falling-in-love experience is fuelled by ecstasy or misery, whereas companionate love is intensified only by pleasure. Put another way, passionate love is driven by passionate experiences, good or bad, whereas companionate love is driven by positive experiences and dampened by painful ones. Normally, passionate love is experienced at its peak when we fall in love, and companionate love or loving follows in the several decades of marriage. In the next chapter we shall explore the falling-in-love state, but the bulk of this book will consider loving or companionate love, which sustains marriages over several decades. We know a great deal more about falling in love than about loving, but an attempt will be made to remedy this.

It may be said that the whole drama of modern marriage is the peak experience of falling in love, which couples try to recapture subsequently and never quite succeed. We have yet to establish the importance of sustained love over the decades that modern marriage spans. In previous centuries, couples came together for a reproductive cycle of love as described in the previous chapter. Today that model remains only in outline as procreation becomes a much smaller part of the totality of love, and the personal encounter of the couple looms much larger. This book tries to interpret this transition from a reproductive to a personal love.

CHAPTER 7

Falling in Love and Courtship

The natural history of development is for the child to separate gradually from its parents, develop the secondary sexual characteristics of puberty around about 12 or 13, leave home at 18 and, after a few years of living alone, marry. This timetable has been interrupted by cohabitation, but the overwhelming majority of men and women marry. Before marriage there is the period of courtship and falling in love and this chapter is dedicated to that experience.

The age of marriage dropped after the Second World War, but has been steadily rising since the 1960s. The mean age for men in 1961 in the United Kingdom was 25.6 years; in 1991 it had risen to 27.5. For women, the ages were 23.1 and 25.4 respectively for the same years.[1] In the United States in 1988, the mean age for men was 25.9, and for women, 23.6.[2]

Before discussing the courtship process, it may be asked what social factors drive young people towards each other and marriage. One very obvious factor is sexual attraction, but this takes place within a framework of social norms. Here is a young man speaking in Mansfield and Collard's study about marriage:[3] 'I suppose I accepted it as being inevitable because I suppose 90 per cent or whatever it is of the male population in this country is married. I suppose I accepted it as inevitable that I would marry.' This is a view resulting from peer pressure following the norms of society. Busfield and Paddon express it in similar terms:[4]

> Much of the pressure to marry comes from the simple fact that being married and having a family are regarded as

> proper and normal conditions. The argument might sound circular as if we are back to asserting simply that people marry because they are expected to do so.... It is not that people marry because they are expected to marry, but that by marrying they come to occupy roles that are socially acceptable and legitimate. Marriage slots people into their rightful place as adults in society.

I mentioned above that leaving home in the teens was a goal for men and women, but a number do not leave their family homes. For these men and women marriage then means a home of their own. Here are some views about this home expressed by the newly married. 'Coming home after work and sitting in our own house, giving the orders, I am not being told what to do, I can decide what I want to do, when and how, Heather can decide the same.' 'As an adult – as well as a married couple, you know, we have got our own home and we have got our own views and we have got our own way of doing things and we have got our own front door, you know, and what we say and do behind it is our business.'[3]

Then there is the relationship with the parents, which seems to change after marriage. 'I can't explain it ... when we go round there or they come round here they seem different, they seem to welcome us differently and treat us as if we are different people. Although I am still their daughter I am married now, you know; that seems to make a difference to them.'[3]

Courtship seems to be the preliminary for an intense yearning to be recognised as a normal, independent adult, and to secure the future appears to be the most common motive for marriage. But sometimes this yearning for independence may arise out of conflict with the parents. Pincus in her work with adolescents writes,[5]

> Where adolescent difficulties have been particularly severe, courtship or marriage may be a desperate attempt to deal with the conflicts about dependence or rivalry. The

> partner may be important as an instrument, rather than in his own right as a person to love; as offering an opponent to the parents, or a way of escape, rather than as a life partner. Many of the very young couples who reach helping agencies seem to have married out of conflict with their parents rather than from any real feeling for each other.

Mansfield and Collard show that there are social and psychological background factors such as independence, separating from parents, being treated as individuals, and having a home of one's own, which form the background to courtship.[3]

DATING AND COURTSHIP

The above social and psychological factors lead to two separate processes; one is dating and the other is courtship. This two-tiered system of heterosexual interaction is said to have begun at the beginning of the twentieth century. Bailey attributed the rise of dating both to the creating of adolescence as a distinct period of life and to the emergence of mass culture.[6] Adolescence meant that dating allowed the selection of a mate to be delayed and a mass culture provided a uniform set of rules of etiquette to be followed by all. Others refer to the shift from rural to urban society, the emancipation of women, the emphasis on companionate marriage, the widespread ownership of cars, the rise of the movies, and the reduction of community control.[7, 8, 9]

In the twentieth century, dating has been a vehicle for getting to know someone before settling into an exclusive pairing. Dating focused on success and increasing one's popularity without becoming emotionally involved, which belongs to courtship. Courtship focused on finding someone who exhibited the traits of emotional maturity, honesty, genuineness and a desire for family life.[10]

One of the issues that has concerned contemporary society is the mark-off point for sexual intercourse. Traditionally, sex was confined to marriage or to committed relationships, but increasingly sexual intercourse has spread to dating with increasing confusion of what its meaning is. Is sexual intercourse meant for procreation? Is it a signature of a committed relationship or is it an expression of sexual pleasure that the intimacy of dating permits? There is no clear answer to these questions, but in fact hardly anyone reaches marriage nowadays as a virgin.

Dating is the ultimate evolution of the man/woman relationship to the point of personal preference, from a stage several centuries ago when mate selection was almost entirely determined by the families involved. The next step is to examine the transition to courtship, when a young man and a woman begin to keep steady company. Courtship has been studied extensively in the United States and what follows is a summary of a detailed analysis by Cate and Lloyd.[11]

EARLY STUDIES OF COURTSHIP

The early studies interpreted their findings on the basis that a single dimension of relationship dictated the process of courtship. One of the earliest models for mate selection was Winch's complementary needs.[12] In lay terms this means that opposites attract. For Winch, the basis of attraction and selection has two phases. The social characteristics of age, social class, religion and so on determine the field of eligible candidates, but the actual selection is made by complementarity. Thus those who fall in love are alike in their social traits, but complementary in their psychological needs: for example, one partner having the need to be dominant and the other submissive, someone who needs to be nurtured being attracted by someone who needs to give help, or someone who has a high need to achieve being matched by someone who has the need to abnegate. Although this theory is very attractive, it has not been supported by research.[13, 14, 15]

The alternative single-basis model is the similarity model. This holds that mate selection operates according to the lay wisdom that 'birds of a feather flock together'. In other words, the theory holds that individuals select marital partners on the basis of whether they are similar to each other. The research evidence seems to support this theory and marital partners have been found to be similar in attitudes and values,[16, 17] personality,[18] physical attractiveness,[19] and similar social characteristics such as age, religion, race, ethnicity.[20, 21]

Similarity might produce compatibility through (a) the reinforcement of each other's strengths (but it should be pointed out that there is also the possibility of reinforcing each other's weaknesses), (b) confirmation of people's sense of esteem or worth, (c) the implication that the partner may provide rewards in the future. As with the complementarity models, similarity has received criticism. At the heart of this criticism lies the view that because we tend to interact with people living close to us who are likely to be socially similar, this limits the opportunity to select those who are not similar to us. In other words, because we live near and are likely to interact with those who are already very similar to us, our chances of meeting someone similar to us are heightened more by proximity than by systematic choice. Another criticism comes from the view that similarity evolves through time in the interaction of the couple, rather than in the original choice.

STAGE MODELS OF COURTSHIP

Stage models of courtship suggest that courtship goes through phases, unfolding the process from being strangers to being lovers ready for marriage. There are four such models.

1. Reiss's Wheel theory.[22] According to this model, the first stage of courtship is that of forming rapport – that is, feeling at ease, the ability to communicate and to understand each other. Once rapport is there then couples proceed to self-revelation – that is, revealing one's values, beliefs and attitudes. This revelation builds a feeling of mutual

dependency so that the couple begin to rely on each other; they become of unique significance to one another. Finally the couple assess whether their relationship provides intimacy and their needs for fulfilment.

2. Kirckhoff's and Davis's Filter theory.[23] This model suggests that the first factor for selection or filtering is that of social characteristics, such as religion, education and class. The second stage is similarity in attitudes and values. Once potential partners are narrowed down on these bases, the final selection is on need complementarity.
3. Murstein's Stimulus – Value – Role model.[24, 13] The first stage of this SVR model is the presence of a stimulus. Particular attention is paid to physical attraction. Much research has shown the power of physical attraction.[25, 26] Other desirable stimuli include the reputation and behaviour of the other. The next stage is value similarity and this comes from self-disclosure. Finally there has to be compatibility of role – that is to say, the expectations each has for the other in their potential marriage.
4. Lewis's Premarital Dyadic Formation Framework.[27] Like some of the other models, the first process here is the perceiving of similarities. These include social and cultural values, interests and personality factors. The next stage is achieving pair rapport in which positive feelings are expressed. This is attained through ease of communication, positive evaluation of the other, and validation of self. This is followed by self-disclosure and role-taking, which leads to achieving interpersonal role-fit and finally arriving at dyadic crystallisation.

These stage models are all American and have intuitive appeal, but have been heavily criticised, not least because there are no studies replicating the original models. Another criticism is that they fail to do justice to the complexity of the mate-selection process.

Another way of describing courtship is the assumption

that relationships are shaped by different causes and are dependent on the unique interaction of the couple, which suggests that there are multiple pathways to commitment or marriage. An early study of courtship supported the multiple-pathways view.[28] Bolton recognised five types of movement towards marriage. The personality-meshing type was the product of personality 'fit', and couples who reflected this tended to be similar in background and values. The expediency-centred type felt a strong pressure to marry, experienced by one or both partners. This pressure could have come from the urgent desire to leave home or the inability to be alone. The identity-clarification type produced increasing convergence of partners and ideas about roles in the relationship. The relational-centred type is characterised by mutual and early commitment, the instant falling-in-love. The pressure- and intrapersonal relationship type tends to have the attraction focused towards the relationship rather than the partner.

Both the idiosyncratic and the stage descriptions of courtship suggest that the relationship proceeds from similarity and mutual physical attraction, through disclosure to share-fit of roles, but there is still a great deal of variety in the patterns of courtship.

STABILITY IN COURTSHIP

So far, we have examined patterns of courtship, but do we know the factors that contribute to the stability of the process? The first factor that has been found to predict the stability of courtship is love. Previous chapters have shown the various types of love. Based on several studies, courtship development is facilitated through love that is characterised by (a) the need to care for the partner, (b) the feeling of attachment to the partner, (c) the feeling of commitment, (d) feeling that the partner can be disclosed to and, in fact, is disclosed to, (e) the feeling of uniqueness about the relationship, (f) the feeling of belonging, closeness and involvement, (g) the feeling of being sexually involved.

The importance of love vies in significance with commitment as a factor determining stability of courtship. Johnson has provided a comprehensive understanding of commitment.[29] He points out that commitment can be divided into two categories, namely personal commitment and structural commitment. Personal commitment involves attraction to the partner, attraction to the relationship, definition of self in terms of the relationship and a moral obligation to stay in the relationship. Structural commitment consists of irretrievable investment, social pressure to remain in the relationship, difficulty in ending the relationship, and dissatisfaction with available alternatives. Marriage that follows from structural commitment is basically unstable and may soon be followed by divorce.

The next factor to be examined in relation to stability of courtship is the availability of alternative partners (comparison level). Rusbult found that those who broke off their premarital relationships reported higher availability of alternatives than those who stayed together.[30]

The time spent together was also predictive of stability. The more time spent together, the more stable the relationship. Fernlee found that fewer hours spent together per week was predictive of break-up;[31] the more hours spent together, the more likely that the relationship would remain intact.

SIMILARITY

Several theoretical models have suggested that an essential component of courtship is similarity. Data from the *Boston Couples Study* showed that stability was linked with higher similarity in age, academic achievement, educational aspirations and physical attractiveness.[21] Recently Surra and Longstreth reported that similarity in preference of activities also predicted stability.[32]

PREDICTING MARITAL SUCCESS

The importance of this chapter is based among other reasons on the link between courtship and marital success. Cate and Lloyd state their opinion boldly,[33] 'We believe that courtship sets the foundation for the later quality of marriage.'

Given that the breakdown of marriage occurs for many couples early in marriage, in fact in the first five years of marriage, many marital problems are likely to have their roots in the premarital stage. Lloyd states,[34] 'Premarital partners often have some inkling of what is to come in marriage (both good and bad), but because of the romanticised nature of courtship, partners are able to ignore the bad and glorify the good.'

What are the factors which relate to marital success? Age at marriage has been persistently shown to be related to marital stability.[35] Teenage marriages are particularly prone to divorce.[36, 37] The relationship between age at marriage and marital happiness is well established. The older the couple are on marrying, the higher the level of marital happiness.[16, 38, 39, 40] However, it has also been shown that those who marry after the age of thirty are more prone to divorce than those marrying between twenty and thirty.[41]

Length of courtship is related to marital adjustment. Partners who have dated for longer periods of time and who have been engaged longer, report higher marital happiness.[16] Longer courtships allow the partners the time to test their compatability.[33] But courtship can also be 'too long'. It has been shown that long, troubled courtships, characterised by slow commitment and several break-ups, are predictive of lower marital happiness and divorce.

The level of education is related both to marital adjustment and to stability.[16, 40, 37] Early research work in the 1950s showed that the higher the educational achievement of husbands and wives, the greater the stability of the marriage. Subsequent work has confirmed this finding. Level of education, age at marriage and length of courtship have been described as 'premarital resources which contribute to adequate role-functioning in marriage'.[41]

The quality of the childhood environment is also positively related to marital adjustment. This is a relationship that is very strong in character. Happiness in the marriage of one's parents, greater attachment to one's parents and siblings, and lower conflict in childhood with one's parents are all associated with greater happiness in one's marriage; [42, 15, 43] but some studies have shown that it is the wife's positive relationship with the family of origin, rather than the husband's, that is the key factor in marital happiness.[44] Not only is there a positive association between parental stability and happiness and that of the offspring's marriage, but there is also a positive association between parental divorce and divorce in the children's marriages.[45, 46]

PERSONALITY FACTORS

As we shall see in Part III, personality plays a major part in marital happiness and stability. Vaillant assessed a sample of college men in the 1930s.[47] Forty years later he evaluated marital stability and satisfaction of fifty-one of these men and found that the maritally satisfied were significantly more mentally healthy in college than those who were subsequently divorced or maritally dissatisfied. Terman's longitudinal study of 500 gifted children produced similar results. A measure of the emotional stability of the gifted children at ages 7–14 predicted marital happiness nearly twenty years later.[48] Kelly and Conley carried out another longitudinal study.[43] They first assessed 300 engaged couples in the 1930s and then reassessed 200 of these couples in the 1980s. Personality was a powerful predictive factor; for both wife and husband, marital adjustment was predicted by lower neuroticism, higher impulse control and greater conventionality.

All the above are long-term studies. There are also short-term longitudinal studies. Burgess and Wallin conducted a five-year longitudinal study of 1000 engaged couples and found that premarital levels of emotional stability, consideration for others, companionableness, self-confidence and emotional dependency predicted marital happiness.[16] Adams carried out a longitudinal study of 100 engaged couples and assessed them again between the second and third year of marriage and found that premarital levels of tranquillity, frankness and steadiness in men and frankness, stability and contentedness in women predicted marital happiness.[42]

Finally, there is the question of aggression. O'Leary et al. studied premarital physical aggression.[49] They followed 272 couples from one month pre-marriage to the third year of marriage. Couples who reported physical aggression at pre-marriage, 18 months of marriage, and 30 months of marriage were significantly more dissatisfied with their marriage at 30 months than were couples reporting no aggression in their marriages.

FALLING IN LOVE

The accounts of love described in Chapters 2–6 show the wide variety of background possibilities of the process of falling in love. In these chapters, love is shown to be an attachment process, to be made up of different kinds of love, to express a triangular form of commitment, passion and intimacy, to have an evolutionary basis and to contain passionate and companionate levels.

Courtship leads to falling in love, which is definitely an expression of passionate, intense love. In their study of experiences of falling in love, Aron, Dutton et al. refer to Tennov's idea of Limerence in which falling in love is experienced as an unwanted intrusive thinking of love, with an intense need for exclusivity, reference to ecstasy and a longing for the state itself.[50] In other words, people are in love with love. In contrast, affectional bonding may typify love from the start or occur after Limerence and is associated with a feeling of compatibility, pleasurable sexual experiences, shared goals and great contentment.

Shaver concluded that the most common antecedents to being in love were that the loved one provided something the person needs, wants, or likes.[51] As already seen, falling-in-love research has proceeded on the basis of:

1. Similarity; people falling in love are likely to have similar attitudes[52] and personality traits.[53]
2. Propinquity; familiarity with each other in terms of having spent time with each other,[54] living near each other,[55] more exposure to each other,[56] and thinking about the other.[57]
3. Desirable characteristics of the other, especially the other's appearance.
4. Reciprocal liking – that is, being liked by each other, both in general as well as when it is expressed through self-disclosure.[58]
5. Social influences, including general social norms and approval of others in the social network – that is to say, being approved of by the relatives and friends of the beloved.
6. Filling needs, particularly needs as stable personality traits.

The above six are background characteristics of general attraction, but for falling in love there is in addition:

7. Arousal; physiological arousal in which there may be palpitations, sweating and excitement.
8. Specific cues; some characteristics of the lover – voice, eyes, posture – which are sufficient to release a strong attraction; perhaps explains falling in love at first sight.
9. Readiness for entering a relationship; this may include loneliness or lowered self-esteem necessitating a boost to one's ego.

10. Exclusiveness; this characteristic refers to being alone with the beloved.
11. Mystery; found in the situation and as a perceived trait in the other person.

Aron and Aron studied the falling-in-love experience against the background of these eleven factors and concluded that falling in love was very frequently reported to have been preceded by the other's being perceived to have desirable characteristics and particularly to like oneself; moderately frequently by mentioning of one or more of the falling-in-love literature variables, such as readiness, arousal; low to moderate frequency by perceiving the other as similar and having spent time with the beloved. The special emphasis of these authors is on mutual liking and desirable characteristics. This view fits in with the authors' study that falling in love occurs when the individual perceives the other person as an opportunity for rapid self-expansion.[59] This requires the perception of two conditions: (a) that the other possesses resources that would expand the self (desirable characteristics) and (b) that the relationship is possible (the best sign of which is perceiving that the other wants such a relationship – reciprocal liking).

However the person reaches the falling-in-love stage, it is a state filled with excitement, a sense of joy and pleasure, with heightened awareness of oneself and of the other, who is idealised. This idealisation means that time is spent together, the positive features of the relationship are emphasised and the negative features diminished. There is a readiness to forgive and forget and to experience great pleasure in being together. This is the state of ecstasy in which the couple enter marriage and expect to remain for ever.

CHAPTER 8

Marital Satisfaction

We left our young couple at the peak of their love experience, at the wedding ceremony. What happens to this love afterwards as measured by marital satisfaction?

In order to answer this question, social researchers have divided marriage into several stages. One of the earliest proponents of this classification was Duvall.[1] It has been called 'The Family Life Cycle'. The life cycle defines sequential stages through a family career, basing the stages on the major developmental tasks faced by the family.

LIFE-CYCLE STAGES

I. Married couples (without children).
II. Childbearing families (oldest child birth – 30 months).
III. Families with preschool children (oldest child 2½–6 years).
IV. Families with schoolchildren (oldest child 6–13 years).
V. Families with teenagers (oldest child 13–20 years).
VI. Families as launching centres (first child gone – last child leaving home).
VII. Middle-aged parents (empty nest – retirement).
VIII. Ageing family members (retirement – death of one or both spouses).

Against a timetable of family stages, the next necessity was a measurement of marital satisfaction. Blood and Wolfe combined five components of married life into a single scale.[2]

The five constituents were standards of living, understanding, love and companionship, together with the congruity of the expected number of children; the wife's satisfaction was measured by the importance she attached to these five components.

Another investigation used a single self-rating scale. Rollins and Feldman asked the question, 'In general how often do you think that things between you and your spouse are going well?'[3] The response was 'all the time, most of the time, more often than not, occasionally, rarely or never.'

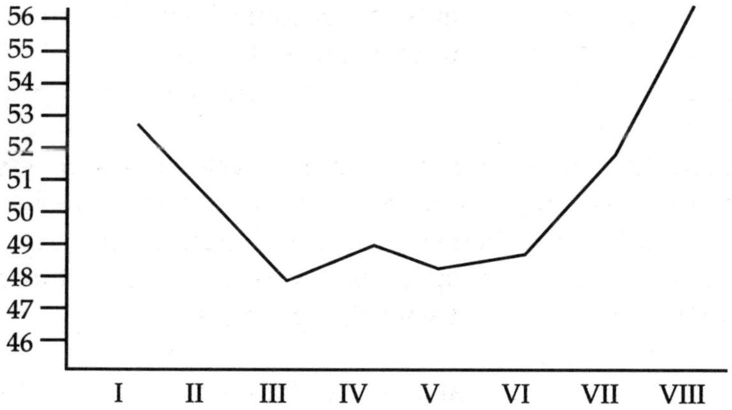

FAMILY LIFE CYCLE
Mean scores on marital satisfaction by stage of family life cycle according Rollins–Feldman

These approaches were both American and showed a consistent U model of marital satisfaction. Several studies have repeatedly shown a curvilinear pattern with satisfaction low when the children arrive, and remaining low whilst they are adolescent, and then beginning to pick up when the children leave home.[3, 4, 5, 6, 7]

Why does marital satisfaction drop over the first twenty-five years of marriage? Several explanations have been offered. Rosenblatt[8] and Houseknecht[9] suggested that 'children compete for the amount of time spouses are able to share with each other in communication, that the presence of children played a strong role in determining the amount of discussion shared between spouses as well as shaping the level of marital satisfaction perceived by wives'.

As the children grow older, early adolescence may also adversely affect marital satisfaction. Research indicates that pubertal maturation is associated with increases in parent–child distance, adolescent autonomy and parent–child conflict.[10] Mothers are especially vulnerable to the adverse psychological effects of frequent or intense conflict with their children.[11] As the children move into adolescence, they begin to de-idealise their parents, to become less dependent on them and to form a separate or individual sense of self. This leads to conflict over the times of returning home from parties, dating and discipline.

The middle stages of the family life cycle are also likely to be the years when parents are reaching mid-life, which may bring with it diminished self-esteem, doubt, uncertainty and depression; these may spill over into the relationship and provoke disenchantment with it, regardless of changes in the adolescents.

It can thus be seen that a certain loss of satisfaction enters into the marital relationship from the time the children arrive until they leave.

These are American findings; have they been replicated in Britain? In a study by Walker,[12] similar findings were found. The British study examined a number of individual characteristics over six stages and these are shown separately below.

As with the American studies, marital satisfaction declines and reaches its nadir around the time of the adolescence of the children and then picks up again. In the British study, there is a continuous decline in satisfaction with the expression of love and the sexual side of married life. The wife expects more in the way of companionship, in the amount of understanding the way she feels and in the expression of

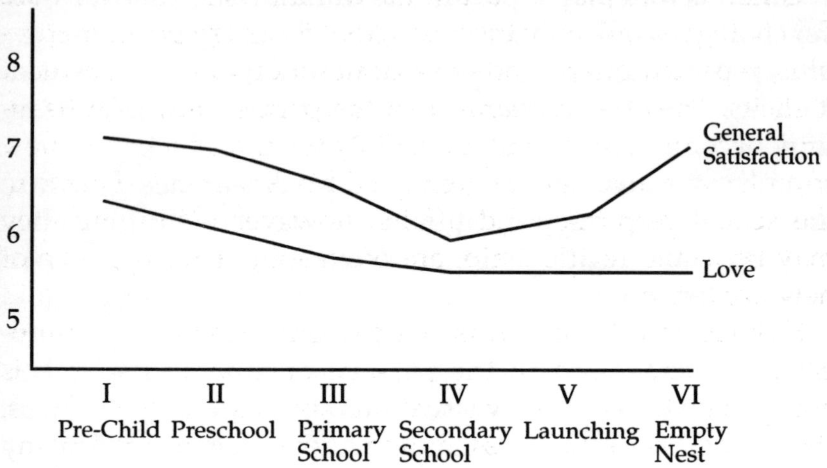

Marital satisfaction and love over family life cycle.

love, than she receives, though she is relatively more satisfied with the material aspects of marriage and with her experiences of motherhood. It can be seen that the British study distinguishes between satisfaction and love. Recent research at One Plus One suggests that there is a distinction between marital satisfaction, based on marital interaction, and personal love in the feelings for each other. It was also found that, in general, working-class marriages showed lower levels of satisfaction throughout. Those who married under the age of twenty showed an early decline in satisfaction compared with those marrying later.

It can thus be seen that a number of studies, both in the United States and in Britain, show a decrease in marital satisfaction starting from the beginning of marriage. In the British study a specific drop in love and sexual satisfaction was noted.

Apart from the arrival of children, how can we explain this decrease in marital satisfaction and its equivalence in love? Clearly the giddy heights of being in love cannot be sustained over decades and the return of satisfaction after the children leave home suggests that, although children are a source of satisfaction, they also dilute the intimacy of the couple.

Other factors play a part in the diminution of satisfaction. Psychologists talk of habituation; that is, a very positive stimulus, repeated often, leads to a diminution of the excitement it elicits. Thus the appearance of the partner, however beautiful, becomes less stimulating. Only the introduction of new stimuli can evoke new excitement. This is particularly true in the sexual response, and affairs, however disturbing they may be to the relationship, are often sought for the sake of new excitement.

Habituation, however, is not the only reason for diminished excitement. With the passage of time, the spouse is going to be tested in new situations such as economic stress, the in-laws, serious illness, moving house, ageing and many other everyday events. Some of these will be handled efficiently; others will be a source of disappointment. This disappointment will spill over into the relationship and will reduce the gratification experienced.

Longitudinal studies indicate that, over time, change is more common than stability. In particular, it has been found that the younger an individual is when he or she marries, the more likely he or she is to alter beliefs and values in subsequent years, so that they become unrecognisable, leading to the remark 'This is not the person I married'. Changes in marriage may also be due to the fact that during courtship men and women summon the will to be extra nice, co-operative, loving and sexy, which they do not sustain once the routine of marriage is reached.

Finally, when we look at psychoanalytic explanations, we find that dynamic psychologists postulate that when we marry, we engage the conscious and unconscious parts of our partner. A deprived individual not only marries a partner who is suitable in socioeconomic terms but may seek an emotional response of affection from their partner. As time passes, these unconscious needs emerge and the spouse begins to see in their partner a needy person, who is quite different from the man or woman they married. These unconscious needs for emotional affection and security make heavy demands of which there is little warning at the beginning of the marriage.

It can thus be seen that, although many couples cohabit nowadays in the hope of anticipating subsequent marital difficulties, this is unlikely to overcome all the problems that lead to the reduction of satisfaction over time. Apart from children, the couple have to face change in their values and beliefs, the dilution of excitement with habituation, challenging new situations that may disappoint, and new needs arising out of the unconscious. All these offer a tremendous challenge to the relationship and a number of couples succumb to the strain.

Before closing this chapter, there is one more research finding that merits attention and that is the gender difference in marital satisfaction.

> There are few findings more consistent, less equivocal, more convincing than the sometimes spectacular and always impressive superiority on almost every index – demographic, psychological or social – of married men over never-married men. Despite all the jokes about marriage in which men indulge, all the complaints they lodge against it, it is one of the greatest boons for their sex.[13]

On the other hand, more wives than husbands report marital frustration and dissatisfaction. More report negative feelings; more wives than husbands report marital problems; more wives consider their marriage unhappy, have considered divorce or separation, and have regretted their marriage; and, as we have seen, fewer report positive companionship.[13]

We have seen in this chapter that marital satisfaction drops dramatically in the early years and until the children have left home, and that wives are proportionally more dissatisfied. It remains to be seen over the next four chapters what factors contribute to the viability of the relationship.

CHAPTER 9

Basic Needs

In the last chapter it was shown that the heightened, ecstatic state of falling in love wanes gradually over the childbearing years and reaches its nadir when the children are adolescent, from which point there is a climb to higher satisfaction, understood here as love.

But what keeps the couple together for these twenty-five years or so? There is no textbook to describe the loving or companionate love during these years. The author has analysed, in several publications, [1, 2] what he considers loving to be during these years, and this will be described in the next few chapters. In the meantime we need to look at what research has found out about basic human needs that have to be met in intimacy.

Murray visualised the personality and interpersonal relations as an intricate interplay of needs and press.[3] According to Murray a need is an internal force which structures perception, appreciation, intellect, thinking and action, so as to produce a recurrently desired state. These desired states include affiliation, aggression, dominance, exhibition, nurturance, order, play, sex, succour and understanding. The term 'press' he uses to denote an external opportunity or obstacle to express these needs.

Recently Maslow has looked into the same issue and has visualised the personality as operating on a hierarchy of personal needs, varying from basic security up to more advanced needs for belonging, esteem and self-actualisation.[4]

These theories refer to a large number of basic needs that

have to be met in personal relationships. Jung,[5] Rogers[6] and Kelly[7] reduce this multiplicity to one basic tendency, namely self-realisation. Yet another theorists, and the ones we are going to concentrate on, posit a dualistic meeting of needs. Though the dualism is described in different ways, it is generally understood as a distinction between a general motivational tendency towards agency/power/excitement and a contrasting one towards communion/intimacy/joy. Bakan summed up this dualistic approach in two words: agency and communion.[8] Agency refers to the person's attempts to consolidate their individuality, to separate from others, to master their surroundings, and to assert, protect and expand the self. Communion refers to the person's attempts to lose their individuality by merging with others, to participate in a 'larger organism' of which they are a part, and to surrender the self through contact, openness and co-operation.

In the chapters that follow, this background dualistic concept of separateness and closeness should be kept in mind in the various categories of characteristics that define loving. The loving that occurs in the aftermath of falling in love has been described by the author under sustaining, healing, growth and sexuality.[1, 2] Under sustaining I describe five factors that are crucial to the moment-to-moment relationship of the couple. These are communication, availability, demonstration of affection, affirmation and resolution of conflict. Under healing is the way the two personalities of the couple interact, so that there is a potential healing process between the two. Under growth is the way that the couple react to each other's development over time, and finally there is the central place of sexuality in their loving.

There is no agreement as to what are the essentials of loving in the lives of couples, and the author has drawn these characteristics from research evidence and clinical experience. Readers may be interested to compare what is stated here with their own experiences.

PART II

Loving as Sustaining

CHAPTER 10

Communication

Central to the theme of this book is that personal relationships, expressed in the intimacy of marriage for the majority and in other forms such as permanent cohabitation for a minority, have shifted from emphasising action in terms of social roles – such as bread-winning and leadership for men, childbearing and rearing and homemaking for women – to an emotional interplay where feelings predominate. This does not mean that action is not important, but it does mean that, in the final analysis, men and women evaluate each other by the quality of feelings through which they experience one another. In this exchange of feelings, communication stands supreme. The way women and men talk and their understanding of each other is a principal way of expressing their feelings to each other. In this chapter, I shall describe some aspects of gender communication, self-disclosure and non-verbal communication.

GENDER COMMUNICATION

There are many stereotypes of how men and women talk to each other. Women are supposed to talk too much, interrupt often and nag, and men are purported to be the strong and silent ones. Amongst the many linguistic experts, Deborah Tannen, in her book *You Just Don't Understand*,[1] has come nearest to explaining some of the main differences in the way men and women communicate and what follows owes much to her research.

INTIMACY AND INDEPENDENCE

Conversation, according to Tannen, is connected with two things: intimacy and independence. Intimacy is the key in a world of connection when individuals negotiate complex networks of friendship, minimise differences, try to reach consensus and avoid the appearance of superiority. In the context of independence, status is of great importance. Status is a means of telling others what to do. Though everyone needs both intimacy and independence, women tend to focus on intimacy, and men on independence. The implications of this are extensive. Tannen says, 'It is as if life blood ran in different directions.'

Men, in conversation, are often concerned with position and power. Is the other person trying to be one up or put me down? Is he trying to establish a dominant position by getting me to do his bidding? Whereas women are more concerned with connections in the relationship. Is the other person trying to get closer or to pull away? Since both elements are often present it is easy for men and women to emphasise different aspects of the conversation. Tannen again says, 'If women speak and hear a language of connection and intimacy, while men speak and hear a language of status and independence, then communication between men and women can be like cross-cultural communication, prey to a clash of conversational styles. Instead of different dialects it has been said they speak different "genderlects".'

The different approach to talking, between men and women, is vital for meaning. Much meaning in conversation is not about the words spoken, but about the way these words are interpreted. Thus the sexes decide whether what is spoken is said in the spirit of different status or that of symmetrical connection. Let me illustrate these differences by some examples. Many men are inclined to call women 'Nags'. Why is this? Women often do what is asked of them, whereas men are likely to resist even the slightest hint that they will do what they are asked, which they interpret as orders. Women tend to repeat their requests, hence the reputation for nagging, because they are convinced that their man will do what he is asked if he really understands that she really wants him to do it. The man, however, who does not apparently want to obey orders, will delay doing what he is asked until he chooses, in order that he may think he is in control and doing it of his own free will. The result is nagging: each time she requests, he puts it off, leading to repeated requests.

Another example is giving help. Many people who offer help are surprised when it is refused. In so far as help aids the person who is helped, it shows generosity and caring, but at the same time it may convey the message that the helper has superior assets, which makes the receiver look inferior. My help may send the message, 'I am more competent than you'. The same applies to protection. However, a protective gesture from a man to a woman denotes traditional norms and so may be more acceptable; when it is the other way round, a woman protecting a man, this may be resisted because women normally protect children, and men are put in the position of feeling childish.

An extension of protection is the solution of problems. Men and women are often frustrated by the way they respond to each other's signals of help. For a man, life is problem-solving. Men, listening to a woman's problem, itch to offer a solution and they often complain that women refuse to take action to solve the problems they complain about. But, while women are grateful for a man to mend their practical problems, they may not want a fix for their emotional ones. For most women, talking about a problem is a request for understanding. What they want to hear is, 'I know how you feel', or 'I felt the same way when something similar happened to me'. In other words, trouble talk is meant to reinforce rapport. Women feel frustrated when they do not get this message, but instead a different one, namely 'You have the problem and I have the solution'. By giving advice, the man appears to be more knowledgeable, more reasonable, more in control – in a word, one up. Women tend to show understanding of another woman's feelings. When men give reassurance, women feel that their feelings are belittled or discounted. They feel a distance from the man, not intimacy.

Finally, in connection with giving help, there is the point of asking and giving information. There is the standard story of the couple who are in the car and getting later and later arriving at their destination as the husband, who is the driver, goes round and round in circles, refusing to ask for instructions. For men, asking and receiving information in these circumstances is a sign of inferiority. Men, who often see relations as hierarchical, construe the eliciting of information as a sign of weakness. The person who is giving the information is seen as the expert, superior in knowledge, and the receiver as uninformed, inferior in knowledge and one step down the ladder of the superiority–inferiority index.

When relations are seen in terms of hierarchy and status, then apologising is a very pertinent matter. A regular story in marriage counselling is that husbands find it difficult to apologise. Wives apologise more easily and more frequently. Wives do not always say 'sorry' as an expression of regret, they may say 'sorry' as a token of feeling sorry for the predicament that has befallen the other person. But the difficulty that men have in apologising often has to do with their interpretation of reality in terms of status. Saying sorry means that they accept they are in the wrong and thus they lose face.

MEN AND WOMEN TALKING

Women are believed to talk too much, but Tannen insists that study after study shows that it is men who talk more at meetings, in mixed-group discussions, and where boys and girls are in close proximity in educational settings. When a public lecture is followed by questions from the floor, or a radio programme opens the phones, the first voice to be heard is likely to be that of a man. So who does talk more, men or women? This difference is resolved when speaking is divided into public and private. Men feel more comfortable when speaking publicly, whereas women feel more at ease when they speak privately. Another way to distinguish the two is by describing men's talk as report and women's as rapport. For most men, talking is primarily the means of maintaining independence and status in a hierarchical social order. Talk in this way shows knowledge and skill. Men talk to 'attract and keep attention on themselves'. For most women, talking is rapport, a way of establishing connections and negotiating relationships.

If men do talk more than women, why do men persistently believe that it is women who do more talking? Very likely because they hear women talking in circumstances where they themselves would not, such as at home, when their wives speak over the phone or with their friends – in other words, on the occasions of private speaking. Home is the setting for the picture of the silent man and the talkative wife, but this is not the picture when the couple is out socialising. When couples have guests or are visiting, the husband cannot stop talking, leading to another common complaint of wives, 'He seems to have a lot to say to everyone else and nothing to say to me'.

For women, talk is the glue that holds relationships together. For men, relationships are held together by action. Men do things together or talk about activities that interest them, such as sport, work, money or politics.

These differences make the home a place for separate experiences in conversation between spouses. For many men, the comfort of home means the freedom from action, from having to prove themselves and impress through verbal display. They are free to remain silent. For women, home is a place where they are free to talk and where they feel the greatest need to talk to their nearest and dearest. For them, the freedom of home is to talk without being judged. Men's interest in the details of politics, news and sport is reciprocated by women's interest in the details of personal lives. If women are afraid of not knowing what is happening in the world of persons, men are afraid of being left out by not knowing what is going on in the world at large.

When men do talk at home, they can turn the conversation into a lecture, with the husband lecturing his wife on some subject or other on which he feels he is an expert. The act of giving information when the husband lectures gives him the feeling of being of a higher status, while the act of listening appears to give the women a sense of being inferior. But when women listen to men, they are not thinking of status, they are concerned with relationship connections and establishing rapport; however, these intentions, when interpreted through the lens of status, can be misinterpreted, putting women in the subordinate position.

Of course, men are not always talking and women are not always listening. But, by and large, men like lecturing, in an exchange of knowledge and information, whereas women are concerned with establishing and affirming relationships.

CONFLICT

We have seen that, according to Tannen, women use communication to focus on connection and the formation of community, whereas men use it as the means of negotiating power and status. Thus, in her words, 'To most women conflict is a threat to connection, to be avoided at all costs. Disputes are settled without direct confrontation, but to many men conflict is the necessary means by which status is negotiated, so that it is to be accepted and may even be sought, embraced, or enjoyed.'

This different approach to conflict has implications for the stability and satisfaction of married life. Wives want their husbands to feel part of a team, the couple, and may use the language of 'Let's do this or that'. Often this is taken by the husband, not in the spirit of a proposal but, in line with Tannen's view, with the word 'Let's' being interpreted as an order or command. Under these circumstances, men complain that their independence and freedom are being assailed. Their early-warning system is geared to detect signs that they are being told what to do. This surprises women, who cannot easily understand that men naturally resist attempts to control them and to determine their behaviour. This natural tendency to resist suggestions by wives tends to become far more acute when the man has been raised in an authoritarian environment, when as a child he was frequently told what to do.

This view of the sexes has given rise to the myth of the henpecked husband. Men resist any inkling that their wives want them to do things, which they interpret as orders. Women, on the other hand, have been traditionally subject to the needs and demands of others, their children and husbands, and there is no 'rooster-pecked wife' syndrome. Women expect their actions to be influenced by others. Their concern is to keep the ties strong, to keep everyone in the community and accommodate to others' needs. If a man struggles to be strong and independent, a woman struggles to keep the community strong.

If Tannen is right, and there is this idiosyncratic difference between the sexes, it explains a great deal of the conflict that is seen in marriages during the middle years. In the absence of understanding the different approach that couples take to communication, the reason for an argument is found in some conflict between the partners, but, before the actual conflict is reached, there is an innate sensitivity on the part of men that makes them rebel at the slightest suggestion of being told what to do. Sociologists watch this tussle and see it in terms of a power struggle, but there is a more basic issue of affiliation and independence, of togetherness and separateness. Loving, for a man, involves strict appreciation by his wife of his independence, autonomy and status. Loving, for the wife, implies that she is recognised as a partner, a member of a team, that she is in affiliation with her husband.

In this struggle between the sexes, one of the most sensitive elements is interruption. Interruption is particularly painful in close relationships when we seek to be understood. It is generally accepted that men interrupt more than women and this makes sense when conversation is often seen by men as sparring, fighting for position, with issues of dominance and control. Interruption can be a way of transferring the initiative from the speaker to the person who interrupts, who in turn takes control. Men, who see interruption as part of the warfare of power and control of conversation, expect, of course, to be resisted, but women, who do not see conversation in these terms, feel interrupted, dismissed, rejected. Furthermore, in conversations which emphasise the rationality of the exchange, interruption is a point of order to challenge the logic of a statement, but, if the emphasis is on the exchange of feelings, an approach favoured by women, logical interruptions are experienced as dismissals of the feelings expressed. This exchange is often to be seen when a husband continuously interrupts to elicit the rationality of the communication and his wife feels defeated because her emphasis is on emotions and sentiments.

Tannen's theory, which sees communication between the sexes as a battle between power and affiliation, is highly relevant in the world of loving in marriage, because every exchange by a couple leaves a residue of either being understood, reached, affirmed, or misunderstood, alienated or rejected. Thus, at the heart of ordinary conversation are contained the seeds of acceptance or uncertainty, reception or dismissal. When the centre of marriage is a loving reciprocity, the importance of Tannen's findings cannot be exaggerated.

SELF-DISCLOSURE

Tannen offers an overview of the exchange of information between the sexes, in which communication is governed by certain innate expectations of the couple, but the difficulties of status and connections may be minimised if the mutual disclosures of the couple are so clear that they remove the anxieties of men and women. When self-disclosure is done well, it takes a lot of the guess-work out of interpersonal communication. Ideally, disclosure should inform and affirm each whilst reducing the inherent fears of men and women outlined above. Self-disclosure is about telling another, in this case the spouse, about oneself. It concerns offering one's thoughts and feelings for the perusal of the other and hoping that a truly open communication is established.

Altman and Taylor consider self-disclosure a vital aspect for relationship progression.[2] At the beginning of a relationship, breadth of disclosure on many topics is the rule, but depth, related to intimacy, develops as the relationship continues. In the maintenance of continuing relationships, self-disclosure plays a vital role. We need to know and be known. Jourard,[3] who is considered the psychological father on the subject of self-disclosure, felt that the physical and psychological health of individuals, as well as the quality of the relationship, depended on the ability of self-disclosure to remove the social masks with which people relate.

A consistent finding of self-disclosure is its reciprocity.[4] Disclosure by one partner prompts self-disclosure from the other.[5] This applies to the initial stages of a relationship, but how does it work in established married relationships, which we are considering here? The evidence is somewhat contradictory. Morton found spouses to be less reciprocal in self-disclosure than strangers,[6] but Hendrick[7] and Komarovsky[8] found spouses to be highly reciprocal.

Self-disclosure in marriage is a subtle matter. Is it good to tell one's partner every little secret? Gilbert suggested that there was a dichotomy between security and intimacy needs in a marriage, with security threatened by too much self-disclosure, and intimacy fostered by it.[9] Self-disclosure depends on the knowledge and trust one has of one's partner. Are they likely to accept, understand and tolerate every bit of information imparted to them, or are they likely to create havoc with particular aspects of it? After a certain point of self-disclosure is reached, the costs of intimacy may be too high so that it is no longer wise to indulge in it. Self-disclosure means different things to a married couple at different times in their relationships. For example, if a piece of self-disclosure is used against one at a later date, then one becomes circumspect about what one reveals.

Nevertheless links have been drawn between self-disclosure and marital satisfaction. Burke et al. found that the greater the likelihood of disclosure, the greater was the marital and general life satisfaction.[10]

Different reasons were given by spouses for not disclosing to each other. Wives who did not disclose did not want to bother their husbands, or felt their husbands *would* not understand; husbands, on the other hand, felt their wives *could* not understand. Hendrick also found a positive relationship between a couple's marital satisfaction and self-disclosure.[7] The same research found that the more the wife disclosed, the more satisfied the husband was and vice versa. Hendrick also found a negative relationship between self-disclosure and years of marriage, probably because, as couples continue in their marriage, they become sensitive to the aspects of their behaviour which displease their partner and they keep these to themselves. Another area of research found different expressions of self-disclosure in happy and unhappy marriages. Komarovsky found that high levels of disclosure are not always associated with marital satisfaction.[8] Couples who disclosed a great deal but were still unhappy, revealed negative material. In these unhappy situations, wives were more likely to divulge negative information than husbands. In a similar finding, Levinger and Senn showed that marital satisfaction was highly related to the disclosure of positive rather than negative feelings.[11] Satisfied couples tend to disclose positive, important things, and less happy couples tend to talk about negative things of every level of importance.

In general it can be said that disclosure is good for a marriage – but not disclosure about everything, especially negative information, not all the time and not for every couple. As already shown, communication needs change during the life cycle of a relationship. Self-disclosure is high at the beginning and thereafter there is a balance between security and intimacy needs. Sometimes self-disclosure may deepen intimacy; at other times it may threaten security, but clearly the goal for couples is to achieve a degree of mutual trust, so that they can reveal their innermost secrets without threat. However, this requires hard work and is not always achieved. Spouses worry about what their partner will think of them if they reveal something negative and, if their self-esteem is low or their partner is judgemental, then disclosure can have negative effects. In the end, each couple will discover what suits them in the way of disclosure at different stages in their relationship, seeking all the time the highest degree of mutual frankness that is possible.

So far it has been suggested that self-disclosure is a primary element in initiating and developing relationships. Altman has also proposed privacy as a factor of importance.[12] In this context it is postulated that relationships contain both openness and closedness, both accessibility and inaccessibility, and also stability and change. Particularly in marriages of long duration there are periods of stability with a balance between openness and closedness, and periods of change when openness becomes more pronounced. The level of mutual revelation is not the same at all times. For example, at a time of crisis, disclosure of feelings is more pronounced, as a couple exchange the pangs of pain and anxiety. At other times, when life is going through a patch of routine, there is stability with a minimum of communication. Thus marital relationships, like all relationships, are characterised by forces towards contact or openness, and at other times by separateness or closedness; and forces towards stability or consistency and towards variety or change.

This complementarity produces satisfaction and a feeling of mutual closeness. The trouble comes when one of the couple needs different reactions from that offered by the partner. A wife wants to share an urgent matter with her husband, who says 'Not now, dear – later'. Some wives, put off in this way, become more and more disturbed and pin down their husband when he cannot escape, often in bed at night. In counselling, husbands often complain that they are kept awake until the early hours of the morning by their wife who wants to know the answer to some particular matter there and then. Very often the issue in question is whether their husband loves them. In desperation the husband says, 'Of course I love you, I am here.' But this does not convince the wife, who replies, 'You have nowhere else to go and where would you find a better cook and housewife?' And the exchange continues to the early hours of the morning with the husband feeling exhausted.

This example has the wife in charge, demanding answers from her husband. Some of the most interesting but contradictory research has been carried out in the gender differences of self-disclosure. Several studies have suggested that women disclose more than men,[7] whereas other studies reveal no gender differences.[13, 14] Just as important as the amount of disclosure is the person to whom the revelation is made. Women will disclose to same-sex friends, whereas men will disclose more in potentially romantic relationships. Jorgensen and Gaudy,[15] assessing over a hundred married couples, found that both disclosures given to a partner and disclosures that one perceived were given by a partner were positively related to marital satisfaction. At the heart of mutual disclosure lies not only information, which enlarges our knowledge of the person we love, but also the mutual trust engendered by the fact that we are entrusted with the inner being of that person. Ultimately, through self-disclosure, we return to a state where we feel that we are known and understood as our mother and then our father knew and understood us, completely and thoroughly. By stages we get to the point where our inner world is appreciated without communication, when we are instantly understood by a look, a touch. Then the absence of communication is not a barrier but a mystery of union, when we are truly one.

When one listens to the problems presented by couples in difficulties, one of the commonest is the inability to communicate and with this comes an alienation that deeply erodes their love for one another. So far, we have seen that communication between spouses depends on understanding the emphasis they place on the words exchanged, whether it refers to status or connection;[1] and that communication is deepened further by self-disclosure, which binds the couple, but, after many years together, may also threaten. It is now appropriate to move to the third dimension, non-verbal communication.

NON-VERBAL COMMUNICATION

Normally we emphasise verbal communication, but non-verbal signals, such as looks, touch, smiling, head nods, postural shifts, and gestures, all have their meaning. For married couples, the level of non-verbal involvement can provide an important indicator of the quality of the relationship. Beier and Sternberg interviewed couples with different degrees of agreement and disagreement.[16] Those with low levels of disagreement displayed patterns of (1) sitting close to each other, (2) higher levels of mutual gazing, and (3) more frequent touching of the partner.

Touch in close relationships may be used in a number of ways to show positive feelings. Jones and Yarbrough showed a variety of ways that touch can be used in close relationships.[17] Firstly, there is support, which serves to nurture, reassure, or promise protection to the spouse. Secondly, appreciation signals gratitude from the person who is doing the touching, often accompanied by the word 'Thanks'. Thirdly, inclusion touches, such as holding hands or putting an arm round the partner, emphasise the closeness or intimacy between the participants. Fourthly, sexual interest is shown by touching any part of the body, but especially the chest, pelvis or buttocks. In general, high levels of mutual gazing are present in couples who are in love,[18] and married couples show more frequent affectionate touches.

Conflict or apathy in a relationship is often reflected in decreased non-verbal involvement between the partners. One word of caution is needed in the assessment of non-verbal affection between married couples: their intimacy may be so well established that they do not need to touch one another. What happens, however, as the married relationship extends, is that they can infer the inner world of each other from a minimum of clues. A change in facial expression may tell the wife something important about her husband's reaction that would be lost to strangers. In the same way, in bed, couples signal to each other that they want to make love with a touch, without words, which is well understood.

Touch, in the form of hugs, embraces, and holding each other tightly, is also the response to fear, grief or rejoicing and sportsmen are often seen holding one another after they have scored a goal. Within the family, married partners embrace each other for reassurance, rejoicing or celebration. Hugs, kisses and laughter are ways of indicating the sharing of good news. Research has shown that husbands with high marital adjustment are more accurate in decoding their spouse's non-verbal messages and that these husbands are better at sending positive messages. In general, non-verbal communication deepens with the passage of time and is a shorthand of loving which needs no words. It is also of value when two people do not share the same language or when words become impossible through illness.

MODELS OF MESSAGE EXCHANGE

So far we have looked at gender differences of language, self-disclosure and non-verbal communication. But research workers have gone further and proposed several models of actual message exchanges.

1. Behaviour-exchange model. This model is based on the belief that couples assess their relationship in terms of costs and rewards. At the heart of this world is a comparison between positive and negative exchanges. Positive exchanges would include agreeing, joking, compromising and affirming, whereas negative exchanges consist of nagging, criticising or complaining. The greater the ratio of positive to negative exchanges, the happier the marriage is presumed to be. This ratio is certainly important, but couples in unhappy marriages appear to be more sensitive to negative exchanges. They notice and remember the bad times more than happy couples do.[19]

2. Behaviour-competency model. This model proposes that marital unhappiness takes place when spouses do not know how to express feelings to each other, how to argue constructively or how to develop ways of coping with normal life stresses.[20] This is an optimistic model, because couples can be taught these skills.

3. Social-learning model. This model puts the emphasis on social reinforcement,[21] which means giving a reward that strengthens the behaviour. Examples of positive reinforcement include attention, and affection in terms of a hug or a kiss or a smile. Positive reinforcement is offered by a spouse in the form of a pleasant reaction after the spouse has done something welcomed by the partner. Negative reinforcement implies the removal of an unpleasant stimulus after the behaviour has been performed. For example, a spouse nags the partner to do something and when this is done the nagging stops.

4. Structural model of interaction. This model owes a great deal to Gottman,[22] who tested and supported three hypotheses. The first one argues that unhappily married couples are more rigid and inflexible in their communication than happy ones. The second suggests that unhappy couples express more negativity, both verbally and non-

verbally, than do happy couples. The third infers that, although there is no difference in the reciprocity in positive messsages between happy and unhappy couples, the latter more often reciprocate negative messages. So that, in all types of marriages, a compliment produces a compliment; but a sarcastic remark begs a sarcastic remark only amongst the unhappily married. There is thus clear evidence that happily and unhappily married couples communicate differently and part of healing is to change this pattern.

CHAPTER 11

Availability

In Chapter 2 we saw that the baby forms a basic bond with the mother, which lays down a pattern of affective attachment from cradle to grave. This attachment gives the child a basic security, affection and a safe centre from which to explore the world around it. Thus closeness and availability become central in our life of love, and the amount of time we spend together with our spouse is a crucial feature of marital happiness.

Another theorist, Homans,[1] has shown that, except when two people are rivals, the more frequently two persons interact with each other, the greater their affection for each other. Greater affection, in turn, leads to greater interaction and so a positive cycle is brought about.

Turning to marriage, exchange theory maintains that shared leisure activities reflect rewarding interactions that draw spouses together and contribute to marital happiness. Exchange theory is frequently used in the sociology and psychology of relationships. Essentially, an exchange is an 'act of giving or taking one thing in return for another as an equivalent, i.e. trade or barter'. In personal relations, the balance between rewards and costs is the crucial factor maintaining the relationship.

It is hypothesised that marital interaction has a positive effect on marital happiness.[2,3] This proposition has been confirmed by Hill,[4] who found that greater companionship and more shared activities are associated with greater marital happiness. Levinger and Roper (cited in Orthner and

Mancini)[5] found that companionship is reported to be a top priority in marital life.

Couples who are dissatisfied with their marriage are also found to have spent little time in joint activities.[6] Kingston and Nock argue that, although the absolute amount of time couples spend together has no effect on the quality of interaction, the time does provide a resource that can be used to create positive interaction.[7] Therefore, they conclude that the greater the amount of togetherness, the happier the marriage.

There is no doubt that the research literature provides evidence of the link between physical togetherness and marital happiness, which in this book is interpreted as the presence of love, and so togetherness is treated as a contributory factor to love. As previously stated, the awareness of the presence of the spouse gives a feeling of security and a basis from which to carry on with one's own activities, whilst feeling at peace. In counselling, the complaint about the absent husband who is perpetually late in the evening, works at the weekends or for some other reason is not available, is very common. Wives feel 'widowed' by their husband's absence and, at times, unloved.

Another growing concern has been the impact of time constraints on marital happiness, due to the increase in labourforce participation.[8, 9, 10, 11] Less time for leisure and less time for one another have changed family patterns. Research workers have taken a close look at the reciprocal relationship between marital happiness and marital interaction – that is, the time a couple spend in joint activity.

What follows are the findings of two American studies, by White[12] and Zuo[13]. White's study begins by referring to Burr's remarks that the proposition that spousal interaction had a positive impact on marital happiness was so obvious and so commonplace that he could not find it explicitly stated or tested in the literature.[2] Before White's study in 1983, research had begun on this relationship, but there was some confusion as to whether spouse interaction was a cause, a consequence or a part of marital happiness.

The data of White's study come from a nationwide telephone survey of 2034 married men and women. Measurement of spousal interaction was estimated in relation to a list of five activities. The men and women were asked how often they and their spouse ate their main meal together, went shopping together, visited friends together, went out in the evening together, or worked around the house together. In their sample, the least interaction was shopping (42 per cent) and the greatest was eating together (90 per cent).

The work involvement of both husbands and wives has a negative effect on marital interaction, although the link is more pronounced when husbands work long hours than when wives do. Spouses' interaction is significantly reduced when husbands work long hours and when either husbands or wives have irregular work schedules – for example, evening meetings, or shift-work.

The presence of children is an important factor in the interaction of spouses. The number of children in the home, but not particularly preschoolers, significantly reduced the amount of husband–wife interaction.

Finally a traditional division of household labours does significantly reduce spousal integration. In summary it was found that a traditional division of labour in the home, a large number of children and a busy husband reduce interaction, whether or not wives are working.

When it came to the measurement of marital happiness, more areas were studied. These were: the extent of understanding, the amount of love and affection received, agreement with the spouse, sexual relationships, the spouse's relationship with children, the spouse as a breadwinner, the spouse as someone who takes care of things around the house, the spouse to do things with, the spouse's faithfulness, and happiness with home.

The findings of this study confirm that there is a positive relationship between interaction and a marital satisfaction, but a major finding of the study was the importance of marital happiness for marital interaction. The study shows that the most important determinant of interaction is not time constraints, such as work hours or the presence of children, but the quality of the marriage. This study confirms the impact of marital interaction on marital happiness, but the even stronger effect of marital happiness on marital interaction.

Zuo repeated the study and confirmed White's findings.[13] In his words, 'The amount of time that a couple share in joint activities is not solely a function of macro-social structures (that is, work, children, labour division). It is also a result of the extent to which individuals are happy with their marriage... The present study indicates that individuals who have a satisfactory marriage find ways to create time for one another.'

The amount of time couples spend together is not the only factor that matters. In fact, couples adjust to a balance of closeness and separateness on a daily basis and over a long time. The interaction needs to be meaningful. A couple can sit together and the husband goggles at television or reads the newspaper and does not take the slightest notice of his wife or children. A meaningful interaction is not only one in which couples are in each other's presence, but also one in which they derive pleasure from this presence. They can be silent in each other's presence but feel that they are in touch with each other's inner world. This means that availability is not only physical but also emotional – that is to say, the couple are in touch with each other's mood and feelings and they can respond to each other in a reciprocal manner of understanding. Couples can be in contact but angry or tense, in a state of misunderstanding or conflict.

Research workers concerned with interaction have found that the physiological state of spouses – that is, their blood pressure, heart-beat, pulse and respiration, or their state of arousal – matters in the relationship. Couples become aroused when they are threatened, in what has been called the 'fight or flight' syndrome. Biologically this arousal prepares us to stay and fight or to run away. This biological theory of arousal shows that, despite availability, there is a fundamental difference between husbands and wives as to how they interact. Husbands are physiologically aroused more easily than wives, particularly in tense situations and are slower to calm down afterwards.[14, 15] This finding contradicts the view of the highly emotional wife. Extreme physiological arousal leads the husband to withdraw from the marital relationship and can lead to the collapse of the marriage. The arousal of the husband, his withdrawal and the pursuit by his wife is a negative cycle often described in counselling situations.

Pursuing the study of what maintains a loving relationship in a companionate marriage: after communication, availability – and positive availability at that – plays an important role.

CHAPTER 12

Affection

Reciprocal affection is an important element of love. We have seen, in the model of love as attachment, that the young baby experiences affection when it is touched, stroked, hugged, talked to, and picked up when in distress, and these signals remain pertinent throughout life for married couples. After wanting to be with one another, couples yearn for demonstration of affection. But demonstration of affection falls after the initial excess. Counsellors are accustomed to hearing the following conversation in their offices.

> WIFE: He never tells me he loves me.
> HUSBAND (looking puzzled): I told you I loved you twenty-five years ago, why do you want to hear it again? If I change my mind, I will let you know.

But silent presence is not enough. Women who have affairs often complain of the lack of affection in their lives.

What follows are observations, including examples, based on a chapter called 'Vision of Romantic Love' in the book *The Psychology of Love* by N. Branden.[1] He describes certain behaviours which reflect successful couples' lives. Couples who remain happily in love over long periods of time more consistently exhibit these behaviours.

1. *They tend to express love verbally.* The words used are personal and can simply be 'I love you' or they can refer to the special nickname reserved for each other. 'A woman said, "Saying the words is a way of touching. Words nurture

feelings, keep love strong and in the forefront of the relationship". Her husband commented, "Saying 'I love you' is a form of self-expression. It is putting a bit of yourself out there, so my feelings are in reality, not just inside me."'

2. *They tend to be physically affectionate.* Touch is one of the earliest means of experiencing security, trust and affection. We were held by our mother and held on to her in our earliest years, and when we were in distress we ran back to cling to her. 'Touch involves hand-holding, hugging, kissing, cuddling and comforting.' Both sexes enjoy the affection of touch, but women in particular crave to be held. Some women complain that their husband cannot contain touch for affection only; he wants sex and they only want affection. Thus the man wants to touch the sexual areas and the woman only wants to be embraced.

3. *They express their appreciation and admiration.* 'Happy couples talk about what they like, enjoy and admire in each other. As a result they feel visible, appreciated and valued. A wife remarked, "My husband has always been my best audience. Whether I am telling him about what I did at work that day, or a remark he liked that I made to someone at a party, or the way I dress, or a meal I have prepared – he seems to notice everything. And he lets me see his pride and delight. I feel I am standing in the most marvellous spotlight. That kind of awareness – and talking about it – is what love means to me."' Women, and men as well, appreciate being admired with regard to the clothes they wear, the food they produce, the car they have purchased, the decoration they have done and even small things like the light bulb they have changed.

4. *They offer each other an emotional support system.* 'They are for each other in times of illness, difficulty, hardship and crisis.' The importance of the availability of spouses in times of illness and crisis cannot be exaggerated. To be there when needed is a special demonstration of

affection. Wives once again complain of husbands who get paralysed when they are ill, who were absent or drunk when they had their babies, and could not support them when their relatives were ill; and these complaints abound when marriage deteriorates. These deficits are stored in the memory and gradually dilute the love for the partner or become the excuse for an affair.

'In happy marriages, men as well as women understand the importance of nurturing. Nurturing is acting to support the life and growth of the partner. To nurture is to accept each other unconditionally, to respect their mutual independence, to encourage and support their social and emotional growth and to care about each other's thoughts, feelings and needs.' Parents are accustomed to nurture their children, but often believe that adults can look after themselves. But adults are in a process of development and growth too, and need support from each other. 'A man said, "I think that one of the most important things we look for in love is one person who will be truly devoted to our interests and well-being. And that is what the other person naturally expects in return. Without that, what is love? What is marriage?"'

In the past, it was the wife who was expected to nurture the man, be there when he came home from work, attend to his physical and emotional needs and generally support him in return for her economic maintenance. In contemporary marriages, both men and women want to be nurtured, a task which some men do not find easy. The busy executive, working wife may be a giant at work, but emotionally she needs to be heard, understood, reassured, affirmed, and her self-esteem boosted. Often this support is missing from a husband who is dazzled by her professional competence and does not realise her emotional needs.

5. *They express love materially.* All the above characteristics need words and physical touch, both of which may be difficult for either partner. Husbands in particular some-

times find it difficult to verbalise intimate thoughts and feelings. There are other ways of expressing appreciation: with gifts and actions. Buying things for a spouse may be appreciated but it can also rebound. Women do not always want to be given gifts. A diamond is not necessarily a woman's best friend. Things can cheapen a relationship. Sometimes actions speak louder than words or gifts. Husbands traditionally show their affection by doing things in the house, but there are sad tales in the consulting room of kitchens started and left unfinished years later, or the DIY man who causes more havoc than order. Nevertheless actions can be substitute deeds for affection. With regard to gifts, price is not relevant; it is the intention that matters.

6. *They accept demands or put up with shortcomings.* Loving another person often means living with their limitations and doing things for them that we would not dream of doing for anyone else. In this loving relationship, the partner's virtues outweigh their shortcomings. What often happens in the middle years is that the couple take each other for granted. In this way, spouses begin to feel used. The husband complains that he is only wanted for the money he brings in, and the wife, for her services as a cook, housekeeper and provider of sex. These marriages are exhausted and the couple become ghosts of their initial romantic falling-in-love state. Such couples become alienated and the wife might turn to her children and friends for succour, and the husband might fall back on his work, and his mates at the pub or club. Sooner or later an affair will intervene because both partners are hungry for attention.

The frequent demonstration of affection is a necessary catalyst for the loving maintenance of a relationship. This affection is often linked with sex, but it has to be considered as a separate entity in its own right. For affection is an experience that starts well before puberty and extends after sexual intercourse has ceased, and is a crucial element in companionate marriage.

CHAPTER 13

Affirmation versus Negativity

Of course, couples cannot always be showing affection for one another. At times they will express negative feelings. Research has shown that there are marked differences, in the balance between positive and negative remarks, between happy and unhappy couples. Listening to couples in the consulting rooms, the phrase 'The trouble with you is ...' reverberates. Spouses in difficulty are obsessed with the negative traits of each other. In fact, spouses who wish to complain about each other's behaviour, or to point out a quality that they find irritating, should try to convey the information in the least upsetting way possible. They should couch their criticism in terms that can convey positive feelings for each other. Thus a sentence could run 'That was fine but ...', 'Well done but ...'.

Markman found that marriages in which partners were disposed to interpret each other's behaviour positively, predicted their satisfaction with their relationship several years later.[1] How do spouses in happy and unhappy marriages interpret each other's behaviour? Spouses in happy relationships make interpretations that maximise the favourable implications of positive behaviour but minimise the implications of negative behaviour. It is the other way round in unhappy marriages, which de-emphasise the favourable implications of positive behaviour, but concentrate on the unpleasant implications of negative behaviour.

To give an example of the above causal attribution, as it is technically called, a happily married man attributes his wife's warm greetings to the fact that she is a warm, affectionate, wonderful person and attributes a sharp rebuke to the fact that she has had a hard day at work. Whereas an unhappily married man receives the warm greetings with surprise and attributes it to something good that has happened to her, unconnected with him, whereas the sharp rebuke is due to the fact that she is insensitive and bad-tempered.

Causal attribution theory[2] posits the proposition that, when marriage is good, then behaviour is interpreted as coming from the inner part of the personality, it is repeatable, total, and meant to be unselfish and giving praise, whereas negative behaviour is external, incidental, unintentional, unselfish and no blame is attached. When the relationship is negative, the behaviour that is positive is transient, unrepeatable, accidental, unintentional and not worthy of praise; but when the behaviour is negative, then it comes from the inner person, is repetitive and total and therefore, intentional, selfish and blameworthy.

This theoretical position – in which happy couples expect loving behaviour and are surprised by unloving patterns, and unhappy couples expect rejection and are surprised by love – is continuously in evidence in the consulting room, where unhappy couples have come to expect negativity and are not going to shift from this expectation in a hurry. They know their partner is bad for them and, whatever they do or the counsellor says, they remain convinced in their negativity. That is why so much counselling is too late, because by the time the couple come for help they are set in their expectations of each other. Individual spouses put it a different way, which is 'Whatever I do, I am wrong and they are right'. Their spouse has made up their mind that anything that they do that is right is an accident, which is not meant, and all that they do wrong is intended all the time, eliciting the feeling 'I told you so ... the trouble with you is ... nothing good can come from you ...'. Whereas happily married couples always give each other the benefit of the doubt. Thus distressed spouses operate in a very different affective climate from non-distressed couples. For example, those in less happy marriages tend to misunderstand each other more frequently than other couples, following their inner basic expectations. There is also a clear tendency for the communication accuracy of the husband to be the critical discriminator between couples high and low in marital adjustment. Wives are much more likely to assume positivity when none was intended, whereas husbands are more likely to assume negativity when none was intended.

Extensive research shows different patterns between distressed and non-distressed couples in negativity.[3,4] Distressed spouses appear to be hypersensitive on a subjective emotional level to their partner's immediate behaviour. Not only does negative behaviour occur more frequently in distressed marriages, but when it occurs it has a deleterious affect on daily ratings of marital satisfaction. In contrast, happier couples appear to be less affected by the negative behaviour of their spouse.

Distressed couples reciprocate negative behaviour to a significantly greater degree than do non-distressed couples, indicating a tendency to escalation. It is the 'Yes, you did'/'No, I didn't' perpetual cycle. Distressed couples maintain long cycles of negative interaction, which become more and more intense as the conversation continues.

Distressed husbands and wives tend to underestimate the frequency of a spouse's positive behaviour.[5] In general, the more adjusted couples understand each other better and have lower levels of negativity. In this, better empathy and affirmation – that is to say, rewarding each other's positive behaviour – play a part. Rewarding each other in marriage is not too common. In too many marriages there is silence when things are going well and loud criticism when things go wrong. Love needs an equal voicing of affirmation and constructive criticism, and happy couples actively appreciate each other.

CHAPTER 14

Conflict

In the counselling situation, it is common to face couples who are arguing a lot and cannot resolve their conflicts. Conflict has been defined by Peterson as 'An interpersonal process that occurs whenever the actions of one person interfere with the actions of another'.[1] Couples often find themselves in situations of conflict. The reasons for the conflict are multiple, such as money, doing the chores, not having enough affection or sex, managing the children, joint activities, or personal choices.

Rapoport described conflict in terms of debates, games and fights.[2] Marital conflict occurs in all these forms. The best form is a debate in which views are exchanged and a common decision is taken. Next is the world of games, in which the competition is strong and so is the bargaining to maximise the gain. Finally there are 'fights', in which partners want to win outright and defeat their partner.

Arguments may be about specific issues but they become complicated when to the specific issue are added all the complaints they have about each other and so no resolution can take place because the exchange becomes a slanging match. Ideally couples should stick to the subject under consideration and resolve it, without expanding the issues to an all-out war.

When couples argue, there are a number of possible outcomes. The first is that the couple avoid talking about the problem. All modern insights suggest that it is better to face a conflict and talk about it rather than let it fester. The second situation is domination. The more powerful personality compels the partner to yield and the yielding is often out of fear; but giving in out of fear causes resentment, which expresses itself in other ways. In the past, when males dominated relationships, it was often the wife who had to yield, but with women's emancipation this situation is no longer operative. The third solution is compromise. Compromise takes place in most happy relations, with one spouse giving up a little and the other reciprocating, so that the conflict is limited. This can only occur when each partner accepts responsibility for his or her actions, is willing to change and does not project all the blame on to the other. This ability to accept responsibility for one's actions requires a mature personality with good self-esteem, who does not feel defeated if he or she accepts responsibility. The fourth approach is the solution in which a compromise is found in which both partners leave the conflict with their needs completely or partially met. This is very satisfying and it really implies that both husband and wife are prepared to listen and appreciate each other's point of view or need and the ensuing compromise respects both. The fifth approach and the most fundamental is that both husband and wife change in their behaviour to meet each other. This is long-term alteration in behaviour, which is done out of love for each other.

One of the basic differences in the approach to conflict, mentioned already, is how a couple view the reasons for the disagreement. A typical example is when one partner is late for an appointment. When they arrive at their destination, the person who was late offers an excuse, such as that the roads were busy. Their spouse, however, does not accept that. They see the lateness as a characteristic of the personality of their spouse. They are always late; it is their nature. The one offers an excuse, the other interprets it as a permanent feature of their personality. It takes time to reach the view that it is the personality of the spouse that is at fault, but when this conclusion is reached despair also sets in because no change is expected. Couples come to counselling when it is too late because they are convinced that their partner cannot change.

There are some interesting findings of gender differences in apportioning blame. It has already been seen that, in patriarchal-power conditions, the man is supposed to be the superior. As recently as ten years ago Hendrick found that, although husbands and wives agreed on the problems that wives contributed to the marriage, there was very low agreement on the problems that husbands contributed.[3] There is a further gender division. In marital conflict, women are more likely to engage and men to avoid. As already mentioned,[4] it has been suggested that men avoid conflict because they become physiologically aroused during arguments, and the unpleasantness of palpitations, butterflies in the stomach and sweating lead to the avoidance of conflict and to withdrawal. Withdrawal by the husband results in escalation by the wife and a recognisable vicious circle ensues.

A number of differences have also been found between distressed and non-distressed couples. Fincham et al. found that non-distressed couples tended to view their spouse's behaviour as more benign – that is, more unselfish than their own – whereas distressed couples felt their own behaviour to be more benign than that of their partner.[5] In other words, unhappy couples tend to think the worst about each other. Not only do such couples think the worst about each other but they are certain that they are right. Halford et al. note that 'The most outstanding feature of unhappy couples is their inability to terminate negative interaction ... In contrast happy couples manage to de-escalate such a process or refrain from starting it at all.'[6]

Continuing the differences between distressed and non-distressed couples, Billings noted that distressed couples showed greater reciprocity of negative behaviour and 'Among some distressed couples, the proportion of hostile communication escalates as the conflict continues'.[7] Thus the way that distressed couples perpetuate their conflict is by being oversensitive, exchanging negative remarks, escalating the negativity, becoming worse and worse as the talk continues without a satisfactory termination. Counsellors watch these endless exchanges in their consulting rooms and often find it difficult to bring them to an end. Koren et al. confirmed from questionnaire and observation data that distressed couples were more critical of each other and less responsive to each other's suggestions.[8]

Kelly et al. showed that conflict influenced satisfaction.[9] 'Conflict over time erodes the affection that partners have for one another'. Rands et al. collected data on conflict resolution and marital satisfaction from 244 married couples and found that couples who were very intimate and had little conflict were the most satisfied.[10]

Thus research has established that there are differences in the way satisfied and unsatisfied couples argue. The former have fewer quarrels, can give in gracefully, agree and terminate a quarrel before it gets out of hand. The latter argue more frequently, reciprocate negativity, enlarge the argument, escalate it, and blame each other, without being able to reach a mutually satisfying agreement.

There are many theories to explain conflict but the one selected here is relevant to the theory of love as attachment. In her book *Violent Emotions*,[11] Suzanne Retzinger proposes that at the heart of conflict is a threat to the social-emotional bond between the couple. She proposes that at the heart of conflict is a feeling of shame. She extends the feeling of shame, so that when the person becomes uncomfortable, insecure, uneasy, tense, confused, feels small, worthless, inadequate, stupid, foolish, silly, weird, helpless, weak, funny, idiotic, restless, stunned, alone, disconnected, alienated, impotent, then all these states constitute the feeling of shame which is central to her theory.

Using Bowlby's theories, she maintains that anger is the signal used to repair lost or threatened bonds. She goes on to postulate that what happens in escalated conflict is a threat to the attachment bond by the couple heaping on to each other demeaning criticism, contempt, disgust, blame and feelings of being devalued, all of which elicit shame. She maintains that, in order to bring about a de-escalation of the conflict, this shame should be acknowledged and the threat to the bond of attachment repaired. When the shame is unacknowledged, the partners project the problem and the blame on to each other in an endless vicious cycle.

In this theory, conflict is seen as a way of restoring threatened bonds via the experience of shame. Shame is not a feeling that is easily recognised, and guilt is the more common feeling that is spoken about. But when we see couples fighting each other, it is clear that in persistent fighting they are trying to protect something precious, which is the intactness of the relationship (with mutual self-respect), and the feeling that fuels the rage is that their partner is not taking them seriously. Persistent fighting is about much more than the issue involved, it is about the integrity of the relationship, Bowlby's bond of love. Spouses are saying with their anger 'You don't love me any more. If you did you would pay attention to my grievance'.

In this theory, persistent conflict is about threatened bonds. The difficulty is that the couple are obsessed with the righteousness of their case and often persistent conflict is a prelude to separation and divorce. Careful intervention may sometimes help them to see that their anger is a cry for help from each other to feel recognised, wanted and appreciated again.

To summarise, then: the occasional conflict is an inevitable part of marriage, but frequent and persistent quarrelling is a sign of dissatisfaction and a sign that love is under threat. At the centre of a quarrel appears to be a battle to be won, but the battle is to appreciate and remedy the wound that the partner is experiencing.

PART III

Personality and Loving

CHAPTER 15

Biological Origins

The personalities of the couple are central to loving. In the absence of an absolute commitment to permanency, the latter is only achieved if the couples progress in their relationship through mutual understanding, complementarity, meeting of needs and concerted action. These experiences are heavily dependent on the personalities of the couple. In this and in the next two chapters, I shall look briefly at what we know about the personality that is relevant to marriage. Central to marriage, cohabitation, indeed all sorts of intimate relationships, is a dual approach to the personality, ranging from those who believe that persons of similar temperament come together and those who think that opposites attract. Mention has already been made of this distinction. What we have to find out now is exactly what is joined together in a relationship, how we can describe the personality. There are two major sources of description of the personality, one emanating from biological sources and the other from analytical psychology. Both will be briefly described.

BIOLOGICAL ORIGINS OF THE PERSONALITY

These have their roots in ancient Greece, which elaborated the four temperaments – choleric, melancholic, phlegmatic and sanguine – words which are still used today. Since the nineteenth century, the terms extroversion and introversion have become fashionable all over the world. Today, these terms reflect a system of understanding the personality as rooted in the physiology of the brain. Experimental work has shown that extroversion is linked with resting states of low cortical arousal and introversion with states of high cortical arousal. At first sight this seems the wrong way round. The extrovert should be the one with an excitable cortex, but in fact the cortex is used mainly to inhibit the lower neurological centres and to control the messages that come from the rest of the body. The link between extroversion/introversion and relationship is that extroverts seek stimulation in terms of sex, alcohol, drugs and gambling and so they are more inclined to extramarital affairs, to become alcoholic, take drugs and gamble excessively, all of which plays havoc with the relationship. Introverts, through their moodiness and anxiety, may also contribute to marital problems.

The dimensions of extroversion and introversion are not absolute; they constitute a continuum in which a man or a woman finds a place in a circle of characteristics.

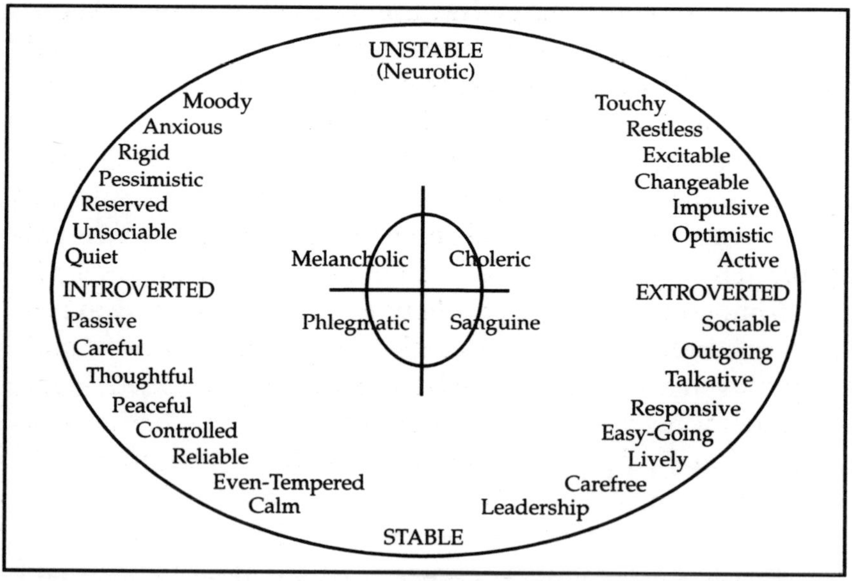

In Britain, Eysenck has been the foremost worker to emphasise the division of the personality into extroversion and introversion in one plane and neuroticism and stability in another.[1] In the diagram, the circle denotes the characteristics of extroverted and introverted people and also adds the dimension of stability and instability as neuroticism.[2]

The word neurotic is used in two ways in psychology; in the biological sense of people who are anxious, moody or depressed; and in the analytical sense of having emotional conflict and difficulties. This division also charts the way neuroticism is treated, either with medication or psychologically with various psychotherapies.

In the biological distribution of anxiety, we also have personalities whose anxiety is expressed through various phobias – for example, fear of heights, open and closed spaces, and many other situations. The obsessional personality is preoccupied with things over and over again, carries out meticulous and organised work, is fussy about details and at the same time can worry about shutting doors, putting the lights out, leaving the oven on, not switching the gas off, etc. Then there is anxiety itself, in which the personality is apprehensive about everything; and finally the histrionic personality, which exaggerates, turns crises into tragedies and dramatises the ordinary events of life. These manifestations of anxiety at their extreme end are the bread and butter of psychiatrists, but couples have to learn to live with each other's features in their everyday life. Anxiety is very common and so are the fears, obsessions and preoccupations of people. They do not normally contribute to marital difficulties. What contributes to problems is change. Thus an extrovert personality who is sociable, outgoing, talkative and lively may marry someone who is passive, controlled, calm and undemonstrative, and may find the relationship initially congenial, only slowly to change and to find the introvertedness of their partner irritating.

PSYCHOPATHIC PERSONALITY

While extroversion/introversion and neuroticism are widely distributed in the population, another type, the psychopathic personality, probably of biological or genetic origin, can and does play havoc with marriage, or indeed with any intimate relationship. Much has been written about this condition in psychiatric circles and an excellent review is to be found in Tyrer and Stein,[3] from which the remarks that follow are taken. The incidence of this condition varies from 2.1–3.4 per cent and is higher for males than for females.

These men and women have:

1. Callous unconcern for the feelings of others and lack the capacity for empathy.
2. Gross and persistent attitude of irresponsibility and disregard for social norms, rules and obligations.
3. Incapacity to maintain enduring relationships.
4. Very low tolerance of frustration and a low threshold for discharge of aggression including violence.
5. Incapacity to experience guilt and to profit from experience, particularly punishment.
6. Marked proneness to blame others and to offer plausible rationalisations for the behaviour bringing the subject into conflict with society.
7. Persistent irritability.

Clearly not all these criteria are present in the same person, and for classification purposes three or more are sufficient. In the field of marriage the overt psychopath cannot sustain relationships, but there are men and women who have less intense but similar characteristics, with whom spouses persevere for a long time. Sometimes they are rewarded because these features decrease with the passage of time. The psychopathic personality inhabits the courts and the prisons, is frequently involved in divorce and is a source of distress to himself and society. Sometimes psychopathy is disguised by a peculiar charm that is deceptive and leads to the initial union.

CHAPTER 16

Psychodynamic Origins

As stated in the previous chapter, the word neuroticism has two meanings. The first is the presence of anxiety and mood changes in a biological sense, and the second the presence of personality characteristics that arise from childhood. In this chapter, I deal briefly with the second, the world of psychodynamics.

Why is a psychodynamic theory important for contemporary marriage? Essentially the feelings we experience as a child are a transaction between ourselves and the intimate environment of childhood. Marriage, or any intimate relationship, is a reliving of this closeness and we experience our partner with the same feelings as we did our parents in childhood. Part of mature marriage relations is to learn to distinguish between the past and the present and to treat our partner as a separate person from a parental figure.

The second thing that psychodynamic theory tells us is that, where the original experience between ourselves and our parents was negative and painful, we used what are known as defences – that is, we operated in an unconscious way to relieve our stress by making our parents responsible for the pain. We repeat this as adults and we push on to our partner, again unconsciously, unwanted feelings for which we should be responsible, but for which we make our partner responsible. Thus it is not *we* who are angry, jealous, envious or sexually irresponsible, but by the technique of projection, we blame our partner. Dynamic psychotherapy for marriage is concerned to help people to see these projections on to each other and reclaim both positive and negative feelings.

FREUDIAN PSYCHOLOGY

Those who want to study the origins of Freud's works have many books to which to resort. Here the briefest outline will be given. Essentially Freud saw the origins of the human personality in the two drives of sexuality and aggression, which as instincts propel the unconscious part of the psyche, the id. These instincts are pushing for gratification and are opposed, equally unconsciously, by the super ego which is the source of moral authority in all of us. In between lies the ego, which is the conscious part of ourselves and which mediates between the id and the super ego.

These two drives, aggression and sexuality, have a desire to be gratified, and the parents play a crucial role in which the boy loves the mother and ultimately has to give her up, and the girl loves the father and, likewise, has to give him up. In the resolution of the Oedipus and Electra complexes is situated the centre for maturation, and for orthodox Freudians the unresolved conflicts from these situations go on haunting the individual in adult life and, for some, marital problems reflect these unresolved issues.

Gradually these initial theories of Freud gave way to what has come to be known as the object-relations theory, which owes a great deal to British analysts. This theory does not see the parents as the persons on whom the drives of the child are unleashed. On the contrary, they see the emerging personality of the child as an interaction between the behaviour of the parents and the response of the child.[1]

Whether we accept the orthodox Freudian view or the object-relations theory – and the majority of theorists and practitioners adopt the latter – conflict between the child and parents is inevitable, just as conflict between spouses is also inevitable. One of the essential features, as already stated, is the ability to accept responsibility for one's actions and not to blame others for damaging activity. When we cannot cope with the anxiety of trauma, we unconsciously use defences, and these continue to be used in adult life and are present in marriage. It is worth looking at these defences, which Anna Freud described as regression, repression, reaction-formation, isolation, undoing, projection, introjection, turning against the self, reversal and sublimation.[2] Of these, projection is one of the most important; in it, for example, because we cannot accept our aggression, we project the feeling on to somebody else, often our spouse, and we make them responsible for our anger. All this happens unconsciously.

THE WORK OF E.H. ERIKSON

A later worker, the American analyst Erikson,[3] gives us the experience of the child in terms we can understand. Erikson divides the person into eight ages, but I will concentrate on the early ones. Erikson speaks of acquiring 'a sense of' a given positive characteristic versus its opposite characteristic. In the first year, he refers to the sense of basic trust versus mistrust. Thus the roots of trust are acquired from the consistency of being held, fed and looked after and this trust grows into verbal veracity with the spoken word and the general trust that develops slowly, whereby we trust each other physically, emotionally and socially. We hardly need reminding that mutual trust is essential for a loving relationship in marriage.

In the second and third year, Erikson describes a sense of autonomy as against the sense of shame and early doubt. The child learns to feed, dress and walk at this stage and to control himself and his surroundings. Erikson's words are: 'From a sense of self-control without loss of self-esteem comes a lasting sense of goodwill and pride: from a sense of loss of self-control and a foreign overcontrol comes a lasting propensity of doubt and shame'. Autonomy at two or three is the precursor of that balance of dependence and independence that is central to all relationships and figures crucially in marriage.

In the third and fourth year, Erikson speaks of the child's initiative versus a sense of guilt. He says, 'There is in every child at every stage a new miracle of vigorous unfolding, which constitutes a new hope and a new responsibility'. 'Initiative adds to autonomy the quality of undertaking, planning and "attacking" a task for the sake of being active and on the move'. 'The danger of this stage is a sense of guilt over the goals contemplated and the acts initiated in one's exuberant enjoyment of new locomotor and mental power: acts of aggressive manipulation and coercion which soon go far beyond the executive capacity of organism and mind and therefore call for an energetic halt to one's contemplated initiative'.

By the age of four and five, the child's self-esteem is beginning to build up and the combination of self-esteem and initiative leads to the ability to take charge of life. In adult life, self-esteem and initiative allow us to reach out to life and to other persons and to take initiatives that are profitable in terms of monetary results, and loving in terms of personal relationships. The opposite of initiative in adult relationships is passivity through fear of doing the wrong thing. Before the child enters school it does not have to earn its self-esteem, but receives it unconditionally simply for existing and being unconditionally loved.

Finally in this childhood period, Erikson refers to industry versus inferiority. Industry is, of course, school life, where the child acquires another form of self-esteem. This second form of self-esteem is achieved by one's efforts in the industry of school life. Love is now earned through achievement. We shall see again the difference between the person who can feel good only through work and those who can feel loved for themselves in their personal relationships. These two aspects of self-esteem are fundamental in marriage, where feeling loved for simply being there contrasts with having to earn love, by being proficient in earning money, being a success, or running the home successfully. The way we grow up in our experience of being loved plays a major part in the way we allow ourselves to be loved within the intimacy of marriage.

ADULT REPERCUSSIONS OF CHILDHOOD

In this chapter the view is expressed that there is a link between childhood experiences of love and adult love responses. This is not to deny that genetic factors play a part in our development, but to accept the commonly held view that both nature and nurture play a part in our personality.

Are there some observations we can make about childhood experiences that have repercussions in the adult intimacy of marriage? By and large the following points can be made. We see in adults who had deprived childhoods a hunger for love. These men and women have been repeatedly let down by parents or parent substitutes, were usually serviced physically but did not receive affection, were not affirmed and often were heavily criticised so that they lack self-esteem. Lack of self-esteem means that they do not feel lovable and do not experience love when it is offered to them, are surprised when they are loved and find it very difficult to retain love, so that they want to be constantly reassured that they are lovable. Lack of self-esteem is also accompanied by uncertain confidence and lack of trust in oneself. These men and women find it difficult to approach others, to get close to them and to stay in intimacy.

Part of a mature upbringing, as we have seen, involves a proper respect for the other. Psychoanalysts refer to the narcissistic personality, who is obsessed with him or herself, wants constant attention, is driven by an enormous desire to be loved but cannot contain it, and who flits from relationship to relationship. At the extreme end of narcissism is the person who shows their deprivation by clinging to their spouse. Such relationships are called fused, or, in lay terms, possessive. Such a person finds it very difficult to be alone, needs physical and emotional closeness and is very suspicious of being left for another. Another description of the suspicious personality is the paranoid person, who also finds it very difficult to trust, expects to be let down and attacked, and at their worst believes that everyone is against them, including their spouse. We find that those who are not mature remain dependent on their partner and rely on them for physical, social and emotional facilitation. In these marriages there is great difficulty in obtaining a balance between dependence and independence.

Following Erikson we can see that, as we grow up, we have the possibility of receiving the right experiences of love, in terms of trust, autonomy and feeling loved, or the wrong ones of being abandoned, lacking in self-esteem and feeling unloved.

ATTACHMENT THEORY

Still remaining in the dynamic mode, reference has been made in Chapter 2 to attachment and its continuation in adult life. Basically, research has shown that about 50 per cent of us have a normal attachment ability, 25 per cent of us have an anxious attachment and are frightened of being abandoned or let down, and finally the other 25 per cent have avoidant personalities. The marriage-counselling rooms are littered with avoidant personalities; here, men and women, but particularly men, are described by their spouses as finding it difficult to get close to them, show affection, and be intimate; they feel suffocated with closeness and spend a good deal of their time at work, from which they get their self-esteem. The avoidant personality often just manages to conceal their difficulty in intimacy when they are in courtship, but returns to their aloofness once they settle down, and their wife often complains 'This is not the man I married'.

COMBINATION OF BIOLOGICAL AND PSYCHODYNAMIC

One of the most frequent combinations that is met in the

consulting rooms is the presence of the extrovert personality, a man or a woman who is bubbling with energy, outgoing, lively, and appears to need nothing, but who is nevertheless hungry for affection and attention. The signals he or she gives are of contentment and satisfaction but there is a basic restlessness that is hidden and their partner cannot see it. Very often their partner is an introvert who finds it difficult to demonstrate affection, who is dependent on their extrovert partner for support and becomes very confused when they realise that their spouse needs them. One of the most helpful things that can be done in these circumstances is to point out the needs of the extrovert spouse, to show their partner that, behind the mask of satisfaction, there is a needy person who yearns for care. When the way is opened, then a new balance can be reached in the relationship.

CHAPTER 17

Healing

We have seen that a proportion of men and women who enter marriage have been subject to traumas in their childhood, or that as many as 50 per cent have anxious or avoidant attachment patterns. Can the intimate relationship of marriage help them to overcome their difficulties? This is a crucial aspect of loving in contemporary marriage. A good deal of research has shown that personality and neurotic disorder feature highly in marital breakdown. (For a dated but still highly relevant review by Dominian, see *Marital Breakdown*.[1])

The alternative to marital breakdown is to see love in marriage as a healing, supportive experience. This is an optimistic view and indeed some may call it an idealistic one. We are so familiar with marital breakdown that little research has been done into the healing effects that can exist in contemporary relationships. But in the course of my lecturing, I find an enormous interest in the subject of healing and much intuitive assent.

There are, however, two studies that hint at what is possible. The first is to be found in *Social Origins of Depression* by Brown and Harris.[2] In this book, part of an extensive series of studies by Brown and others on the causes of depression, it was found that for women whose husbands or boyfriends were their confidants, prior experiences normally associated with depression later in life, such as early loss of mother, three or more children under fourteen and lack of employment, can have their impact lessened.

The second study, Quinton et al.,[3] was a prospective follow-up study of two groups of women first studied in the mid 1960s, when they were children. Ninety-four girls were reared in institutions and fifty-one were in the general population. Both groups were interviewed in detail when aged 21–27 years old and home observations were undertaken for those with young children. The institution-reared women showed a markedly increased rate of poor psychosocial functioning and severe difficulties parenting in adult life. However, those women enjoying a harmonious marital relationship with a non-deviant husband were much more likely to show good parenting and fewer psychological difficulties.

What remains is to look at the mechanism by which healing can take place. The first stems from the traditional psychoanalytic view. For an extensive review of psychotherapy for couples from the dynamic point of view, there is Ruszczynski's study of the work that emanates from the Tavistock Institute of Marital Studies.[4] Dynamic psychotherapy for couples is a complex phenomenon, but one of its features is for the therapist to interpret the interaction of the couple and the defences they use towards each other – that is to say, principally the projections they give to one another. Couples treat each other as parental figures and expect behaviour that is consonant with the way they were treated as children. Part of the work of the therapist is to interpret these transferences and help the couple to see each other as they are and not as parental substitutes.

Therapists dealing with couples are pessimistic about couples doing this work for themselves. Here is a typical view: 'Much as it is true that our partners cannot heal the hurts and injuries of our past in the way that psychotherapy can do . . .'.[5] Nevertheless in the rest of the sentence the author goes on to say, 'good relationships are in fact often experienced as nourishing and reparative.' I think the difficulty that professional therapists have is that they reflect on the couples they see in practice, who are usually those embattled in deep conflicts. There are millions of couples who are not so wounded and who do heal each other to a greater or lesser extent.

Let us look at how this healing occurs. With a hundred years of psychology behind us, husbands and wives today realise more than ever that their partner treats them as a parental figure. Women find it far easier to see themselves in the role of mother and to see their husbands as a little boy, despite his manly appearance and conduct. Husbands find it far more difficult to see themselves as fathers, with their wives in the role of little girls. But there is no doubt that both partners can continue in the parental role. It is important to assess the parental role that one has been put in, and avoid colluding with it. Each partner should be made responsible for his or her own life; one partner should not avoid the task of growing up by letting the other make decisions for them, make up their minds or step in and do things they find difficult.

Secondly, it is important to recognise the defences our spouse uses. But says the expert, 'You can't do that' because they are unconscious. Defences are indeed unconscious. Spouses use denial, projection and rationalisation, and we confront a blank face when we take our stand. At first we may hesitate, but the point about defences is that they are repetitive and predictable. Handling the repetitive defences of our spouse is a special task of healing. The mistake most of us make is to resort to moralistic language, which is reciprocated. When our spouse repeatedly denies some damaging action they perform, we call this failure to own up lying. When they offer an explanation of why they cannot do something we have asked them to do, we call them lazy. When they put their interest before ours, we call them selfish. The homes of millions of couples reverberate with this moralistic language, which is tossed to and fro as a form of abuse. 'The trouble with you is ...' 'No! The trouble with you is ...'

But not everyone joins in this battle or they do so initially and then proceed further to find out what lies behind the defence. Then is the time to gently confront the defence with reality. This confrontation is not always welcomed and may, of course, be denied, but it can reach the spouse and, if it is accompanied by support, encouragement and help, it may be accepted. This is after all what happens in successful therapy. If spouses are accused in moral terms, they simply dig their heels in, further protecting their character. An essential part of healing is to avoid using moralistic language and to explore defences. When reality breaks through, then, as I said, help is given to overcome the difficulty. Most of the normalisation of marriage is the continuous breakthrough of defences so that a new form of adjustment is reached.

The next form of healing follows a non-dynamic psychological model. This is by shaping each other's behaviour through rewards and punishments. This is in fact how most of us relate to each other. When we are pleased with what we experience we reward the person and in this way encourage the repetition of the particular conduct. The reward can take any form in marriage, from expressing pleasure to sexual intercourse. When the behaviour is unpleasant or painful, then we respond in a punitive manner. In marriage, spouses withdraw from each other and either withhold behaviour that pleases or actually deliver something unpleasant.

There is a third model based on what psychologists call cognitive therapy. In this approach, we appeal to the learning mechanism of another person, to show them that their behaviour is wrong or unacceptable, and we offer alternative ways of doing things. This is an attempt to change people by appealing to rationality, but, although it sometimes works, we have to remember that two other factors, the unconscious and learned habit, are powerful obstacles.

Now let us lok at some common healing situations.

DISORDERS OF ATTACHMENT

I have mentioned that about 25 per cent of people form anxious attachments, and about the same number form the avoidant variety. People with anxious attachments are constantly afraid of losing the person they are close to, of being abandoned. Short of losing them, they are apprehensive about their being injured or falling ill. The response to the person with the anxious attachment is initially to ensure that they are not made unduly anxious. If they are terrified of losing their partner to another man or woman, there is little point in their spouse flirting or becoming excessively involved with another person. Their partner should try to be as reliable, predictable and punctual as possible and make the spouse feel secure.

A basic fear in anxious attachment is the fear of disintegration that will ensue if the person is left alone. In order to overcome this fear, they should be encouraged to be less dependent on their partner and learn to cope and fend for themselves. The person with anxious attachment has to gain inwardly a sense of greater confidence in their capacity to survive by themselves in case they lose their partner, and that means stretching their potential while their spouse is alive and available.

In avoidant attachment the spouse's anxiety is not about loss but about closeness. They are afraid of intimacy, which feels like an intrusion or a suffocation. They keep their distance and avoid emotional contact. Such a person makes a genuine attempt to be intimate during courtship, but afterwards begins to show fear of closeness and does not want to be touched or to become emotionally involved. Although they are aloof, they yearn for companionship. The response to such a person is to try to reach them as far as they will allow it. After that, every effort should be made to overcome their resistance by making emotional contact rewarding. Their partner can encourage short periods of physical closeness, touch, kissing, hugging, first in private and then gradually in public. The whole point about the person with the avoidant attachment is that he or she has to learn to experience physical intimacy safely.

DISORDERS OF TRUST

Some men and women grow up with a very low level of trust

about other human beings. They have been neglected, let down, abandoned, tossed from person to person, so that they become suspicious, mistrustful, afraid that they will be let down and, at the extreme level, paranoid. It is out of the ranks of such people that jealousy is most commonly found and the morbid jealousy found in Othello is an example of its extreme manifestation.

The mistrustful person does not extend their suspicions to such a degree, but they tend to be secretive and guarded. They will keep their papers locked up; they will hide the things that matter to them from their spouse. They are reluctant to disclose their inner world in case the information they reveal is used against them. These are the people who are described as keeping their cards close to their chest. The mistrustful person is not easy to reach. They need to be reassured that their confidence will not be betrayed. At the same time, they have to be confronted about their anxieties. Basically, they are afraid of being let down and exploited. These fears have to be challenged. They need to be trained to discern between people they can trust, such as their spouse, and others, who may let them down. In building up trust, the spouse has to be careful not to promise beyond their capacity, so that they do not let their partner down and reinforce their fears.

DISORDERS OF AUTONOMY

At the heart of disorders of autonomy is to be found the man or woman who grew up in a home dominated by one or both parents. For years they had to submit their will to parental wishes, out of fear or the threat of being dismissed or humiliated. They grew up resenting such authority and they refuse to take orders from anybody. The difficulty with such a spouse is that the simplest request is interpreted as a demand. Clearly such a person is extremely sensitive to any approach made to them. The tone of the request is vital and their co-operation should be sought before anything is asked of them. A request can be preceded by the indication that it is not a demand. But life has to go on and the spouse has to make it clear that he or she is not an authoritarian parent, but is simply asking what is necessary for survival. An understanding should be reached that distinguishes the spouse from the parent figure and encourages requests to be treated on their own merits. This is achieved more quickly if the spouse handles the sensitive partner with respect, listens to their opinion and pays attention to it, and generally considers them as responsible adults, which dilutes the feeling of being treated as an incompetent child.

DISORDERS OF DEPENDENCE

The whole aim of development is to finish up as an adult who is reasonably autonomous, self-reliant and self-directing. A number of people attain intellectual and physical adulthood, but remain emotionally dependent and insecure. Such a man or woman often marries an apparently domineering, assertive, competent partner and there is a collusion between the two, which can prove disastrous for the relationship when the dependent person matures and no longer needs the stronger partner. The secret of a successful outcome is for the so-called 'strong' partner to realise what is going on early in the relationship and to encourage the partner to grow up. That means in practice that, when appealed to for advice, the pros and cons of a situation are discussed, but the decision is taken by the dependent partner. In the same way, when they ask that things that they are afraid to do be done for them, an attempt should be made to encourage them to tackle the object of their fear, rather than taking over parts of their life. In general the dependent person should be supported and encouraged to tackle the things they are afraid to do, and be rewarded as they achieve a new step of independence. This is the opposite approach from the one in which the strong partner controls and regulates the life of their dependent spouse. In fact, the strong partner should not be afraid to show from the very beginning that they too have needs, which their partner should make every effort to meet.

DISORDERS OF MATURITY

The dependent person is a frightened child. The immature spouse is an irresponsible child, clothed in adult garments. As mentioned already, at their extreme they have been called psychopaths. But immaturity does not need to be so marked and many a spouse has some immature characteristics. These characteristics are the need for immediate gratification without the capacity to delay, postpone or forfeit it. They are impulsive, covetous and hoarding, but unable to enjoy or appreciate the things they have. They are attracted by glitter, material acquisitions and the power of money. They can be generous but are often mean. They are very sensitive to criticism, with excessive and unreasonable outbursts of anger. They may resort to violence and often sulk. They tend to lie because they are afraid of responsibility of any sort. They can often be very charming, promising the moon and delivering very little. They can be belligerent one moment and crying on their knees the next, begging for another chance.

In the presence of such a person it may be thought that the best thing is to give up and try afresh. Indeed, such spouses clutter the divorce courts under the category of unreasonable behaviour. If an attempt is made to try to cope with such immaturity, then the only tenable response is kindness, coupled with firmness. It has to be realised that one is dealing with an irresponsible child, even if they are creative adults. Firmness is the only way out. Such men and women have to be reprimanded for their bad behaviour, told in no uncertain terms that aggression will not be tolerated, and that they will be rewarded only if they behave themselves. A certain number of them mature with time, but they do represent hard work.

CHAPTER 18

Loving and Growth

> 'Nowadays the majority of couples can be expected to live together for some fifty years or more. There are those who claim that no two people can endure each other for such a period and that a change is necessary. Boredom is offered as one of the reasons for divorce. In fact, if couples are offering to each other the right ingredients in their social, emotional, sexual, intellectual and spiritual life, they do not want to change partners. A marital relationship is a major investment of one's life, and it should not be lightly discarded if the spouses are mutually compatible. A new partner might be more exciting, but every relationship needs a good deal of energy expended to make it work and so the original effort should be carefully nurtured. In addition, it is exciting to see the person with whom one lives change and grow. Loving implies that one can live with the change and assist the partner to realise their potential, in other words to be a facilitator.' [1]

Thus, although the core of the identity of our partner will remain the same, the details will alter, and sometimes there will be substantial change. Acceptance and growth go hand in hand. According to Lyons,[2] 'Growth requires the continuing conscious effort to recognise the reality of each partner by the other as well as the capacity to forgive each other for not turning out to be all that was originally projected'.

The development of the personality, according to Jung,[3] is a movement towards wholeness by means of the integration of the conscious and unconscious parts of the personality. It is a central tenet of the dynamic approach to marriage that couples are involved in this mutual process of 'individuation'. Part of the mutual growth is acting as a mirror to each other. We can find out what we are by the way our partner responds to us. We are also influenced by our partner and, with time, we grow more like them. We can understand growth as love in marriage a little more precisely if we see it as the tension to work out what has been repeatedly stated in this book, namely the balance between autonomy or separateness and intimacy or togetherness. Couples can be totally autonomous or enmeshed. One of the salient issues of love in marriage is to work out a position that is satisfactory for both spouses, which at the same time respects their wholeness – that is, their psychological integrity.

If falling in love is about meeting one's undeveloped side in one's partner, then growth is about developing the missing parts with the help of one's spouse. Growth is creative, in that one becomes a richer person by commanding a greater repertoire of psychological facilities. It is also dangerous because we can outgrow our need of our partner, who becomes redundant in our life. In working out a balance between autonomy and intimacy, some individuals find that their need for intimacy is coupled with the fear of being swallowed up by their partner, and the need for autonomy is linked with the fear of being alone and abandoned. In the remaining part of this chapter, I shall look at this balance of opposites. It is not possible to examine all the dimensions of the human personality – this would require a book in itself – but the reader can insert the factors which are appropriate to their relationship.

MATURITY–IMMATURITY

At the heart of emotional maturity is a development from childlike reactions to adult behaviour. Children need a good deal of and instant gratification. Adults have to exhibit denial of gratification and the delay of its achievement. In marital life, this dimension is a matter of several issues. Spouses need to learn to delay their pleasure until that of their partner is met. This means learning to put the other spouse first in consideration when it comes to food on the table, resources and money, their pleasure versus ours and so on. Putting the other first has to be balanced by considering one's own needs, otherwise one can become a martyr or a doormat. Psychologically, this tension is resolved by giving to a point where the spouse as an 'other' is recognised. The 'otherness' of the spouse must not be eliminated by taking the spouse for granted, nor must the partner be a source of fear and awe. Little by little the spouses have to learn that each other exists, has needs which have to be respected and that, on each occasion when there is tension between these needs, care will be taken to reach a conclusion that does justice to the minimum requirements of each other.

Maturity for spouses enters the intimacy of their sexual relationship. The commonest tension in sexual relations is that husbands want quantitatively more sex and wives want qualitatively better sex with emphasis on affection. Growth is a matter for the husband to learn more about affection, preceding and after sex, and for wives to understand the instinctual drive behind the needs of their husband.

Maturity for spouses also operates in relationship to their children. Parents, often mothers, tend to put the needs of their children before their own. Up to a point this is how it should be. But parents do not cease to have their requirements, which must not be ignored.

REGRESSION–MATURITY

Within the dimension of maturity that is being adult, responsible, patient, tolerant and non-judgemental, couples need to be able to tolerate moments or short bursts of regression – that is, behaving in a childlike manner. Regression means the pursuit of self-indulgence, moments of irresponsibility, from spending too much on a favourite item to speeding in a new car, being intolerant and dismissive, and wanting one's own way. Accepting that there are moments when we all want to go back to our childhood is part of the tension of regression and maturity. This is a very different matter from giving in to the immaturity of the partner. Transient moments of immaturity are part and parcel of ordinary marriage, whereas immaturity, as a permanent feature of the personality, which no attempt is made to change, is unacceptable.

DEPENDENCE–INDEPENDENCE

Reference has already been made to the subject of dependence and independence in the section on healing but this pattern is so common and so important that it is repeated here in the context of growth. At the heart of childhood dependence is the need to rely on parents for food, material resources, emotional support, guidance, assessment, decision-making, the relief of pain, encouragement and reassurance. There are couples in which one partner starts the relationship by being emotionally dependent on their spouse. This is a very common pattern of relationship. They want their spouse to do things for them, make up their minds, handle their finances, drive them around, shop for them and so on. Little by little such a dependent person develops their own resources. A wife who relied on her husband to drive her, handle her money, decide where they went for their holidays, pay the bills and generally look after her, may slowly learn how to drive, cope with her own money, have her own friends, make her own decisions and choices, and become more independent. Frequently her husband will welcome her steps towards autonomy and take pride in them. Sometimes there are husbands who are unsure of themselves and have needed the dependence of their wives to bolster their self-esteem. The gradual independence might then be viewed with suspicion and sabotaged. Ultimately there has to be a balance between needing each other socially, emotionally and sexually, and being independent.

RESPECT–FALLIBILITY

As has already been mentioned, we tend to marry a person who fulfils part of ourselves which is missing. This is a form of complementarity in which our need for praise, support, reassurance, boosting of self-esteem, encouragement, perseverance, hope and trust are met by a partner who is high in these characteristics. When our needs are met, we feel comfortable and appreciate and respect the qualitities of our spouse. Our respect is not only for the emotional qualities our partner possesses, but also for their intellectual and spiritual capacities. Respect and admiration are part of the loving exchange between partners.

Nevertheless, frequently we find that our spouse does not possess all the qualities we desire. This is because, in falling in love, we idealise them. We exaggerate their resources and we minimise their frailties. When we come to live with them, we discover, sooner or later, the truth or the reality. Then we have to forgive their fallibility and limitations and we still have to respect them, even if we are disappointed.

SENSITIVITY–ACCEPTANCE OF CRITICISM

Mention has already been made of the oversensitive personality who cannot easily tolerate criticism. An essential part of the tension between spouses is to work out solutions to differences of opinion, courses of action and decision-making. In these dialogues it is vital to hear and see another point of view. In counselling we often meet spouses who interpret differences of opinion or view as a criticism and then become so busy protecting their self-esteem that they are blind and deaf to the case made by their partner. For them a different approach is not an alternative view but an attack on their position.

Slowly spouses begin to move from positions, 'So you

don't like what I said', 'You don't think my idea is good', 'You never agree with me', to seeing that both can have good ideas and that the way forward is to incorporate the best in each other. In this way not only do both gain but they enlarge their mutual worlds. In order for partners to accept the views of each other, these views and feelings must first be acknowledged as the fruit of each other's labour. They should be appreciated, not ignored, because if the views and feelings of a person are ignored, then the person feels dismissed. Having paid attention to the contents, these can be evaluated. It is not a question of right or wrong, but a point of view seen from different angles. Ideally a composite decision should be taken that does justice to both spouses. In practice, this is not always possible. What happens is that partners take turns to have their positions accepted and over a long period there is a fair distribution of mutuality.

In this vein the dimensions of togetherness and separateness, the pursuit of excitement and tranquillity, material aggrandisement and contentment with the good-enough, creativity and familiarity, trust and mistrust, secrecy and openness, can all be examined in the duality of autonomy and intimacy.

The whole point of growth of love is the ability to act as a sensitive responder to each other, to acknowledge what is present and to unveil what is hinted at, which means opening the partner to the unconscious hidden parts of themselves. We can reveal ourselves in a variety of ways, of which love and aggression are the two most common, and in between there is a whole array of confusion and uncertainty. Love in mutual growth needs to unpack the hidden world of each other. Dynamic psychology emphasises feelings and the unconscious. Freud pointed out that the way to the unconscious is sometimes through dreams. Although spouses sometimes share their dreams, they do not usually spend time unravelling their contents. They have neither the skill nor the time to do so effectively. But there are many other ways that spouses can facilitate each other. They can listen to each other's dreams in the sense of their ideals, hopes and aspirations. The spouse wants to write a book, create a marvellous garden, change their job in midstream, start a new venture, acquire a faith in some ideal, or pursue a new form of study. All these innovations, from the humblest to the most major, are ways by which the unconscious speaks, and they need a spouse who can contain the anxiety they generate, and reassure the doubts that accompany the aspirations. One of the commonest and most ordinary moments is when a spouse starts a sentence, then abruptly stops with words such as 'You will not be interested ...', 'It's really stupid ...', 'You will laugh at me ...'. These are moments which should not be lost because a creative germ might be aborted.

All of us know something about parenting, either by experiencing it at the hands of our parents or by parenting ourselves. There are many aspects to parenting, but one feature is the way we encourage, facilitate, stimulate, act as holders of our children's anxieties and fears, soothe their pain and in this way encourage their development. Spouses can show their love for each other by being facilitators to each other as parents are to children. This is totally different from keeping each other in the dependent position of being a child. Dependence, as already mentioned, implies living by kind permission of the spouse. Growth, on the other hand, is developing one's potential intellectually and emotionally by finding one's spouse a source of gentle encouragement to bring out what is hidden.

CHAPTER 19

Maintaining Relationships

In the course of my counselling work I have come to see that sustaining, healing and growth are the necessities for nurturing love over the whole life cycle of marriage. In the previous chapters covering these areas, I have supported these inductive, clinical views through the research findings of sociologists and psychologists.

I want to devote this chapter to two works which concentrate on how couples maintain and repair their relationships. Much has been written about the beginning and ending of relationships and this research is reflected in this book.

However, there is a massive lack of knowledge about what maintains the majority of marital relationships and the whole focus of this book is to try to remedy this.

The first study is by Dindia and Baxter.[1] They collected 100 marital partners, fifty couples, whose mean age was thirty-eight, married for a mean of fourteen years, and put the following proposition to them in writing.

> We are trying to determine what spouses do when they are trying to maintain their relationship in a healthy state. This usually happens when one or both spouses think that the relationship is good the way it is and he and/or she wants to preserve the relationship from going downhill. What do you do or have you done in the past when you are trying to keep your relationship from going downhill?

The study went on to examine not only what couples do to maintain the relationship, but also what they do to repair it.

The participants were given 49 strategies, which were coded, and the couples were allowed to chose 10 maintenance strategies and 10 repair strategies. The analysis is very detailed and what I have done is to include the strategies and to comment on the findings.

STRATEGY TYPE

I. CHANGING EXTERNAL ENVIRONMENT

A. Barren/Hostile
B. Fertile/Benign

In this strategy the couple will be driven closer when they face adverse external conditions, such as a mutual enemy, or (B) the opposite when they create a positive external environment such as a romantic candle-lit supper. These strategies are rarely used.

II. COMMUNICATION STRATEGIES

A. Talk
B. Symbolic contact
C. Openness/Honesty
D. Talk about the day
E. Share feelings

These communication strategies, as might be expected, are heavily subscribed, both for maintenance and repair, with the actual quantity of talk heading the list. Open, honest communication came second, sharing feelings third, talking about the day in the evening fourth and symbolic contact such as a telephone call last.

III. METACOMMUNICATION

A. Talk about problem
B. Interim progress reports
C. Time out

These are used mainly for repairing the relationship. The commonest was talking about the problem, the next frequent was interim progress reports, which means chatting about how things were going, and the third was an explicit decision temporarily to stop talking about the problem.

IV. AVOID METACOMMUNICATION

This is an attitude which avoids communication, in which the couple keep quiet and let the problem disappear by itself. This approach is rarely used.

V. ANTISOCIAL STRATEGIES

A. Arguments
B. Ultimatums
C. Equilibrium tests
  1. Insolent
  2. Sullen
  3. Hypercritical
  4. Obstinate
D. Extreme tests
  1. Imply relationship has no future
  2. Break contact
  3. Be cold
  4. Refuse self-disclosure
  5. Refuse favours
  6. Threaten exclusiveness/common space/future

This is all antisocial behaviour, which marriage counsellors see frequently in couples who have difficulties, but these behaviours are not used as ordinary procedures to maintain or repair relationships.

VI. PRO-SOCIAL STRATEGIES

A. Maintain equilibrium
  1. Be nice
  2. Be cheerful

3. Refrain from criticism
4. Give in

B. Opposites
1. Imply relationship has future
2. Maintain contact
3. Be warm
4. Provide favours
5. Ensure exclusiveness

Pro-social strategies on the other hand, such as being warm, nice, refraining from criticism, providing favours, giving in, are often used, particularly for maintenance, but also for repair.

VII. CEREMONIES

A. Commemorative
1. Original celebrations
2. Reminiscence

B. Ceremonies re end of relationship

C. Piacular

D. Communion/Celebration

E. Reassurance rituals
1. Expression of affection
2. Compliments
3. Gifts

This group contains ceremonial or ritualistic strategies, including celebrating anniversaries or birthdays and recalling past pleasurable experiences. Piacular behaviour refers to making up after an argument. Communion rituals involve, for example, having dinner together. Ceremonies connected to undoing the relationship refer to remarks such as 'What would you do if I wasn't here?' The reassurance rituals are self-explanatory. These strategies, particularly those expressing affection, are frequently resorted to for maintaining relationships.

VIII. ANTI-RITUALS/SPONTANEITY

This approach refers to actions meant to introduce novelty or stimulation in the relationship. They would be welcomed by spouses with an extrovert personality and may be initiated by them. Bringing home a surprise or doing something unexpected would come into this category, which is frequently used for maintenance.

IX. TOGETHERNESS

A. Time together
B. Shared activity
C. Spend time with network

Spending time together has already been mentioned under togetherness in the dimension of sustaining. This study confirms that it is a vital element in maintaining relationships.

X. SEEKING/ALLOWING AUTONOMY

Autonomy is the opposite of togetherness and this has been referred to in the last chapter as part of the balance between autonomy and intimacy. This is a balance that is important for maintaining the harmony of relationships.

XI. SEEKING OUTSIDE HELP

A. Seek outside help
B. Joint use of prayer/religion
C. Individual use of prayer/religion

This strategy refers to seeking outside help, which is rarely used, and to resorting to prayer, which is used by those who have a religious orientation.

Readers may like to compare their own maintenance and repair strategies with those found in this study and perhaps add their own. There were no gender differences, except the well-known one that wives were more likely to seek external assistance in times of difficulty. From the ten categories offered for selection, communication, metacommunication (talking about the problem), warmth, ceremonial expressions of affection, and togetherness stood out as the main means of maintenance and repair. In this book, in common with all main commentators in Western society, I have taken the view that marriage is changing from the traditional type, of a contract of social roles, to a companionate variety in which love is the key to its viability, expressed in the quality of the relationship. My colleagues from One Plus One, Marriage and Partnership Research, which I head, will be publishing a very original study that analyses the concept of companionate marriage far more clearly.

In another study, which was initiated in 1979, sixty-five couples in England were investigated in their premarital and first three months of marriage, and the resulting book was published under the title *The Beginning of the Rest of your Life.*[2] At the heart of this study is the finding that the *raison d'être* of married life was the togetherness of the couple. Forty-seven of the sixty-five couples were reinterviewed five years later, three-quarters of them then being parents. The main finding was that the sense of togetherness remained the central theme of their married life.

The investigators asked what was the basis of their sense of togetherness; was it just companionate life, understood as feelings and emotions present in the relationship? Analysing the results of the interviews, the research workers have come to the conclusion that their couples have a wider sense of the meaning of companionate, which the authors of the forthcoming book call partnership. The anchor of marriage of their couples was based on the state of their partnership.

Partnership was evaluated on three factors, namely: the BELIEFS of the couple – that is to say, the values they held concerning division of labour, male/female differences, and roles; SHARED BEHAVIOUR – that is to say, how they spend time together and separately, particularly the way they shared their social life and their social networks and the actual division of labour; and finally the essential part of companionate marriage, their RELATING TO ONE ANOTHER, which includes communication, confiding, their sexual life and their level of intimacy.

This model, which is merely briefly outlined here, has a very rich sense of description of married life and explains how couples do remain married when their relationship fluctuates but their sense of partnership is strong. In my book, the relationship element has been analysed in detail and the other aspects of partnership have been referred to indirectly, but if the new model finds favour, we will have a richer description of companionate marriage.

CHAPTER 20

Patterns of Marital Relationships

So far, I have maintained that at the heart of loving is an essence of sustaining, healing and growing, which is made up of the interaction of different personalities. A distinction has to be made between the individuality of the personalities of the husband and the wife and how they blend together as a married couple. In this chapter, I look at three patterns of marriage found in America, but seen also elsewhere in the world. The point about these patterns is that the couple, in addition to trying to sustain, heal and grow, find a particular way of interacting that suits them. These descriptions, called typologies by social scientists, try to express the fact that, although every marriage is unique, in fact marriages fall into a few basic types.

INSTITUTIONAL AND COMPANIONATE

Nearly fifty years ago the American workers, Burgess and Locke categorised marriages as 'Institutional' or 'Companionate';[1] this book has been based on the belief that the change from the former to the latter is a major event of our time and we have to study and recognise this shift if we are going to make sense of present-day marriage and ultimately reduce the level of divorce.

The institutional variety lays emphasis on the importance of rules and authority. In this type the husband is the head of the family, the enforcer of law and discipline, the breadwinner, the person who takes decisions, and the ambassador of the family to the outside world. The wife is the childbearer, child-rearer and homemaker. The way such couples behave is influenced by the way society, religion and the law may react and what other people may think. Such couples do not have strong feelings for one another, but are very attached to the roles they have to carry out. If these roles are discharged well and they remain faithful to each other, then society and they themselves consider the marriage to be good.

The companionate marriage, which is the subject of this book, emphasises mutual affection and common interests, and love plays a prominent part. The upsurge of divorce is a declaration by many people that, when affection, love and mutual respect cease, there is no marriage left. In this marriage, men and women both tend to work and husbands participate in the upbringing of their children. Although wives work, they are often still primarily responsible for homemaking and taking care of the children. The main emphasis of companionate marriage is on the quality of the relationship, in which affection, love and compatibility are uppermost. This type of marriage needs different skills, which we have not yet learned, and depends a great deal on the meshing of the personalities. (Hence the emphasis on these in Chapters 15 and 16 and on healing in Chapter 17.)

SUBTYPES OF THE INSTITUTIONAL AND COMPANIONATE VARIETY

Cuber and Harroff studied 400 upper-middle-class Americans and focused on couples who had been married for at least ten years and had never contemplated divorce; this left 211 people within this group.[2] The workers found two varieties of companionate and three of institutional marriage.

The first companionate type was called *vital*. The vitals are very close and interconnected in all life matters. They try to do things which are of mutual interest to each other and have no fun without each other. The second companionate type is very similar to the vital and is called *total*. The difference between the two is that the total couples go to extremes, sharing everything together. Privacy is a foreign idea to them. In the total marriage, the couple experience life as one. There are three institutional types. The first is *conflict-habituated*. In this marriage, the couple fight frequently but settle nothing. They move from fight to fight. Such marriages are high in conflict and they appear incompatible, but they stay together. The second institutional type is called *devitalised*. In the devitalised marriage, the couple have a close relationship, but they have grown apart since the early days. They do things out of routine and duty, and spend more time with the children and the community. The third variety is the *passive–congenial*. In this type the couple are civil to each other, they have common interests and they focus on things such as professional responsibilities, property, children and their reputation.

Cuber and Harroff drew up these descriptions on an intuitive basis. They did not measure these characteristics.

FITZPATRICK'S TYPES

Fitzpatrick, an eminent worker in the United States, whose book *Between Husbands and Wives* contains a wealth of detailed analysis of patterns of marital interaction based on extensive measurements,[3] describes five patterns of marital interaction and their mode of communication. Here, I use the five brief descriptions inserted at the beginning of the book.

COUPLE I: TOM AND JENNIFER

Tom and Jennifer have the same philosophy of life. They believe that their marriage is very important and that both should sacrifice some personal independence for the good of the marriage. They believe in stability; they stress the importance of being able to predict each other and their life together.

Marriage provides them with a stable, committed relationship that helps to tie them into their community. Tom and Jennifer spend a lot of time together, working on their home and in leisure pursuits. They make time for each other during the day by keeping a regular daily schedule and eating their meals together. They avoid conflict in general and say that when they do disagree, they try to argue only over very important issues.

Part of their philosophical agreement about life involves the nature of male/female roles; Tom sees himself as analytical, assertive and dominant in the marriage, and Jennifer sees herself as warm, expressive and nurturing. They are good at predicting one another's moods and feelings.

Because they share the same values and have a commitment to conventional male and female roles, Tom and Jennifer do not engage in power struggles in their conversations. Norms and conventions that they follow have already established that Tom is the head of the household and controls decisions in certain spheres of influence. Jennifer, too, has her spheres of influence – the home and the children. But when they do engage in power struggles, they tend to exchange orders rather than to negotiate. In general they sweep discord under the rug, but this is a fairly effective strategy for Tom and Jennifer because they have very few conflicts.

Tom and Jennifer feel that they can express their innermost thoughts with each other. Tom believes he can express his anxieties and vulnerabilities to Jennifer, and that he is willing to listen to her when she wants to talk. Their actual disclosure patterns to one another are muted and they actually disclose more positive than negative feelings – matters that are hardly risky to reveal. However, when Tom and Jennifer talk, they are very responsive to each other; they lean towards each other, smile, talk a lot, interrupt each other and finish each other's sentences.

Tom and Jennifer present themselves to others as a couple; their conversation is peppered with the word 'we' ('we' think this, 'we' do that and so on). When they talk about their marriage, certain themes emerge. They see communication and verbal openness, being in love and displaying affection and sharing time, activities and interests as very important in marriage. They downplay distinct individual traits, habits or skills because they reject the idea that marriage is a product of separate identities or roles.

Tom and Jennifer are somewhat stoic; they both think some problems are just inherent in marriage, and they are willing to moderate their expectations of marital happiness. They believe that sometimes relationships are beyond their direct, personal control.

Tom and Jennifer think of their marriage as being extremely well adjusted. They say they are very happy, they have never thought about divorce and they agree on all major marital and family issues.

This couple are called *traditionals*.

COUPLE II: SCOTT AND MISSY

Scott and Missy have the same philosophy of life; they believe that love and marriage primarily exist for the psychological gratification that the relationship gives to spouses. They believe that a marriage should be based on the satisfaction that each partner derives from the relationship. This couple stress the importance of having a good time and believe that in this quickly changing world it is vital that each individual has a strong sense of self, that is not lost just because that person is married. For this couple, the most freedom in marriage stems from allowing each partner some privacy and independence. Scott and Missy try to spend a lot of time together, but they do not keep regular daily schedules and they both have outside friends and interests.

Scott and Missy thrive on conflict; neither is afraid of openly expressing their views. Part of their philosophical agreement on life involves the nature of male/female roles;

they both believe in egalitarianism. But Scott and Missy tend to see themselves as androgynous or capable of combining masculine and feminine characteristics in their personalities. In other words, Scott sees himself as both assertive and nurturing, whereas Missy is analytical and expressive. Because they are deviating from the conventional norms about male/female roles that have existed for centuries, naturally Scott and Missy are more likely to engage in conflicts, bargaining and negotiation. They are venturing where few couples have gone before, redefining and renegotiating roles, rules and norms of marriage.

Scott and Missy both believe that they can disclose their innermost thoughts, feelings and anxieties to one another, but each wants the other to open up even more. They disclose both positive and negative feelings about each other. They are very responsive to one another in conversations, picking up on each other's topics. They tend not to finish each other's sentences; rather, they tend to interrupt with questions.

When Scott and Missy talk about their marriage, certain themes emerge; they often blame their marital problems on environmental influences, on elements of their current situation that are beyond their control.

Scott and Missy talk about their separate identities and roles as well as each person's individual interests; they rarely refer to themselves as a couple by using the word 'we'. They do not automatically presume to understand each other; they are reasonably maritally adjusted; they agree to disagree, to work through problems as they arise.

This couple are called *independents*.

COUPLE III: FRANK AND ELEANOR

Frank and Eleanor have the same philosophy of life, and the same ambivalence about that philosophy. They both want to believe that marriage is so important that both should sacrifice independence for the sake of the marriage, but they are unsure of these values and ambivalent about how beneficial such values have been for them. Frank and Eleanor live together, but their bond is one of frozen isolation. Togetherness is a matter of habit and convenience, and not a sign of a real desire to be in each other's company.

Frank's and Eleanor's marriage provides them with a stable relationship that ties them into a community yet includes little personal closeness. They try not to spend very much time together, either working around the house or pursuing leisure activities. Their major points of contact occur at meal-times or other regularly scheduled daily events.

Frank and Eleanor will go to great lengths to avoid conflict. A strong bond between them is their commitment to conventional male and female roles; each has a sense of the duties and obligations connected with being husband and wife and each tries to live up to these obligations. Frank sees himself as analytical, assertive and dominant, but Eleanor is unsure of her femininity. Neither does very well at predicting how the other sees himself or herself.

Frank and Eleanor feel that they cannot express their innermost thoughts to one another and they do not. They do not open up to one another or to outsiders. They are extremely careful in their conversations with one another. They tend not to interrupt each other, and generally they do not talk very much with one another.

When Frank and Eleanor talk about their marriage, they talk about having separate time, activities and interests, and about each of them having distinct personalities. They see their marriage as the product of factors that are outside their control, factors that are part of normal stages of life. Frank and Eleanor tell their friends that their marriage is happier than most marriages, and it is. The major source of satisfaction for Frank and Eleanor is that they agree on major issues in married life and they rarely talk about divorce or separation.

This couple are called *separates*.

COUPLE IV: JIM AND TAMMY

Jim and Tammy have the same philosophy of life, although Jim, unlike Tammy, is sometimes ambivalent about that philosophy. Both believe marriage is very important, and each sacrifices some independence for the good of the marriage.

Jim agrees with some of Tammy's traditional emphasis on stability and predictability, but he sometimes feels trapped in the marriage. Jim does not value sharing and companionship as much as Tammy does, and he tries to avoid conflict or open disagreement. Both of them have extremely strong commitments to conventional gender roles. Tammy sees herself as remarkably feminine and as the perfect counterpart to Jim's masculine, assertive personality. Both view the marriage as one uniting a 'strong silent male' to 'a warm nurturing female'. They see each other as very different but complementary. Tammy is exceptionally good at predicting how Jim sees himself; although he is emotionally remote, she is good at drawing him back into the marriage.

Jim and Tammy do not openly express their anxieties about each other, but often they do not have to; they can use gender stereotypes to predict how the other is thinking or feeling and often they are right. On the other hand, they rarely refer to themselves as a couple by using the word 'we'.

Jim and Tammy agree about many of the major issues that come up in marriage and family life. According to them, their ability to show affection and to engage in sexual relations is a major source of marital satisfaction.

Since Jim is a separate and Tammy is a traditional, this couple are called *separate–traditionals*.

COUPLE V: ERIC AND MARIE

Eric and Marie do not share the same philosophy of life;

Eric believes in stability and predictability, and Marie believes in personal growth and individual psychological gratification. Because Marie also believes that couples do not have to share complete, total agreement on all issues, she accepts Eric's traditionalism, although she sometimes quarrels with him about it.

Both enjoy spending time together and are capable of having a lot of fun, although Marie tends to value privacy and independence more than Eric does. When they do engage in conflict, Eric tries to keep the conflict muted, but Marie always expresses what she is really thinking and feeling.

Part of their philosophical disagreement about life involves the nature of male/female roles. Eric sees himself as very masculine and in general believes men and women should follow conventional roles. Marie is more egalitarian and thinks people should follow their own individual preferences. Marie thinks of herself as feminine but also analytical and capable of leading.

Because this couple is trying to negotiate an acceptable level of closeness and distance in the marriage, their conversations often show signs of a power struggle and these power struggles continue for fairly long periods. Neither side is willing to give in or give up.

They think of their marriage as being extremely well adjusted. Sometimes Marie thinks about divorce or separation, but Eric says he never does. Despite their disagreements they are very affectionate and companionable.

Eric is a traditional and Marie is an independent and this couple are called *traditional–independents.*

These descriptions can be identified in a lot of marriages and the reader can discern the general tendencies which apply to them. In a study by Fitzpatrick of 700 couples,[3] 20 per cent were found to be traditional, 22 per cent were independents, and 17 per cent were separates. Of the remaining 30 per cent, no mixed type occurred with greater frequency. The first is the traditional type of marriage, which supports conventional ideas about marriage and family life, values interdependence between partners, and favours restricting open conflicts to serious issues only. The second is the independent marriage, which supports unconventional ideas about marriage and family life, values autonomy as well as interdependence between partners, and favours open conflict to resolve major as well as minor differences. The third is the separate marriage, which supports conventional ideas about marriage and family life, but shows ambivalence about these values. This marriage devalues interdependence and avoids open conflict.

EQUITY

Independently of types, social scientists have given the name equity to what would normally be considered fairness. Egalitarian marriages largely survive on the basis that each partner needs to feel that what they put in roughly approximates what they get out of the marriage.

According to equity theory,[4, 5, 6] intimate partners will feel satisfied if their encounter is equitable – that is to say, the things that spouses contribute, such as affection, sex, money, gifts, etc. should over time be roughly equal. Clearly those who feel underbenefited are strong candidates for separation or divorce, but sometimes those who are overbenefited cannot cope with the excess of benefits they receive and feel overwhelmed. Equity is part of the contemporary marriage's requirement, and independently of the type of relationship a couple have, there is need for fairness in the exchange.

PART IV

Sexuality

CHAPTER 21

Sexual Intercourse

The link between love and sexuality is very close. One of the most powerful expressions of love is to make love and there is no doubt at all that sexual intercourse is the background force that keeps marital love alive.

It is estimated that the average couple spends about fifteen minutes a week actually engaged in sexual intercourse,[1] which means that they spend 99.9 per cent of their time doing something else. But these fifteen minutes play an extremely significant role in their married life.

Although love plays an important part in the sexual life of both husband and wife, it is still generally true that women link sexual intercourse more with affection, and men more with the release of physical sexual excitement.

INITIATION

Clinical experience and research show that husbands initiate sexual overtures more often than wives,[2] but gradually wives also initiate. Blumstein and Schwartz found in their study that husbands claimed that 51 per cent of them were likely to initiate, in 33 per cent the likelihood was equal, and 16 per cent said that their wife was likely to initiate. Wives on the other hand said that 12 per cent of them were likely to initiate, 40 per cent that the initiation was equal and 48 per cent that their husbands initiated.

Given that men make sexual overtures more often, are wives more likely to refuse? Research indicates that this is so,[2] but in the majority of cases, overtures meet with success.[3] The reason for the high rate of success is that couples get to know each other and are likely to ask when they feel that their partner is in the right mood or, if they do not always feel in the right mood, they might agree, to avoid rejection, hurting the feelings of their spouse or for the sake of peace.

It has been found that 60 per cent of overtures are non-verbal,[4] such as touching, hugging, kissing and 40 per cent are verbal, which include 'Let's make love' and 'I want to make love to you'. By and large, requests for sex are made non-verbally and refusal is communicated verbally. Byers and Heinlein found that most couples deal with disagreement over having sex by agreeing not to have sex and agreeing to postpone to another occasion or simply disagreeing.[3] The authors conclude that it is easier to say or accept 'no' to a verbal request than to say or accept 'no' to physical advances.

FOREPLAY

Sexual arousal differs in men and women. Men are aroused by visual stimulation, and the nude body, in particular, is of special interest. Visual stimulation extends to literature, and pornography on the whole is of much greater interest to men than women. Women, on the other hand, are likely to be aroused by emotional or social factors. As has already been indicated, men engage in sex for fun and particularly to discharge sexual tension, whereas women are concerned to express feelings and their commitment to the relationship. Both, but particularly men, are aroused by fantasy.

Sexual arousal leads to preparation for intercourse or foreplay. In his sexual studies nearly fifty years ago, Kinsey found that couples in the United States had about ten minutes of foreplay before they started sexual intercourse.[5, 6] Hunt reported that this time had increased by the 1970s.[7] Foreplay is not only a way of working up to sexual intercourse, but also a means of expressing affection. It usually consists of kissing, genital or breast stimulation and it may also include cunnilingus (oral stimulation of the female genitalia) and fellatio (oral stimulation of the male genitals). In their recent British sexual survey, Wellings et al. state that oro-genital contact has increased.[8] American studies also show this increase. This may be due to the desire to use such an approach to reach orgasm as a way of avoiding penetrative sex to avoid the risk of sexually transmitted disease, or it may be that sexual experimentation, prior to intercourse, has increased, or a combination of both. The fact is that couples tend to maximise the pleasurable potential of sexual intimacy and are more relaxed about it.

On the other hand, some wives may not enjoy sex at all and simply do it to satisfy their husbands. The author has met two wives, one of whom counted the cobwebs on the ceiling and the other who prepared the menus for the next week whilst having sex. Thus whilst the overwhelming majority of couples are sharing an intensely pleasurable experience, there are always some who participate in the preparation but do not enter into the pleasure.

When the arousal is successful, men experience an erect penis, an increased heart rate and a rise in blood pressure, and women vaginal moistening, erect nipples and also rapid heart rate and increased blood pressure.

In a small proportion of men premature ejaculation may take place as the orgasm occurs before penetration. These are dysfunctional situations, which need help.

COITUS

After a period of foreplay, the couple are ready for intercourse, which usually means vaginal penetration. As far as sexual positions are concerned, Gregersen suggests that there are 529 possible positions for sexual intercourse.[9] However, most couples use a limited range, with the man or woman above, the sitting position, side by side or rear entry. The position used most often has always been – and continues to be in our day – that of the man above, but other positions are increasingly used. Hunt found that 75 per cent used the woman-above position occasionally.[7] There is little doubt that experimentation is much more widely used nowadays.

Anal intercourse in heterosexual couples is not a frequent mode of penetration. The British survey referred to previously found in the group aged 18–24 an incidence of 8.6 per cent for women and 8.1 per cent for men. In the United States, Voeller came to the conclusion that 10 per cent of heterosexual couples have anal intercourse.[10]

Whatever method of coitus is used, the object of the exercise is to reach a climax. An orgasm is an end point, in which for the man there is an intense pleasure, with ejaculation of semen. Occasionally ejaculation may not take place. The ejaculation in the male is due to muscular contractions. In women, the stimulation of the clitoris plays an important part in the orgasm, which consists of a series of rhythmic contractions which are highly pleasurable. There may be three to fifteen contractions in the woman.

Husbands and wives do not always have orgasms. Men are more likely to have an orgasm than women, but this does not mean that women do not enjoy the sexual act. In the British survey, respondents were asked to comment on the sentences 'Sex without orgasm cannot be really satisfying for a man' and also '... for a woman'. Forty-eight per cent of all men (not just married) agree or strongly agree that orgasm is necessary for male satisfaction, and 43 per cent of women believe the same on behalf of men. Surprisingly a third of all men disagree with this view. As far as the woman's orgasm is concerned, more men believe that it is important for women's sexual satisfaction to have an orgasm than women do. Darling et al. found that, in order of significance for women, lack of foreplay, fatigue and preoccupation with non-sexual thoughts deter them from having an orgasm.

Orgasm for women nevertheless remains important as part of sexual satisfaction. In the study of Darling et al.[11] not only is the presence of orgasm important but so is the timing. In this study it was found that women who experienced orgasm after their partners were less satisfied than those who experienced it just before or simultaneously. Of the 709 nurses studied, 45 per cent had their orgasms before, 19 per cent simultaneously and 36 per cent after their partner did.

Positions for sexual intercourse are not the only factors that engage couples. Variety also matters. Although some couples have sex on the same day, in the same position and with the same foreplay, others experiment. In the past it was usually the husband who suggested variations. Nowadays, wives also contribute to variety. A study in the United States by Greeley showed some of the experimentation of married couples.[12] Thirty-two per cent abandoned all their inhibitions, 19 per cent swam nude together, 21 per cent watch blue films, 20 per cent buy erotic underwear, 22 per cent make love outdoors, 34 per cent go to a hotel or motel to spend time alone and 39 per cent take a shower together. But Greeley found 46 per cent of married couples never abandon all their sexual inhibitions.

FREQUENCY OF COITUS

There is a wealth of information about the frequency of sexual intercourse in married couples. This information is available in the United States and the recent survey *Sexual Behaviour in Britain* gives up-to-date information here.[8] Early data from Kinsey found a median frequency of sexual intercourse in the married of 2.45 per week for the age group 16–25, and 1.95 for those in the 26–35 age group.[5, 6] Some twenty years later, Hunt found a higher rate,[7] and Blumstein and Schwartz also reported a higher rate.[2] The latter found that 45 per cent of their couples married for two years or less had sex three times a week, and some 38 per cent had intercourse between one and three times a week.

In Britain, frequency of intercourse was measured per month. The median frequency for those women aged between 16–24 was six times; 25–34, was five times; 35–44, was also five times; 45–49, was twice; and the median frequency for all age groups was four. Both American and British studies are aggregates. In practice, couples vary from having no sex to its being a daily occurrence.

One of the features that these figures show is the decline of sexual intercourse over time. However, although frequency may decline, we now know that its satisfaction continues and it extends well into the seventh decade, and in individual couples even later.

James found the frequency of sex in the first month of marriage to be seventeen times,[13] but by the end of the first year, it had reduced to eight times per month. The same worker suggested that while the rate is reduced by one-half in the first year it then takes another twenty years for it to halve again. It is suggested that both duration of marriage and age influence the rate.

When the reasons for the dramatic fall of sexual frequency in the early years is studied, then the arrival of children, work, commuting, housework, financial worries, fatigue and familiarity all contribute to the decrease. The frequency of sex is of course a subject of dispute between spouses and the one who wants more underestimates the amount and the one who wants less overestimates.

COMMUNICATION

It has already been shown that self-disclosure is a means of bringing about closeness between couples. The same applies to sexual satisfaction. Using their clinical experience, Masters and Johnson and Kolodny showed that good communication about sex is linked to a satisfying sexual relationship.[14] What this means is that couples have to acquire the freedom to talk to one another about what pleases and what displeases, about where they want to be touched, stroked or rubbed, about what causes irritation, how frequently they want sex and how they like to experience it.

PERSONALITY

It is clear that some men and women enjoy sex more than others. Some individuals possess an extremely negative attitude towards sex, including sex guilt[15, 16] and anxiety towards sex.[17] Eysenck found that those who score highly on neurotic sex, sexual shyness, sexual disgust and prudishness, are dissatisfied with sex.[18] Marriage-counselling clinics are filled with couples in which one partner dislikes sex.

Eysenck has shown that there are two dimensions to sex. One is sexual drive or libido and the other is sexual satisfaction. Libido reflects the absolute interest in sex, which may be high or low, and sexual satisfaction refers to the degree that it is pleasurable and fulfilling. Some men and women appear to be addicted to sex as they might be addicted to alcohol or drugs, without much satisfaction but a great deal of necessity.

According to Eysenck, individuals who are high in extroversion tend to engage in sex more often and with more partners. Those who have more sex and tend to be extrovert are also more interested in aggressive sex, pornography and sexual permissiveness.[19] As we shall see, the extrovert person is the person who is also likely to stray extramaritally.

Although Eysenck's theory is grounded in biology, it is nevertheless true that psychological factors in childhood, such as sexual trauma and sexual abuse, may contribute to sexual personality problems.

SEXUAL SATISFACTION

American couples seem to be reasonably satisfied with their sexual lives. Greeley discovered that approximately one-third of husbands and wives said they were satisfied 'a good deal' and another third 'a great deal' with their sexual life.[12]

There are some social-class differences in American findings. For example, working-class wives are less satisfied with some sexual activities, such as oral-genital ones.[20] The British survey also states that there is an overall trend showing that for both men and women the proportion reporting anal, oral and non-penetrative sex increases in higher social classes.

Greater satisfaction is reported by younger age groups, but in at least one study the middle-aged married adults said that they enjoyed sex more now than at an earlier period.[4]

One of the most consistent findings is the link between sexual satisfaction and frequency of intercourse; the more frequently a couple have sex, the greater is their satisfaction. As already mentioned, the presence of an orgasm is associated with satisfaction, but the latter can be achieved without it.

In general, couples who are satisfied with their relationship enjoy their sexual life and their sexual life in turn promotes their marital happiness.

CHAPTER 22

Sexual Difficulties

There are three sorts of sexual difficulties encountered in marriage. The first is the reduction of sexual intercourse as a result of the deterioration of the marital relationship. The second is dissatisfaction with sexual intercourse itself and in particular with aggression linked with sex. The third is the presence of sexual dysfunction of a physiological nature against a background of normal marital relationship.

SEXUAL ACTIVITY AND MARITAL RELATIONSHIP

It is natural to expect the quality of the marital relationship to affect the extent and frequency of sexual involvement. This is particularly true for wives, for whom sex is often the aftermath of a preceding emotional atmosphere. When a wife feels cross or indifferent, she is unlikely to wish to engage in sexual overtures. To a certain extent the same applies to husbands, but there are differences. Men have a sexual drive that is independent of the relational atmosphere and they need to discharge their sexual energy at regular intervals. In these circumstances, what often happens is that a poor relational situation is aggravated by the pressure of the husband to have sex, which is resisted by the wife. This is a regular occurrence in counselling situations, in which the husband looks for a resumption of sex as an indication of the improvement of the relationship, and the wife delays sex until there is an amelioration of the relationship. This is a standard problem which needs a lot of patience and skill to negotiate. Blumstein and Schwartz found that when there was conflict in the relationship, couples kiss less often when they have sex.[1]

As already mentioned above, when there is conflict in the relationship, it is the wife who more often withdraws from sexual involvement. This was confirmed by Rubin,[2] who studied working-class couples. The wife often feels that in these circumstances she is used, and the refrain 'You don't want me, all you want is my body' is often heard.

THE LINK BETWEEN SEXUAL INTERCOURSE AND DIFFICULTIES

In the previous chapter we saw the link between frequency of intercourse and sexual satisfaction, and the presence of an orgasm and sexual satisfaction. In this context, wives are annoyed by being pressed for sex when they do not want or desire it, and men are more inclined to be disturbed by feeling rejected sexually.

There is an intimate link between sexual variations or fetishes and sexual difficulties. Sexual fetishes are practices in which sexual arousal is associated with the presence of an additional element. Sexual fetishes are often the domain of men, occasionally of women, who are sexually aroused, for example, when they see their partner in seductive underwear, or are excited by the common elements of fur or rubber and, for example, want their partners to go to bed wearing only a rubber raincoat. On other occasions it may be a husband wants to wear feminine underwear when having sex. In addition to these fetishes, some men and women prefer to be aroused by pain, commonly to be beaten or to inflict pain. The presence of these variations can be accommodated by some wives; indeed, the wearing of exotic underwear is treated as normal. Others find such requests repellent and are deterred by them. Very often the difficulty for the wife is the feeling that her husband does not find her personally sexually attractive, but is only interested in the fetish. When wives find such requests unacceptable, husbands may resort to prostitutes for satisfaction.

Sexual aggression or coercion, in which sexual penetration is achieved by physical or psychological force against the desire of the woman, is not uncommon. Rape by a stranger is an event that hits the headline, but sexual assault also takes place within marriage. Russell discovered that 8 per cent of her survey had been assaulted by their husbands or ex-husbands.[3, 4]

Although physical sexual aggression stands out, it is the more psychological variety that women often experience. Women are often pushed to have sex when they do not want to, for a variety of reasons. Men have traditionally expected their wives to give them sex, and those who assault believe it is their right to have sex,[5] and wives consider that they are under obligation to submit.[3] In fact the emancipation of women will gradually have a profound effect on this matter, to the point where wives will only have sex when they freely consent to it. In some instances, the man wants to have sex to prove that he is a man; Frieze discovered that 78 per cent of the women she saw who had been sexually assaulted, associated this action with the desire of their husband to prove his manhood.[6]

Traditionally, men have considered themselves as the dominant sex and women the passive and yielding ones. There is evidence that men who are sexually aggressive are very traditional in their sexual attitudes.[7, 8]

In addition to the normal assertive attitude of the male and the yielding of the female to avoid conflict, there have been in the past, and to a lesser extent now, economic forces putting pressure on wives to have unwanted sex. There is evidence that economic dependence can make women more vulnerable in this way. It has been found that women who are disadvantaged by having several children, not having been employed before marriage or having had less education, who in some ways are dependent on their spouses, are more likely to be sexually assaulted by their spouses.[6] Another research worker found no direct relationship between economic dependence and sexual assault, but a link between the first and remaining in the marriage.[3]

Alcohol is often implicated in instances of sexual aggression and, as we shall see, of physical aggression. In the counselling situation, the story of the woman whose husband comes home late, the worse for drink, and both assaults her and forces himself sexually on her is a common tale. The next morning he has often forgotten the whole episode. It is stated that alcohol weakens self-control and disinhibits the person.[9] Of course, too much alcohol may stimulate sexual desire but render the man impotent.

Finally, the family of origin has been linked to sexual assault. Wives who have been sexually abused as children are more likely to be victims of sexual attacks by their spouse.[5] These women often do not enjoy sex and end up by refusing their spouse; the husbands in turn force themselves on to their wives. On the other hand, those who are sexually and physically abused as children expect abuse as the norm and become more reconciled to it. It has also been found that men who attack their wives sexually often come from homes where their fathers had abused their mothers.[10]

Whatever the source of sexual abuse, a woman who is sexually attacked finds that her trust in her husband is reduced. Sexual intercourse is an intensely physically and emotionally intimate experience. The woman who has been sexually assaulted approaches sex with a conditioning of trepidation and apprehension. She is simply afraid, not only physically but emotionally. Sometimes this apprehension generalises to other men or to all men. Just as some women who have been sexually abused are angry and apprehensive about men in general, so women who have been sexually assaulted may generalise their fear. Sometimes these women cannot resume sexual intercourse without treatment. Much more common is a reaction of anger at such an assault; and if the anger is deep and prevailing, it may turn to depression. Sexual assault is intimately linked with sexual problems and dissatisfaction and may be a reason for finishing a relationship.

SEXUAL DYSFUNCTION

The third source of sexual difficulties is when the relationship is good, but there is sexual dysfunction. Care should be exercised with the concept of sexual dysfunction. A man may occasionally be sexually aroused to the point where he ejaculates before vaginal entry or soon after penetration. There are other occasions when he may fail to obtain an erection or to sustain it, particularly after a bout of drinking. A wife may fail to have an orgasm. All this is part of normal sexual life and has to be negotiated with tact, understanding and compassion. Sexual dysfunction is present when the difficulty is persistent.

There is a great deal of knowledge and information about human sexuality and its problems, and this book could be devoted entirely to this issue, but I am looking at sexuality as part of marital love. For those who want to refer to specialised manuals, Bancroft in Britain,[11] and Kaplan in the United States,[12, 13] have provided rich material.

Basically, sexual difficulties may be part of the phase of sexual arousal, sexual excitement and orgasm. The commonest problems in men are premature ejaculation and impotence, and in women inadequate arousal, painful intercourse and persistent absence of orgasm. There is now an army of sexual therapists who deal with these problems, but what has been written in this chapter should be remembered: namely that, before dysfunction is looked for, the relationship of the couple must be examined; because one of the commonest experiences in counselling is the presentation of a sexual problem, only to be told privately that the husband or wife can have enjoyable and normal sex with a third party. Nevertheless, there are a host of authentic dysfunctional sexual difficulties which undoubtedly cause marital difficulties and, when the relationship is intact and a functional problem is discovered, it deserves to be treated in its own right.

ABSENCE OF SEXUAL INTERCOURSE

I will finish off this chapter with some observations about marital love when sexual intercourse is absent. Sexual intercourse may be temporarily or permanently absent. Men may become impotent for physical reasons and not amenable to treatment. Women may not want sex after the birth of a child. Both sexes may not want to have sex when they are depressed. How do couples cope in these circumstances? Perhaps the clue to this question is found in the survey, *Sexual Behaviour in Britain*.[14] I quote, 'Two out of three respondents agree that companionship and affection are more important than sex in a marriage.' Only 16 per cent of men and the same number of women agree that sex is the most important part of marriage. In the part of the questionnaire that asked which factors are most important for making a successful marriage, sex came third in the rank ordering, after faithfulness and respect, for both men and women. In other words, companionship and affection are the basic underlying needs of couples and, if these are present, then often the marriage survives.

There are many situations in which sex is absent from a marriage. The first and the easiest to deal with is the one when neither husband nor wife miss the sexual side of the relationship. They get their gratification from being together, sharing their time, common values, interests and feelings. In these circumstances, touching and hugging play a prominent part in the affection. It should be remembered that our earliest affectionate experiences were not genital sex, but the affection we linked with vision (seeing each other), sound (hearing each other's voice), touch (touching and being touched), and smell.[15] These stimuli continue to provide fundamental pleasure, even when we cease to be sexually aroused by each other, and indeed may be said to be the most persistent sources of joy and comfort in our lives as we recognise and hear those to whom we are attached.

The next situation is when the wife is sexually uninterested and the husband remains sexually interested. This situation can be handled by the husband becoming slowly used to the absence of sexual intercourse. Occasionally the wife may agree to masturbate him and of course solitary masturbation remains an option for this situation. Masturbation is of course not the same as sexual intercourse, although in some marriages the two may coexist. Finally it is in these situations that extramarital affairs often take place and these may jeopardise the marriage.

The third situation is the one when the husband is not interested in sex or cannot perform sexual intercourse. Some wives find this difficult and may also resort to masturbation or an extramarital affair, but on the whole they cope with this situation much better than men. In particular they remain satisfied when their husbands will cuddle and hug them, an experience which women enjoy much more in its own right than men do. Indeed, even when sexual intercourse is present, wives enjoy being cuddled and hugged and may not want to proceed to full intercourse, which is sometimes very disconcerting for the husband.

The fact is that marital love can and does exist without sexual intercourse in many marriages. This situation is managed better when communication is good and the couple are frank with each other about their inner world.

CHAPTER 23

The Various Meanings of Sexual Intercourse

Why does sexual intercourse, with its brief duration, play such a vital role in the love life of a couple?

One begins with the obvious, namely that sexual intercourse allows the discharge of a most powerful drive. It arouses an intense physical and emotional excitement and it is ultimately linked, when all goes well, with an overwhelming pleasure, which is associated with the relief of tension and gives an afterglow which may continue for hours or even days. It could be said that, at the hedonistic level, sexual intercourse provides human beings with a unique experience. But, as poets and writers have tried to express, there is more to sexual intercourse than just pleasure. Sexual pleasure of equivalently intense proportions may be obtained from masturbation and yet human beings on the whole prefer sexual intercourse.

Sexual intercourse has three potential functions. The oldest and most traditional has been for the sake of procreation. This function has greatly diminished in our time. First of all, through contraception, sexual intercourse and procreation have been separated; and second, the amount of sex needed to have the small, modern-day family is very little. The overwhelming majority of sexual activity is non-procreative.

There is also the view that sex is simply for fun and recreation. Certainly, couples use some of their sex life for recreation, but recreation itself cannot do justice to the intensity which sexual intercourse arouses.

The third possibility, and the one that this chapter explores, is its relational meaning.

SEXUAL INTERCOURSE AND CHILDHOOD

As everyone knows, it was Freud who postulated that all love relationships were really sexual. This view is no longer widely held, but aspects of the libido theory are still pertinent. Freud postulated that there was an oral sexual phase in the baby, followed by an anal phase and finally a genital-phallic phase. All these erotogenic zones, as they are called, are lined with smooth mucous membrane, which is extremely sensitive to touch. The remnants of these zones are pertinent in two ways. First, touch through kissing has become one of the commonest expressions of demonstrating affection and so the physical and the personal coalesce here. Similar, but much less common, is the desire for anal stimulation. We associate the mouth with eating; it is an acceptable site of the body. We link the anus with elimination and dirt and it has a less romantic hold. But there are, as has been already mentioned, at least 10 per cent of couples who enjoy anal intercourse, and for some people anal stimulation is very pleasurable. Finally, phallic and clitoral stimuli are highly pleasurable and form a frequent part of foreplay. In all these situations, there is an interaction between the sexual and the personal, in the sense that these actions afford us the opportunity to give and receive pleasure, and the giving and receiving are important constituents of love.

The next person who is relevant is John Bowlby, who has been mentioned several times in this book. Very briefly, his attachment theory is a description whereby touch, vision, sound and smell, four physical dimensions, become the means of affectionate attachment, forming the crucial bond between ourselves and others. This attachment is a source of security, a basis from which to explore the world, and a means of comfort and reassurance. Sexual intercourse is an amalgam of touch, vision, sound and smell and, once again, the physical encounter, which is now completed by genital union, becomes the infrastructure for securing and reinforcing affectionate attachment, a personal dimension for security, comfort and reassurance. In this model, the seeking of sexual intercourse when there is stress, discomfort, depression, apprehension, or uncertainty of self-esteem, is a source of personal reassurance through physical means.

Moving on to Erikson, also already referred to, who postulated that the first year of life is associated with the sense of trust, the second and third with autonomy, and the fourth and fifth with initiative. These are very important human experiences and I want to comment on two of them.

In sexual intercourse there is a moment of complete trust between the couple. They disclose their nude bodies to each other, one of the most private aspects of one's self. In this exposure is an implicit request for respect, safety, the avoidance of pain, all dimensions which are violated in rape and coercive intercourse. This initial trust goes on to a physical closeness in which the couple become as close as the oneness of mother and child, with all the sense of unity that this gives. Trust is an essential part of closeness and it forms the essential characteristic of emotional communication. Trust begins to enter our lives physically in the hands of our father and mother and is mediated in that first year of life through sensitive touch and appropriate nurturing. Sexual intercourse repeats that trust physically and emotionally.

In sexual intercourse, we give access to our spouse to the whole of ourselves, physically, socially and emotionally. There is no other act which combines such a loss of autonomy and at the same time achieves such closeness. In sexual intercourse, there is a physical fusion with the most varied and subtle abandonment or withholding of oneself. The whole pursuit of marital love in the balance between autonomy and intimacy reaches its climax in the balance between abandonment of autonomy and the retention of a self which gives and receives, enhances and is enhanced. These aspects of childhood are a crucial element of sexual intercourse and link the love of childhood with the love of the present.

SUSTAINING, HEALING AND GROWTH AND SEXUAL INTERCOURSE

One of the central themes of this book is that a great deal of marital loving can be decribed by acts and experiences which sustain, heal and help a couple to grow. These three aspects of love have been conceptualised as vital. Time alone will show whether they stand the test of careful scrutiny.

In the meantime I believe that sexual intercourse is the background force that motivates, sustains and celebrates these loving experiences. Take, for example, sustaining. Couples make love to celebrate an episode of togetherness. Time spent together in a walk, over a dinner, an evening out that is enjoyable, call for an act of love. Good communication, in which a couple have disclosed a part of themselves, exchanged vital information or understood each other better, prompts a moment of closeness that is celebrated in intercourse. Demonstration of affection is a particular prelude to sexual intercourse. Affirmation is a moment when a couple feel enhanced by each other. This is a moment of praise in which they feel appreciated by each other and, as their self-esteem rises, so the desire to get close to each other develops sexually; and finally a successful resolution of conflict is a moment of triumph for a couple who seek sexual celebration.

The same applies to healing of the personality. As a psychiatrist I have spent my working life dealing with very vulnerable, wounded personalities. But, to a greater or lesser extent, we are all wounded people. If our relationship shows understanding, empathy and care, we spot the moment of difficulty in our spouse. These moments of difficulty can range from an expression of fear of overt problems to the hesitancies and uncertainties we all experience. It can be a facet of self-esteem and a sense of feeling unwanted or rejected. A response which boosts the self-esteem, reassures, accepts, facilitates and encourages, is a moment of healing. These moments can occur at any time. They may be recognised and appreciated, or not. But when they are recognised, sexual intercourse becomes a way of saying thanks. As we shall see in a moment, sexual intercourse itself is a healing moment when the spouse feels repeatedly recognised, wanted and appreciated.

Finally there is the issue of growth, in which couples recognise, facilitate and encourage each other's social, emotional and sexual development. In this respect, spouses continue to act in the capacity of parents. As I have already said, this does not mean acting in a capacity of sustaining the dependence of the partner. They act as parents by spotting, encouraging and overcoming the doubts of the partner when the latter develops an aspect of themselves which has been hitherto undiscovered or undeveloped. Much attention was paid in the section on growth to the balance of closeness and separateness, and intimacy and autonomy, and these are developments in the personality which take time and are hard to pinpoint at any particular moment. And yet spouses are aware of critical moments of achievement. The obvious ones are achievements such as a new job, a rise in salary, perhaps a new recipe successfully negotiated and so on. Both the long-term and the short-term achievements can be celebrated through sexual intercourse.

SEXUAL INTERCOURSE AS A BODY LANGUAGE

Finally I want to conclude with some observations which I have made on sexual intercourse.[1] In these reflections, I have written that the bodily experience of pleasure and joy becomes a language of personal communication in which the spouses are talking to each other. What are they saying with their bodies, with or without words?

I believe they are saying at least five things. Firstly, through sexual intercourse they are sending signals to each other that they recognise, accept, want and appreciate each other. Sexual intercourse when it is freely entered into is a most powerful expression of feeling wanted. In this way, sexual intercourse becomes one of the most eloquent and succinct expressions of affirming each other's identity.

Secondly, in sexual intercourse, the man who successfully arouses his wife sexually and the wife who arouses her husband, mutually affirm each other as man and woman and each other's sexual identity. A successful act of coitus can do more than all the dieting, dressing, cosmetics, etc. that money can buy.

Thirdly, it is a fact repeatedly stated that marital intimacy is impossible without conflict. After an argument or quarrel, most couples forgive and forget quickly; they often follow this up with intercourse. Sometimes the conflict is particularly painful and the alienation is marked, lasting days and weeks. Often it is an act of intercourse that brings it to an end. In this instance, sexual intercourse is an act of reconciliation.

Fourthly, we all need meaning in our lives. We find meaning in work, creativity, achievement, faith and values. Sexual intercourse is a recurrent act in which we feel wanted for our own sake. It becomes a recurrent act of hope in our lives.

Finally, sexual intercourse is a most meaningful way of saying thank you to each other; thank you for being with me yesterday, today and hopefully tomorrow.

Thus, sexual intercourse, which has on a few occasions the potential of giving new life, has always the potential of giving life to the couple.

IDEALISATION

In case the reader may think that this is an idealised version of sexual intercourse, I am well aware that many acts carried out on occasions when a spouse is tired, assents to sex out of habit or to avoid conflict, may not be fully enjoyable and so on. All this is true, but I think the reason that sex is so important to couples is that its potential is enormous and, although it is realised to a variable degree, it is a moment that acts as a glue to the total loving exchange and, as such, is of the greatest significance.

CHAPTER 24

Adultery

Marriage and marital love are intimately linked with exclusive sexual fidelity. In the survey of *Sexual Behaviour in Britain,*[1] faithfulness was considered to be the first factor of a successful marriage and was assessed by over 90 per cent of men and women as being very important or quite important. Seventy-one per cent of men and 78 per cent of women do not agree that no harm would be done by having sex outside the relationship. The same positive attitude to marital fidelity is held in the United States. And yet the reality is very different. In this chapter, I look at the factors associated with adultery. My own knowledge is based on clinical experience but, in addition to that, I have relied on a major British study by Annette Lawson. Her book, *Adultery,*[2] is invaluable and should be consulted by anyone especially interested in the subject. In her study, which was completed in 1982–3, Lawson found that, during marriage, contemporary men and women become more tolerant of sexual infidelity. At the time of her study in the early eighties, 60 per cent of men and women disagreed to some extent with the statement that sexual relations outside marriage are always wrong. Of those who remained married to the same spouse, only 50 per cent continued to believe that both should remain faithful. Interestingly, about 90 per cent of remarried women thought both spouses should, and 57 per cent of remarried men thought the same. It seems that as current marriages continue, both the experience of married life and changing sexual attitudes soften expectations, but equally the harsh reality of divorce stiffens the resolution to remain faithful. Lawson's own explanation of the reduced expectation is analysed and clarified further. She found that, amongst those who remained married to their first partner, it was those who had an extramarital relationship who had reduced their emphasis on fidelity. Those who remain faithful continue to retain their high standards.

Lawson throws light on changing sexual attitudes with regard to fidelity. She found that over 80 per cent of women marrying before 1960 thought that sexual relations outside marriage were always wrong, whereas only a quarter of 1970 brides and grooms did. In these data, Lawson points out that the gap between men and women has narrowed considerably. As we shall see, this change in attitude is related to the greater incidence of women having affairs, which in turn reflects their greater participation in work and their general emanicipation. These changing attitudes also influence whether an extramarital affair will lead to marital breakdown. However, in my experience they do not lead to any reduced reaction to the event. As Lawson herself states, 'Yet emotions are not necessarily rationally based, and guilt often knows no rhyme or reason'.

DEFINITION, INCIDENCE, TIMING AND EDUCATION

There are three types of adultery. The first, the commonest and most traditional, is the affair, which has sexual involvement with someone else that is kept secret from the spouse. The second has been called parallel adultery, when an extramarital relationship is known to the spouse and tolerated, without leading to the break-up of the marriage. The third is a recreational variety, which wishes for recreation but wants to retain the marriage intact, provided of course that the spouse allows this.

Clinically, one divides adultery into one-night stands, which take place when the spouse is away from home for business, education or recreation etc. These affairs do not normally threaten the marriage. Next are affairs that may last from a few months to a year or two and then end with the marriage restructured but ongoing. Thirdly, there exists the ongoing affair in which the spouse forms a new relationship and leaves home.

The incidence of extramarital affairs varies considerably, depending on the sample tested. They range from 73 per cent, who have had at least one adulterous relationship in Lawson's study, to 3 per cent found by Gorer[3] in England. In the United States the estimates are that about 50 per cent of spouses in marriage had extramarital affairs.[4] The general consensus is that about 25–50 per cent of women have had one extramarital lover, and about 50–65 per cent of men, both by the age of forty. All the research suggests that in the last forty years women are having more affairs than previously.

The number of extramarital affairs, however, differentiates men from women. Fifteen per cent of men, but 25 per cent of women, have had one affair; 40 per cent of men have had four liaisons, but only 25 per cent of women have had as many.

According to Lawson, the timing of the first affair has changed and has become earlier. For women married before 1960 it was after nearly fourteen years of marriage; those married between 1960–9, eight years; and those married in 1970 or later, four years. The same trend is noticed for men.

Lawson found that adultery is related to education, not in absolute terms but in the difference achieved by husbands and wives. The man who has equal or superior education to his wife has the average number of liaisons, but the man whose wife is better educated than he tends to have less while she has more.

THE 'WHY'

Why do men and women have affairs? Before answering this question, I want to look at the association of an affair with stress. It is suggested that affairs begin round about the time of the birth of the first child, when stress is high and sex less available. But Lawson's evidence is against this view as being very important. Only 15 per cent of new fathers or mothers had a first affair in the year before or after the birth of their first child. On the other hand, parental death was offered as a powerful reason, especially for women. A very small percentage of men and a much greater one of women thought that illness or an accident had played a part in their affair. Finally the mid-life crisis is offered as a reason by both men and women. A crisis has to be linked with opportunity and the greater involvement of women in the workplace offers this to both sexes.

In fact, the majority of extramarital affairs take place against a background of marital dissatisfaction and this is particularly important for women. Atwater found this link,[5] as did many American researchers.[6, 7, 8, 9] Dissatisfaction with marital sex is another reason.[10, 11] Apart from these two main reasons, the third is the pursuit of fun and excitement, which contrasts with the hard work and reduced pleasure in a continuing marital relationship. Extroverts fit into this category, needing an excess of stimulation to feel fulfilled.

WHAT DOES AN AFFAIR ACHIEVE?

There is very little doubt that, in general, men have affairs primarily for sexual satisfaction, and women for emotional satisfaction. But of course both sexes spill over into each other's territory. Either may feel that they have no intimacy or emotional satisfaction with their spouse; they feel ignored and unrecognised for themselves; their self-esteem is gradually dropping in the marriage; they become depressed and have an affair to rediscover themselves as worthy persons who can still claim attention. Since, in an affair, the excitement of falling in love can be recreated, it provides a powerful stimulation to the person involved. Affairs provide an opportunity to disclose aspects of oneself hidden from the spouse and to get affirmation about one's image that the spouse fails to give, particularly in relation to the pursuit of autonomy and independence. An affair offers a woman the reassurance that she is still sexually desirable, and through her sexuality she can discover aspects of her personality that are hidden from her husband. In many respects, women can discover power in an affair against the powerlessness in their marriage.

REVELATION AND ITS CONSEQUENCES

Unless an affair breaks up a marriage, most of them last for a set period before the spouse finds out and the affair terminates. Lawson discovered in her study that about two-thirds of the spouses told their partner about the affair. Interestingly, in recent years, confession has become more common. Thus 47 per cent of men who had their first liaison before 1965, confessed. This increased to 59 per cent who had an affair between 1965–74, and reached nearly 80 per cent for those who experienced an affair in 1975 or later.

The commonest reason for telling was, according to Lawson, 'the desire to stop the deceit and to be open'. But of course telling is not the only way for the spouse to find out, as evidence of the affair is often left around. The few who did not reveal, did so to avoid hurting the spouse and, as far as women are concerned, to save the husband's face. The person who is having an affair often feels guilty and uncomfortable about it, even when they legitimise it in their own minds, for a whole variety of reasons. Affairs contradict such deep-rooted beliefs and feelings that it is unusual for them to take place without the feeling that one is cheating and should not be doing so. These feelings may not stop the affair but contribute to the effort to keep it secret.

When the affair is revealed, the spouse often feels shattered, betrayed, helpless, is afraid of being abandoned and is likely to become jealous. There is a general and specific loss of trust, which is hard to rebuild, and, even these days when sexual liberality has emerged, the sense of hurt often remains. Clinically what is often found is the profound difference between theoretical attitudes and the harsh reality of emotional pain. The spouse who has been betrayed feels unloved and rejected, is pushed to ask what is wrong with them and generally feels let down. In the context of the subject of this book, adultery is a central attack on marital love, which can be and often is overcome but which nevertheless remains a painful memory in the relationship. The moment of revelation of the adultery is almost invariably painful and associated with anger, sometimes with depression and, for a few people, as I have mentioned, a shattering experience. Counsellors by the very nature of their work see the marriages that have been particularly badly affected.

As we have seen, the majority of affairs are revealed, but when they are kept secret, women are better at doing this than men.

Despite the increased liberalisation and frequency of affairs by women, there is still a profound difference in the results of affairs between the sexes. By and large, men still feel freer to experiment sexually outside the marriage; women feel less entitled to their affairs and hence women find it difficult to run their marriage and affair parallel to each other, as men appear to do more easily. Women feel more guilt over affairs than men do.[8]

What does revelation do to the marriage? As I said, anger, sadness, anxiety, fear, depression and jealousy may all follow. As far as the marriage itself is concerned, it usually survives but it may break up and adultery is a common ground for petitioning for divorce. Lawson and Samson found that those least concerned about fidelity were individuals who were in their first marriage for at least ten years and who themselves had had an affair.[2] Remarried women whose first marriage had concluded on the grounds of adultery were the most frightened of any repetition. Those who remained totally faithful found the adultery of their partner particularly difficult.

Extramarital affairs play a part in one-third of divorces,[12] but we have no idea how many affairs do not lead to divorce – probably the majority, at least of the first, brief affairs. Clearly affairs that are discovered and continue after the discovery form a different proposition. Men on the whole find the affairs of their wife much more difficult to negotiate. Men were three times more likely to blame the break-up of a relationship on their wife's affairs than on their own.

The most likely outcome of infidelity is for the couple to recognise it as a crisis and to work subsequently for the resolution of the difficulties. Thus for most couples, and in particular for wives, an affair is a signal of marital difficulties, and the aftermath of revelation should be restoration work to the marriage. If this is not done effectively, more affairs can ensue. For some men, extramarital relationships are pursued for fun whilst preserving the marriage, but for the majority of husbands an affair is an indication of marital difficulties. Spanier and Margolies make the point that, although most people see their own affairs as the result of marital difficulties, the affairs of the spouse are interpreted as a cause of marital problems.[8] This observation reminds us that even now society tends to see the person having the affair as the guilty party and the spouse as the innocent victim. In practice this traditional division does not work out very well. One not only sees that the so-called 'victim' has perhaps had an affair in the past, but when one comes to analyse the marriage the victim very often contributes by their behaviour to the affair of their partner. Although strictly speaking, guilty parties still remain in cases where there was no marital provocation, this situation has become less frequent.

Adultery in a strange way is one of the prices that companionate marriage pays, as the stakes of love rise and the expectations become more difficult to realise. We have to do a great deal more work of education and support for contemporary marriage, before more of the large range of sexual and emotional expectations are met within one relationship.

CHAPTER 25

The Impact of Children

Traditionally, having children was the primary purpose of sexual activity. The 1662 Book of Common Prayer stated that the primary purpose of marriage was the procreation of children, whereas the 1980 Alternative Service Book states that the primary purpose of marriage is the mutual comfort, help and fidelity of the couple. This shift also took place in the Roman Catholic Church at the Second Vatican Council.

This shift of emphasis has meant that the arrival of children, although still a source of pleasure, is recognised now also as a source of stress and strain on the marriage. This stress and strain is a barrier to intimacy and a cause of conflict. There is evidence from research that the presence of children and marital quality tend to be inversely related.

From the birth of the first child to the time the last child leaves home, parental roles compete with marital roles for temporal and emotional priority.[1]

In Chapter 8 it was shown that marital satisfaction drops from the onset of marriage, reaches its nadir when there are adolescent children, and thereafter picks up when the couple return to a one-to-one relationship. This loss of satisfaction may be due to the fact that over time marriage becomes less satisfactory,[2] and that the children have an adverse impact on the quality of the marriage. In fact both factors may be operating but the research evidence certainly implicates the children.

Longitudinal studies show a decline in the expression of positive affection from the last trimester of pregnancy through nine months postpartum, as reported both by husbands and wives.[3]

Conflict between spouses increases also from the last trimester through the ninth month of the postpartum.[4] Indeed, marital satisfaction declines after the birth of the first child.[5, 6, 7, 8]

This postpartum loss of marital satisfaction may be due to diminished sexual activity, tenderness on the part of the wife, and less available time for togetherness.

A more detailed study of reduction of marital satisfaction (Cowan)[9] showed that women who become mothers showed a significant decline in marital satisfaction within the first six months of the infant's life. Wives' satisfaction continued to decline when the child aged from six to eighteen months. When the children were eighteen months old, fathers also showed pronounced decline in marital satisfaction. These results led Cowan to say that the negative impact of childbirth is first felt by women and then by men. This negative effect of childbirth on women has been persistent in the research literature.[3, 10, 11]

In a study in Britain, Mansfield, Collard and McAllister found that wives felt differently about themselves when they became mothers.[12] Their sense of self, already shaped by being wives, was further defined through pregnancy, giving up work or changing working hours and organising childcare. Husbands find it more difficult to articulate change and they often expressed the feeling of watching change through their wives.

Generally when the baby was planned, or received as a pleasant surprise, the transfer to parenthood was easier. In this instance, both parents discussed the decisions to be made. As in the American studies the changing identity of wives affected the relationship with their husbands, and it was the latter who were not prepared for the impact of this change in the marital relationship, particularly in terms of the negative change in the sexual relationship.

As far as the marriage was concerned, the lives of husbands and wives diverged after the birth of the child. In spite of the intention of both to look after the baby, the traditional division of labour, with the wife having more responsibility, worked out in practice. The balancing of workload in the home was the most likely cause of conflict in the early years of marriage.

Husbands who were more involved with childcare experienced a stronger identity as fathers and it made a difference to their wife's feelings about family life. It seems that involvement with the children made the husbands more supportive of domestic life generally. What the husband did practically was appreciated, but what was appreciated even more was the way he valued and affirmed the domestic world and the wife's role within it.

After the intense research of the early years, when negative changes occur, research goes quiescent and does not re-emerge until the children are adolescent. But of course as the children grow older they make fewer demands on the parents, who are able to return more to each other. But the intermediate years still make immense demands on them.

Adolescence is associated with increases in parent–child distance, adolescent autonomy and parent–child conflict.[13] Parents have their own anxieties about the safety of their children from drugs, pregnancy and alcohol, and their adolescent children revive fantasies of their own sexual relationships. It is a time of considerable stress.

Finally the children leave home. Research on marital relationships identifies this period of the empty nest as one of elevated marital satisfaction.

This chapter briefly summarises the transition from traditional role-orientated marriages, where children were of primary importance and the roles of the parents were subordinated to the needs of the children, to the companionate marriage, where the needs of the spouses are just as important and the impact of children has both advantageous and disadvantageous effects on the marriage.

The inner world of marriage has changed radically when the adverse impact of children is a major factor in the loving/distancing of the couple. Whereas in the past the role of spouses and parents was unified, we now have to see couples as having the dual roles of partners and parents, and that each of these roles makes competing demands on the other.

Part of the evolving nature of companionate marriage is to anticipate this conflict and to have enough information about what to expect so that disappointment does not plunge the couple into an irreversible belief that their marital bliss is over.

As with every other aspect of contemporary marriage, we need to research what actually happens to the relationship and to use this information to arm couples with how best to cope with the reality of the situation.

PART V

Practicalities

CHAPTER 26

Home/Housework

Before discussing the home–housework contribution to marital love it is worth pausing for a moment and asking where does the source of love primarily come from in marriage. Does it come from the personal dimension described so far in the world of the encounter between spouses, or is it the result of having a home, regular meals, the care of one's material needs and the money to provide it all?

In their study of the early phase of marriage,[1] Mansfield and Collard asked their couples the question, 'What kind of things about being married do you like?' One reply was 'Coming home to my own place, to my own home ... going out to buy things: I don't like shopping for food but if we are going to buy something for the home, then we will do it together ... I like the idea of working for something instead of just wasting my life away.'

In fact Mansfield and Collard write: 'At the start of their married lives, newly-weds are expected to have romantic images of marriage, of the "happy-ever-after" variety'. In fact, throughout their interviews, very few romantic images were revealed, although many ideal images were offered of what they thought and hoped that marriages could be like: for example, there were many references to hopes of following a sharing, caring, companionate model of marriage, expressed for example by one wife as 'the usual things – a nice home and sooner or later a family and I'd like our life together to be the most important thing rather than his job'.

As has been already shown, research indicates that love

can be divided: into the romantic, passionate variety, which engages the couple when they are forming the relationship; and then they move into the companionate type, which has both its peak moments in the sustaining and sexual dimensions, and the moments of love that develop gradually in the healing and growth dimensions. This companionate variety has been shown throughout this book as the experience that predominates in marriage. Whilst it is vividly lived at certain moments and times, marital life as a whole is a daily routine of work, chores, care of the children and socialisation. Thus marital love in my view is a delicate interaction between the central experiences of sustaining, healing and growth, and the life that sustains these moments in the presence of a home, and the contribution of housework, home, work and finally the money that makes it all possible. I would propose that, whilst home, housework, work and money are important for supporting companionate love, they are not the central experiences and, if a couple have the attachment bonds of affection, they may suffer but can brave the afflictions of material deprivation. This is not to say that material difficulties and household work are not important for the relationship – they certainly are – but in my experience, when they go wrong, they act as stressors to attachment whereas attachment remains primary. In her book *Between Husbands and Wives*, Fitzpatrick says,[2] 'It is not lack of money that causes marital problems, but rather how the couples communicate and negotiate with each other about their economic difficulties'. I would say that, in addition to communication and negotiation, the presence of a home and money are significant. Couples find it difficult to sustain their love for each other when they have neither. In fact we find clinically that both their absence and their presence are not absolute factors in the deterioration of marital love. The material forces support the primary relationship of companionate love, but it is the latter that determines the survival of the relationship. It is relevant in this respect that the central factor associated with happiness in marriage is its quality, which is largely that of the relationship.[3]

HOUSE, HOME

It is taken for granted in our Western society that a newly married couple want to have a separate abode. Mansfield and Collard stated, 'Advertisers and marriage pundits alike seem to agree that starting off married life in a home of one's own is a crucial ingredient in the recipe for living happily ever after.'[1] A wife of one of their couples is quoted as saying 'I like living here, just me and John – you can do what you want, you can go out and come in (to your own place) and you can do it how you want to do it and have your friends in – show it off – it's nice, isn't it – I've never had my own flat before, so it is nice'.

In another study from One Plus One (see Chapter 36) a group of divorced and continually-married were compared, and the former were found to have a higher incidence in social class V (the lowest socioeconomic group), which in turn had a high incidence of shared marital accommodation.[4] Shared accommodation is but one factor in a vortex of difficulties including financial and educational disadvantages.

Thus a home offers privacy, the freedom to come and go as the couple please, a secure base from which to explore the world, privacy for sexual activity, and the ability to shape it as the couple wish. Later on when they have children, independent accommodation offers the best environment in which to raise them. For a small minority, the togetherness which the confined space of the home brings about may appear as a restriction, and some spouses long for space for themselves. In most homes this is possible and a sense of togetherness can be achieved even if the couple are in different parts of the house.

The home is decorated, furnished and equipped as the couple desire. In this way it becomes a projection of themselves. This projection is not always easy, as husbands and wives do not always like the same things. Most manage to compromise and to make the home a place of utilitarian purpose and also a source of peace.

Psychologically, it becomes a place of familiarity and therefore of security. People find it difficult to leave and change homes, which is a major source of stress. They also find it problematic for instance to go into hospital, and much effort is made nowadays to nurse people in their own homes.

It is the place where the companionate love is lived out and the links between the home and that love become very marked.

HOUSEHOLD CHORES

The home above all is the place where the infrastructure of living takes place, in the preparation, serving and eating of food, in cleaning and maintenance and in its presentation to the outside world. Traditionally the home was the woman's domain. In industrialised societies some women worked in factories but many did not and it was considered their responsibility and part of their 'love' to stay at home and look after it for their family. Gradually, this traditional image of the man out at work and the woman in the home, cooking and cleaning, has changed, with many more women going out to work and men participating in household chores. What is clear is that these chores have been invested with feelings about the 'love' that is exchanged between husband and wife. Thus Oakley discovered that wives who were unhappy with the division of labour of labour in the home were more likely to complain about the monotony and fragmentation of these chores.[5] Those who were dissatisfied were also likely to complain about the loneliness of this work. Thus, gradually the household chores entered the arena of the way husbands and wives treat each other.

In fact, the division of household labour is linked to marital happiness.[6] When the division of labour was considered to be fair, marital happiness was high, and it dropped when it was considered to be unfair. Furthermore, wives get more depressed when husbands do not offer appropriate help in the home.[7] The contribution of the husband is especially important when the wife is working outside the home.

Research has shown that men and women traditionally engage in different tasks in the home. Thus women still do the cooking, cleaning and looking after the children, which are known as feminine tasks, while husbands spend their time on household repairs, cutting the grass, putting out the rubbish, and car maintenance. The structures of these tasks have different characteristics.[8, 9] Men's responsibilities have a clear beginning and end, discretion as to when the task should be done, and often there is an element of pleasure or recreation associated with the task. Women on the other hand have not this freedom. Cooking, washing dishes and looking after the children have to be performed at regular and definite times with very little choice about whether or when they should be done. I shall return later to the question of fairness, but in the meantime it is important to establish the quantitative amount of labour performed by husbands and wives. Both in the United States and in Britain there is overwhelming evidence, that, despite the development of egalitarian marriage, the reality remains that women perform a great deal more household chores than men. In the United States, Blair and Lichter have shown that women perform on average 33 hours of housework per week (exclusive of childcare) and men 14 hours.[10] In Britain a study from the Henley Centre reported in 1993 almost identical results, namely that women spend an average of 34 hours on housework and men put in only 13 hours. But there are variations. In a study by Blair and Johnson,[11] it was found that in 18 per cent of households with wives employed and 16 per cent where they were not, men contributed over 20 hours per week to household chores.

Although wives do more housework throughout the life cycle of marriage, the disparity between them and their husbands is greater in the early child-rearing years and least in the pre-parental and post-parental years.[12] This same study found that wives' satisfaction with the division of labour was lowest when there were preschool and school-age children, and highest in the pre- and post-parental years. That is, their satisfaction was lowest when their contribution to the household labour was highest. Compared to the wives, there was little variation of satisfaction for husbands across the family cycle. This study also confirmed that satisfaction with this aspect of family life was associated with greater marital happiness, lower marital conflict and less verbal aggression.

Examining further women's satisfaction with housework and fairness, there is important research by Blair and Johnson.[11] They confirm the quantitative disparity of housework between men and women. They found two factors related to the wife's appreciation of fairness of housework. Employed wives who see their housework to be appreciated are more likely to believe that housework in the home is fairly divided than those who feel it is unappreciated. In addition to this acknowledgement, Blair and Johnson found that it is not the absolute amount of contribution by men that makes a difference to women, but their specific contribution to 'female chores' that will increase the perception of fairness by the wives. These authors also argue that, for many women, housework is a demonstration of caring. Finally they hypothesise that housework relates to the ideology of women, with the assumption that women who hold more egalitarian ideologies will consider the contribution of their husband to the household chores to be more important. This hypothesis was not supported by their data. Thus it seems that, even in the 1990s, there is still a deep traditional link between women and housework and, although fairness in this division has entered the negotiation between spouses, it has neither changed behaviour very much nor ideology. This is in line with what one sees clinically. Dissatisfaction with marital relations is still primarily the concern of affection and sex, with household work being a relatively secondary factor. There are of course individual exceptions, with women expecting their husband to contribute heavily to housework, but as yet these are the exceptions. For many families, the wife who works also does the housework and sometimes, when possible and financially allowable, help is obtained.

CHAPTER 27

Employment, Money and Leisure

The traditional model of marriage has been of the husband being employed and the wife staying at home, having the children and looking after them and the home. This picture has altered radically throughout the twentieth century and particularly since the Second World War. Now, married women are working in large numbers. The level of economic activity of married women is inversely related to the presence of children. Married women are most likely to be in full-time employment if they are aged 16–29 with no children. After that, economic activity falls sharply once there are dependent children, particularly if the youngest child is of preschool age. As children grow older, economic activity, mostly of a part-time nature, increases. Nevertheless, in Great Britain, the number of married women with children under five working full-time increased from 5 per cent in 1979–81 to 14 per cent in 1989–91. Those with children under five who worked part-time increased from 22 per cent in 1977–9 to 32 per cent in 1989–91. Those with children five years or over who worked full-time were 21 per cent in 1979–81 and 27 per cent in 1989–91, and those working part-time were 45 per cent and 47 per cent respectively. Thus, currently some 74 per cent of all married women work full- or part-time. In the United States, equivalent high levels of employment are found.

Early American research tended to see women's work as having a uniformly negative affect on marriage.[1,2,3] The rise of women's employment and divorce were associated. It was postulated that a wife's employment could, at any level of dissatisfaction with the marriage, increase the chances of divorce by the fact of her financial independence. It was also thought that work might increase a woman's desire for divorce by giving her the opportunity for alternative sources of fulfilment. Thus there has been a link between divorce and rising employment.[4,5] However, many recent studies of large national samples of American marriages report no effect of wife's employment on the marital satisfaction of either husband or wife.[6,7,8,9] In the paper by Spitze,[10] the statement is made, 'In summary, any effect of wife's employment on marital happiness seems to have changed from a negative to a null or perhaps even a positive one'.

Another approach of research for dual-earner couples has concerned itself with the effect of the wife's occupational achievement vis-a-vis that of her husband. The conclusion of this research is that the quality of marriage experiences is not reduced by the wife achieving more than her husband.[11,12,13]

In their study of the wife's employment and the quality of marriage,[14] Vannoy and Philliber found that 'The husband's support for his wife working is important to his marital quality and the wife's perception of that support is important to her marital quality'. Also the stronger his sensitivity is, the more positive his marital quality, and the quality of marriage of his wife is also higher the stronger the husband's sensitivity. In general, the husband's attitudes are more important for the experience of marital quality for both spouses than are the attitudes of the wife. The only attitude of the wife that matters is her competitiveness. The more competitive she is, the less both husband and wife are satisfied.

Thus the latest research suggests that the increased employment of married women does not have an adverse effect on marital happiness and, if the husband is sensitive and supportive, that helps.

MONEY

The result of employment is monetary acquisition. Money is the basis for so much that a family wants to do that it is really a very great background factor to their happiness. In practice, listening to couples with marital difficulties, money seems to have three meanings: the first is its absolute monetary value – that is, there should be enough for the family to meet its minimum needs; the second is intimately related to love; and the third is linked with the power relationship of the couple.

It goes without saying that money, just like a home, is a necessity for the functioning of a marriage. Nowadays there may be unemployment and economic stress. Common sense and experience suggest that when there are economic difficulties there is increased conflict between spouses. Research has indicated that economic stress may lead to withdrawal and lack of attentiveness between spouses.[15] In a paper by Conger and Elder,[16] it was hypothesised that 'Economic problems would promote interactional difficulties only if a spouse experienced psychological stress by recognising that family resources were not adequate to maintain an expected or desired standard of living'. In practice it was found that, when the perceived needs of the family had inadequate resources, thus producing economic strain, this increased the hostility and decreased the warmth of supportiveness of husbands towards their wives. Men's hostility was associated with greater perceptions of marital instability and lower levels of satisfaction by wives. This combination of hostility by men as a result of economic strain was replicated by the study of Liker and Elder.[17]

When economic difficulties result from unemployment, there are additional psychological stresses from the loss of status, grief reaction, shame, depression and despair that result, all of which aggravate the relationship between spouses.[18]

The second meaning of money is related to love. It is usually the woman who has traditionally felt deprived of resources, and her complaint to her husband is 'If you loved me, you wouldn't keep me short'. In counselling, women complain of many things, but being kept short of money is a recurrent theme. The man, on the other hand, who does not feel valued and loved for his own sake, feels that all he is appreciated for is the money he brings in. The woman who feels unloved regards herself as sexually exploited, and the man who feels likewise considers himself financially exploited. These positions may change as women become more financially independent.

Finally, money gives the holder power. Traditionally men had power over women because they were in financial control. Today, once again, the situation is changing and, as women become more financially independent, they feel they hold more power in their hands.

In brief, money not only produces tension between spouses when there is a shortage, but who holds it and how it is distributed is an expression of love. The mean spouse is unattractive, not only because he (and usually it is he) keeps his wife short but because the meanness is interpreted as a meanness of spirit and of love.

LEISURE

Money is not the only factor that is associated with leisure or joint marital activities but the two are intimately related. In Chapter 11, on availability, it was shown that togetherness was a key factor related to marital satisfaction and love. The peak times of leisure are the weekend, the evenings and holiday time, and most models of marital satisfaction argue for a connection between leisure or companionship and marital satisfaction.[19, 20]

Orthner suggested in his study,[21] 'The primary relational factor of leisure for marriage is that of a facilitator of communication during times of potential stress and relational change'. Holman and Jacquart found that the greater the individual leisure the less the marital satisfaction, but that joint activity was related to marital satisfaction.[22] But simply doing things together is not enough. There must be good communication when the couple are together. In particular, wives who are stressed appreciate a good deal of communication. The authors say that the statement 'The family (or couple) that plays together, stays together' should be amended to include 'if they have a great deal of communication while they play'. Their results also show that highly stressed wives find leisure activities to be a resource for dealing with stress but their husbands do not. This research confirms the clinical finding of the disinclination of husbands to talk when there are marital problems.

PART VI

Health Considerations

CHAPTER 28

Physical Aggression

The last thing that is expected of marital love is that it should be accompanied by physical aggression. Nevertheless, both clinical experience and research provide evidence that physical aggression does occur in marriage and that in its most severe form it can lead to violence that ends in death. In fact, a good deal of homicide occurs within the family.

It was Erin Pizzey who created the first shelter for battered women in England at Chiswick. By the end of the 1970s there were 200 shelters for battered women in Great Britain and they soon developed in the United States.

For a long time it was believed that violence in the home was the concern of the police, but now it is realised that it is the responsibility of everyone working with the family. A clinician like the author learns of violence in the home in the consulting room, but has no idea how common it is. In America, systematic studies have been conducted. One, by Straus, Gelles and Steinmetz,[1] of 2143 households, found that about 12 per cent of women and 12 per cent of men had been the objects of physical aggression in the previous year. A much larger proportion, 28 per cent of men and women, said that they had been the subject of violence at some time in their marriage, and some 3.8 per cent of wives had been severely beaten in the year prior to the interview. We see from these results that both men and women can be aggressive towards each other. Women can shove, punch, scratch, hit or throw things, whilst men hit and are of course much more dangerous through their sheer force.

How do these episodes of aggression come about? Most often the couple are in an exchange where there is verbal aggression, which escalates to physical aggression. Typical examples are a husband who comes home drunk from an evening out with his friends. His wife attacks him verbally and he defends himself. The situation may develop into a fight at this stage. At a later stage in the bedroom, he asks for sex and is refused. This may become the occasion of a brutal attack by the husband. Often these attacks are not remembered in the morning, but the wife has a black eye or signs of being battered. The combination of drink and sex is a common triggering point in violence, but individually they can also cause fights. A husband may be criticised for his impotence or, much more likely, attacked for an extramarital affair. These conversations may take place in the early hours of the morning when both spouses are tired. Often the wife wants to find out the sexual details of her husband's affair. The more he confesses, the more she wants to know. The reverse may also be true. A jealous husband may torture his wife for information of her alleged misconduct. The wife may reveal some information that inflames the husband further; both in this situation, and in many others, the prelude to violence is the escalation of a quarrel.

In addition to drink and sex, violence can often develop when either spouse has low self-esteem or is depressed. The spouse with low self-esteem is on the defensive and cannot accept responsibility for their actions. Whenever anything goes wrong, instead of apologising, they blame their partner and in this way another vicious circle of negativity develops. In these vicious circles, both men and women become physically aroused and as a result they cannot control their anger. Anger is not sufficient to lead to violence. Many couples get angry with one another but do not become violent. Almost invariably it is uncontrolled anger that leads to violence.

Reference has been made to the psychopathic personality in Chapter 15. This personality is often involved in physical aggression. Wives report husbands who hit them and then go down on their knees crying, apologising and swearing that they will never do it again. These resolutions cannot be trusted and such persons often repeat their aggression.

In addition to the psychopathic personality – that is, men and women who have short tempers, and are easily irritated, with a readiness to lash out – are found those who have been attacked in their childhood. There is a strong theoretical and clinical basis suggesting that those who are physically violent were smacked, hit or beaten when they were children. This leads to modelling. When they are frustrated, they deal with their difficulties by resorting to their earliest experiences. There is evidence that those who are physically aggressive come from homes where they either observed violence or were the victims of it,[1, 2] but many engage in violence who have not witnessed or experienced it as children.

At the heart of violence in marriage is often the presence of difficulties with communication. A spouse, often the husband, feels attacked verbally by his wife. He does not know how to defend himself. Often he goes silent or he simply counter-attacks with counter-accusations. This leads to two common scenarios. The first is the husband who goes silent; but the wife continues to attack verbally. In desperation he lashes out physically in an attempt to shut her up. The second has already been mentioned. This is an escalation of an argument in which a couple cannot negotiate, apologise, give in, refute effectively or satisfy their partner. As the escalation increases, so impulse control is reduced and the conflict is resolved with violence. The husband might grip his wife and shake her as a way of trying to make her see his point of view.

Sociologists believe that three family factors contribute to violence. The first is aggressivity itself, the second is inequality and the third is privacy.[3] Gelles believes that in certain conditions men think that they do justice to themselves as men by being aggressive or macho. There are women who in the past believed that a slap across their face was a sign of their husband's power and love. Inequality is expressed through the differences in physical size, strength, status and economic resources. Women have a long history of being inferior in these contexts, and in the final analysis their only defence was to use violence. Finally, the privacy of the home allows the expression of aggression without visible social censure. The home has long been held as sacred by everyone, and within it violence can be perpetrated unseen and unpunished. In addition to these three factors, sociologists have incriminated youthfulness of men, the presence of stress, low income, low education and lack of religious affiliation as factors responsible for physical violence.[1]

Although a single episode of violence is often negotiated and forgiven, repeated attacks are no longer tolerated, particularly by wives, and may become the basis for petitioning for divorce.

CHAPTER 29

Depression

Aggression is an act of verbal or physical violence against a partner and is something that in the final analysis should be preventable. Depression is a change in mood in the direction of sadness, misery, or loss of joy, which overcomes a person and over which they have little control. Depression is connected with affect, and depression is considered to be an affective illness. In an affective illness, the person becomes morose, loses the ability to enjoy life, withdraws into themselves, feels tired and is irritable. Communication slows down in that the depressed person talks little, registers little, and their level of alertness is diminished. Physically, the main symptom is tiredness, but when a depression is really severe there is also loss of energy, poor appetite, loss of sexual desire and weight loss. Psychologically, such a person finds it difficult to concentrate, to pay attention or to engage with other people. He or she finds it difficult to read, watch television or even peruse the daily newspapers.

It is clear that the combination of apathy, poor communication, and irritability has an adverse affect on the spouse, who misses the normal joviality, rapport and relaxed atmosphere of their partner. All this would be worthy of consideration only in a textbook of psychiatry if it were not a fact that some 25 per cent of the general population will have at least one severe affective episode in their lifetime.[1] Depression is in fact, with anxiety, the commonest psychiatric illness and it impinges heavily on marriage. One of the most adverse risks of depression is suicide, and a very high percentage of people who commit suicide have a background of depression.

Apart from the risk of suicide, it has been found that spouses who suffer from depression have greater problems in their marriages.[2] Such marriages are characterised by friction, poor communication and diminished sexual satisfaction. The incidence of depression is greater in women, and the depressed woman shows lack of affection towards her husband. Thus far, we have seen that couples whose marriage is in good shape prior to a depression can deteriorate in their relationship after the onset of a depression.

Do marital difficulties precede depression? The evidence is that a poor marriage can lead to a depressive illness. Paykel et al. found that depressed women often gave an increase in arguments with their husbands as a prior state.[3] In another study, Rounsaville et al. reported that over half of their sample of depressed women presented with marital problems.[4] Brown and Harris also found the lack of a confiding, intimate relationship with the spouse or boyfriend a precipitating factor of depression in the women they studied.[5] There is really extensive evidence that marital difficulties can precipitate a depressive illness; they can also result from such an episode. Thus it behoves whoever is looking at depression to take the state of the marriage seriously.

On the other hand, depression leads to marital disruption. In a controlled study,[6] eight male and twelve female depressed in-patients were studied while in hospital and after recovery, and compared with ten male and ten female non-psychiatric surgical patients and their spouses, and the interaction of twenty depressed patients with opposite-sex strangers. They found that the conversations of couples with a depressed spouse were marked by greater conflict, tension and negative expression. These interactions were also characterised by high levels of disruption, negative emotional outbursts and greater frequency of interruptions.

When it comes to the interaction of depressed patients with their spouses, these differed from the interaction of depressed patients with strangers. The interaction of depressed patients with their spouses was more negative in every respect than interactions with strangers. The depressed patient and their spouse are locked in a negative cycle, with the interaction fused into a system of well rehearsed negation, whereas communication with a stranger was free from this entanglement.

Arkowitz et al. also show that the spouses of depressed patients suffer.[7] These authors showed that, following interaction with their depressed wives, husbands reported feeling more hostile than did husbands of psychiatric and non-psychiatric controlled patients. In another study,[8] Kahn et al. reported that compared with non-depressed couples, those with a depressed spouse were angrier with each other following interaction and reported experiencing each other as more negative, hostile and competitive, as well as being less agreeable, nurturant and affiliative.

Thus depression may be both a consequence and a cause of marital distress. The cause of the marital distress is the withdrawal of the partner from their spouse, their negativity, their low level of satisfaction, their low level of sexual involvement and their lack of appreciation and awareness. Living with a depressed partner is hard work.

But if the depression can be lifted, then the situation can improve, and this applies in particular to self-limiting depression, and reactive depressions which are of short duration, in which the triggering stimulus is removed. The important thing is to seek help for the depression and to apply the various remedies that are available.

POST-PUERPERAL DEPRESSION

Since the time of Hippocrates, women have been described as having the tendency to become depressed after the birth of a child. The lightest of these depressive states is the so-called 'maternal blues', which may last from a few hours to a few days. It is characterised by fatigue, crying, anxiety over the baby, headaches, inability to sleep, confusion, and sometimes hostility towards the husband. This condition has a very high incidence and has been estimated at from 50–80 per cent of all pregnancies.[9, 10] A much small number of women, of the order of 10 per cent, become more depressed, perhaps a week to ten days after the birth of a child. Pitt describes these depressions thus:[11] 'The depression becomes evident after the return home (from hospital) as a prevailing despondency, tearfulness, feelings of inadequacy to cope with the baby, fears for her own and the baby's health, tension and irritability, undue fatigue, diminished appetite, difficulty in getting to sleep and decline in sexual interest.' When this group of patients was followed up a year later, 4 per cent had not improved and continued to suffer loss of sexual desire, irritability, excessive fatigue, depression and disturbed sleep.

'Little attention has generally been paid to this small number of women with persistent depressive features, but they have been noted as contributing significantly to marital breakdown'.[12] In fact, these women appear at any time, perhaps several years after the birth of their child, still feeling depressed, or if not that, having lost their sexual desire persistently since the birth of their children.

Finally in a very small group of women a full-blown severe depression indistinguishable from any other severe depression may emerge at any time during the first year after the birth of a baby. In a study of 54,087 births in a population of 470,000 people, there were 120 psychiatric admissions with severe affective disorder in the first month after childbirth. The condition is rare, but being unmarried, having a first baby, a Caesarian section and perinatal death all increased the risk.[13]

TREATMENT

The treatment of depression is a complex subject,[14] and is not relevant to the subject of this book. It is worth mentioning however that depression can play havoc with marriages and lead to marital breakdown and divorce. It is a condition that has received enormous psychological attention in the last forty years and quite a lot can be done to ameliorate it or remove it altogether. Treatment can be through medication and/or psychotherapy in its various forms, and no effort should be spared to diagnose and treat this problem and in this way reduce marital breakdown.

CHAPTER 30

Alcoholism

Of the three main detractors of marital relationship – violence, depression and alcohol – alcoholism has the lowest incidence, with a prevalence of 5.5 per cent in men and 1.6 per cent in women; however, these figures are likely to be underestimates. By and large there has been a shift away from the term alcoholism to that of dependence, which includes all drugs, including alcohol. Somebody is dependent on alcohol – that is, addicted to it – if he or she has exhibited in the previous twelve months three or more of the following characteristics:

1. A withdrawal state.
2. Drug use with the intention of relieving withdrawal symptoms.
3. Shows a subjective awareness of an impaired personal capacity to control the onset, termination or level of drug abuse.
4. A narrowing of the personal repertoire of patterns of drug use: for example, the tendency to drink alcoholic beverages in the same way on weekdays and at the weekend and whatever the social constraints.
5. Progressive neglect of alternative pleasures or interests in favour of drug use.
6. Persisting with the drug despite clear evidence of overtly harmful consequences.
7. Evidence that return to drug use after a period of abstinence leads more or less rapidly to reinstatement of the dependence syndrome.

Another way of describing dependence is that alcohol is used for its psychic effects, stimulation and sedation and that its use is compulsive. Alcohol reduces anxiety and also reduces tension in social situations and this is probably achieved through mild elation, a boost to the ego, and a drive to be sociable. In addition to the relaxation achieved, drinking may be associated with familiar cues such as being in a pub with usual company or even in the chair in which television is watched. Other cues may be associated with the mood. Thus drinking may be linked with being happy, sad or angry.

Mildly dependent patients will notice restlessness at certain times of the day and will want to resort to drink. If they have tried to reduce the drinking, they have not been successful. More severely dependent persons know that they will become restless at certain times and begin drinking early in the morning. Such people are so preoccupied with the need for a drink that they cannot think of anything else. They become restless, unable to sleep, and consume large amounts of alcohol to go to sleep.

When such a dependent person withdraws rapidly from alcohol consumption because alcohol is not available, then an alcohol-withdrawal syndrome follows. In this condition the person shows tremulousness, and has hallucinations, which may be visual in that he or she sees the proverbial pink elephants on the wall, or senses animals crawling on their skin; this condition develops to a seizure – that is, a convulsion and even delirium. Patients are regularly admitted to hospital in this condition.

More often, the family will see the husband or wife in a drunken state. In this state he or she will show various degrees of excitement, loss of restraint, their speech will be slurred, there will be lack of co-ordination of movement and gait, and eventually such a person becomes drowsy and falls asleep. Sometimes, however, he or she may become aggressive. A typical picture is of a man who returns home drunk and begins to show amorous interest in his wife, which is repulsed. This rejection offends him and he attacks her. The combination of drink and aggression is common.

Under the influence of drink, husbands and wives may become verbally abusive. In particular, those who are dependent on alcohol have a tendency to develop jealousy and are perpetually under the impression that their spouse is having an affair. The other problem is that alcoholic dependence is sometimes associated with impotence, which may make the jealous husband worse. The effects of continuous dependence on alcohol can be disastrous to a marriage. The partner who has to put up with an alcohol-dependent spouse has to witness repeated drunken episodes, loss of control, withdrawal of affection and interest, deterioration in work and economic status, violence and physical adversity. The results can be appalling, with the whole family dragged very low.

Clearly the marital, social and economic disadvantages can be tolerated only for a limited period, and unless the alcoholic spouse is willing to receive treatment the marriage cannot survive. But if the spouse is willing to have treatment then their partner can be very sympathetic and help them to overcome their difficulty.

As in the case of depression, alcoholic dependence may start for social or psychological reasons in the person and spill over to the detriment of the marriage, or the marriage may have overt or hidden difficulties which are not being faced and one spouse takes to drink as an escape from an intolerable situation.

Thus we have seen that problems in a marriage may lead to violence, depression, alcohol abuse or an affair, all of which may be symptoms of the underlying difficulties. Because of the interdependence of spouses and the overt pathology, increasingly it is not easy in all these circumstances to identify an innocent and a guilty partner.

Sometimes wives of alcoholic-dependent husbands complain about them but nevertheless enjoy the power they have over them. They stay in these situations and appear martyrs but they take unconscious pleasure in their predicament. Thus, when their husbands try to overcome their drinking, such wives will put temptation in their way by encouraging them to have a drink which 'will not hurt you' or to go to the pub. These remarks also apply when the wife is the alcoholic. The relationship between alcohol consumption and marital relations is subtle, and although we often see the impossible situation in which a partner is at the end of their tether, there are intermediate situations in which a spouse may drink in excess and in this way give the partner a weapon of control over them.

In the majority of instances, excessive alcohol consumption is utterly detrimental to a marriage and calls for a response. The response can be medical or it can be through the use of Alcoholics Anonymous, or a combination of both. Although some experts allow the resumption of controlled drinking after a period of total cessation, it is safer to treat alcohol dependence as an illness and commit oneself to total and perpetual abstinence.

Needless to say, the treatment of alcohol also involves a thorough assessment of the marital relationship, and whenever necessary the intervention of marital help.

PART VII

Divorce and Its Consequences

CHAPTER 31

Divorce

The concluding sections of this book deal with marital breakdown and divorce, their consequences, and possible future strategies. At one end of the spectrum, marital breakdown is associated with the absence of love in the marital relationship. However, not all relationships that become empty of love end in divorce. In the study of Cuber and Harroff mentioned already,[1] the conflict-habituated and the devitalised are patterns of marriage in which very little love may be left, but they survive. Nevertheless, increasingly these empty-shell marriages do end in divorce. Most commentators believe that there is increased marital breakdown and that there is a growing readiness to resort to divorce.[2, 3]

There are theoretical grounds for believing that, as marriage changes into the companionate variety, with higher expectations of affection and sexual fulfilment, both sexes, but particularly women, will tend to leave it if it does not meet their perceived minimum needs.

INCIDENCE OF DIVORCE

Certainly the incidence of divorce in the last thirty years has shown an exceptional rise. I shall quote British figures to show that divorce has been rising throughout the twentieth century, but that the rise has been particularly steep since the 1960s.

TABLE I DISSOLUTIONS IN ENGLAND AND WALES, 1901–1992

1901–5	2816
1906–10	3118
1911–15	3280
1916–20	7548
1921–5	13,668
1926–30	16,789
1931–5	20,056
1940	7755
1945	15,634
1948	43,698
1950	30,870
1955	26,816
1960	23,868
1965	37,785
1971	74,400
1976	126,700
1981	145,700
1986	153,900
1991	158,000
1992	160,400

From these figures it will be noted that divorce rose after the two world wars, after divorce legislation – particularly the Divorce Reform Act 1969 (which came into operation in 1971), which made irretrievable breakdown its sole ground – and generally after 1960; it escalated in the 1970s, leaving the current estimate in the United Kingdom fluctuating around the 170,000 mark. Since the 1960s the divorce rate has increased sixfold. Haskey points out that, at present rates of divorce, just under 40 per cent of marriages are expected to end in divorce.[4] The general picture in the United States is similar, and the projected figure of marriages ending in divorce is 66 per cent.[5] In his detailed study, *The Relationship Revolution*,[6] Dormor found that this escalation of divorce has affected the whole of Europe; so we are seeing a phenomenon that encompasses the whole of Western society. In this chapter we shall try to understand why this is happening.

In addition to the increase in divorce, there is evidence that divorces are occurring progressively earlier in marriage.

TABLE II DIVORCE: BY DURATION OF MARRIAGE – UNITED KINGDOM PERCENTAGES

DURATION OF MARRIAGE	YEAR OF DIVORCE			
	1961	1971	1981	1991
0–2 years	1.2	1.2	1.5	9.3
3–4 years	10.2	12.2	19.0	14.0
5–9 years	30.6	30.5	29.1	27.0
10–14 years	22.9	19.4	19.6	18.3
15–19 years }	13.9	12.6	12.8	12.8
20–24 years }		9.5	8.6	9.5
25–29 years }	21.2	5.8	4.9	5.0
30+ years }		8.9	4.5	4.1

Source: *Social Trends*, No. 24, 1994

It can be seen that in the thirty years from 1961–91, divorces in the first two years of marriage increased considerably. This is accounted for partially by the change in legislation to the effect that couples can petition after one year of marriage, but also in general because marriages last for shorter periods and divorce is earlier. The table shows that nearly a quarter of all divorces now occur in the first four years of marriage. Overall, the median age of wives at divorce is around 33 and that of husbands 36. Almost half of all divorces occur within the first ten years of marriage. Divorce, however, also occurs after many years of marriage, when the children are grown up.

As we shall see, there is considerable concern about the impact of divorce on children and so it is pertinent to ask how many children under the age of sixteen are involved in divorce. It is estimated that the number of children involved varies between 150,000 and 160,000. In keeping with the statistics of earlier divorce, the proportion of children of divorcing couples under the age of five has increased from 23 per cent in 1972 to 32 per cent in 1987. It has been estimated that, if divorce rates were to continue unchanged at the 1988/9 level, nearly one-quarter of all children would experience a divorce in their family before reaching sixteen years of age.[7]

Women petition for divorce much more frequently than men. Nearly three-quarters of petitions in Britain are filed by women. There may be strictly legal reasons for this massive proportion of petitioning by women, but it also shows that by and large it is women who are dissatisfied with current marriages. The Divorce Reform Act, which came into operation in 1971, made irretrievable breakdown the sole ground for divorce. Such breakdown can be demonstrated by proving one or more of five facts. These are:

1. Adultery.
2. Unreasonable behaviour.
3. Desertion for two years.
4. Two years' continuous separation with consent of partners.
5. Five years' continuous separation.

Haskey shows that the petitions sought by the wife were on the whole based on unreasonable behaviour of the husband, and those granted to the husband featured adultery much more.[8] This is an interesting broad observation, showing women's increasing expectations for companionate, affectionate behaviour and intolerance of violence, excessive drinking, gambling and affectionate indifference, whereas men find the sexual behaviour of their wives a more sensitive area.

REASONS FOR DIVORCE

1. GLOBAL FACTORS

Clearly such major change in behaviour must have macro-social factors that pervade Western societies. There are four such elements. The first and most important is the emancipation of women, which is leading to a different man–woman relationship. Women are emerging from the hierarchical, patriarchal relationship to a much more egalitarian one. They are working in ever-increased numbers and that means they are not entirely dependent on their husbands for survival. Family size has been greatly reduced and women are more free to pursue other acitivities than childbearing.

Secondly, in the post-war period there has been a rise throughout Western society in material standards. Food, shelter, clothing, schooling and education are provided for the majority in sufficient quantity. This meeting of basic needs has paved the way for increased expectations in the world of feelings, emotions and sexual fulfilment. Both men and women want more out of each other and these higher expectations are likely to remain so long as the material benefits persist, unless they are met progressively with sufficient education and support.

Thirdly, the nature of marriage, as this book has tried to show, has changed. The traditional contract of social roles emphasising the breadwinner role of the husband and the nurturing, childbearing, child-rearing, homemaking characteristics of the wife, has changed. These roles remain to an extent, but increasingly love is emerging as the principal feature of companionate marriage. The shift from institutional to companionate marriage has taken place rapidly, without the necessary preparation and support for it, and the vacuum has been filled by divorce. Society was familiar with the skills for institutional marriage but has yet to become familiar with those required for companionate marriage, which have been outlined in this book.

Fourthly, Western society has experienced a hundred years of psychology, and has been particularly influenced by dynamic psychology. As the couple become more intimate, the emotional, psychological factors have become more prominent and, as has been shown in the chapters on the personality and healing, the expectations of couples are deeply influenced by the healing possibilities of psychotherapy. Furthermore, with the advent of psychology has also come a powerful orientation towards personal development that can be divided into two possibilities: a narcissistic self-development that may dilute interpersonal commitment and/or a richer realisation of self that contributes to mutual development.

It can be seen that these four factors have permeated the background against which marriage is taking place. They have altered out of all recognition the social and emotional dimensions which weave the matrix of personal relationships. But this reality has not been crystallised and the education for it has not been widely embraced and so the price of divorce is still being paid.

2. SPECIFIC SOCIAL FACTORS

Moving from these global, macro factors into sociological research, sociologists have found a number of social factors associated with divorce. These are described below but not in order of importance.

a) The first is age at marriage. This factor has been found persistently for the last twenty-five years or more. The finding is that those who marry under the age of twenty are more vulnerable to divorce.[9] This finding has been replicated in the United States.[10, 11, 12] In fact Martin and Bumpass conclude that age at marriage is the strongest predictor of divorce in the first five years of marriage,[5] and Moore and Waite show that this effect is independent of early childbearing.[13]
b) Several studies both in Britain and the United States

show that premarital childbearing increases the risk of divorce in the subsequent marriage, but that by itself a premarital conception does not.[5, 9, 14, 15, 16, 17]

c) The combination of youthful marriage and premarital pregnancy is particularly associated with divorce.

d) There have been numerous studies that indicate that spouses who have homogamous (similar) social characteristics, such as race, religion, education, experienced less divorce than those who have dissimilar features.[18]

e) Higher levels of education are generally associated with greater marital stability.[11, 19, 20]

f) Whilst, as I have stated, higher material well-being that leads to greater expectations leads to divorce, it is also a fact that too low social and material standards may contribute to marital breakdown. Thus it has been found that there is an inverse relationship between socioeconomic status and divorce: the lower the socioeconomic status, the higher the divorce rate.[9, 21] The socioeconomic position is related to education, income, home ownership, all of which have inverse relationships with divorce. There is some suggestion, however, that recently the upper socioeconomic groups are catching up in their divorce rate.

g) More committed church affiliation is associated with lower divorce rates.[16]

h) In America it has been persistently found that black Americans are more likely than white ones to divorce.[22] But black Americans are also associated with the social disadvantages that contribute to divorce.

3. CLINICAL STUDIES

The global and the social factors give us broad associations. Is it possible to go further and show that individual social and psychological factors influence divorce? It should be remembered that men and women have different levels of toleration of distress. Those who are in an older cohort generation grew up with strong social and religious commitments to the permanency of marriage and put up with adversity that younger generations do not. Even within the younger generation, there are marked individual differences as to what is acceptable and so it is not possible to indict any particular behaviour in a one-to-one relationship with divorce. It is possible, however, to stress recurrent patterns of behaviour that form the basis of complaints when marital difficulties exist. In this section I give two different accounts of patterns of difficulties associated with marital problems. The first is a model introduced by the author,[23, 24, 25, 26] and the second is descriptions given by divorcing couples in the United States.

THE AUTHOR'S MODEL

In this model, I divide marriage into three phases. The first spans the first five years of marriage to the age of 30. These early years have been shown to be responsible for nearly a third of all marital breakdown, and what is even more important, what occurs in these years has a lasting effect on the rest of the marriage.[9] The second phase is while the children are growing up and takes place between 30 and 50, lasting about 20–25 years. The third phase occurs between 50 and the death of one spouse.

I then look at each phase under the five dimensions of social, emotional, sexual, intellectual and spiritual. What is implicit in this model is that these five dimensions cover the whole range of what constitutes marriage and that marriage is not a static but a dynamic event, which unfolds over the years, and each phase has its own characteristic features.

Phase I The first five years of marriage

These are in some ways the most important years of marriage, for it is from this stage that the character of the relationship will be imprinted on the couple.

Social

Under the social factors, five characteristics emerge repeatedly in clinical sessions. These are the family of origin, household tasks, money, work and leisure.

It is central to current marriages that the couple should detach themselves from their parents and have an intimate personal relationship. Marriage means separating from one's family of origin and forming a new social unit. It does not mean that the parents are dismissed; they still retain a very supportive role as parents and grandparents. Nevertheless, the couple communicate and reach their mutual decisions through each other. Most of the time a new balance of closeness and distance is established between the couple and the parents. However, this does not always happen. In a percentage of marriages, one or both spouses remain overattached to one or both parents. This means they live near each other, see each other frequently and consult the parents about the intimate details of the marriage. The spouse feels on the outside, cut off, isolated, and resents being bypassed. Decisions that should be mutually reached are taken in consultation with the parents and in brief the husband or wife has not achieved emotional detachment from the parents. If things go wrong between the couple, the dependent spouse goes straight back to the parental home.

Having established a home, the newly married couple will decide how to run it. Here the chief problem lies with the contribution of the husband. During courtship the future husband may promise the moon. In reality in the marriage the wife is saddled with the home, her work and the children. The evidence shown in this book is that by and large she accepts this triad. There may however be resentment and tiredness which, with the arrival of children, may erupt into overt discontent.

In the midst of housekeeping, indeed of marriage as a whole, will be found the presence of money. Money, as has already been shown, has three meanings. It has an absolute monetary value: there may or may not be enough of it for the standard of life expected. Secondly, it has an emotional value. The man or woman – it has usually been the latter – who is kept short of money, feels or says, 'If you loved me, you would not keep me short'; and finally money is associated with power, freedom and independence. The financially independent person is beholden to no one.

Work is intimately associated with financial resources. Work plays two roles in marital difficulties. The spouse who works too much is not available to relate to his or her family. The unemployed lose their self-esteem and identity and become more irritable, which leads to quarrelling.

Leisure time is spent in a balance of time available for self and for the family. Here, for example, the problem may be of the husband who uses his leisure time to continue his bachelor life, playing football or other sports, or going to the pub, and has all the advantages of marriage without making himself available to his wife and children.

Emotional

Perhaps the greatest emotional problem in this first phase of marriage is to contain the disappointment of how the spouse is perceived. In courtship and in short cohabitation the spouse is idealised. He or she is projected with ideal qualities, some of which turn out to be realistic, others not. Whether the marriage will survive depends on how disappointed the partner is and their capacity to tolerate and forgive the shortcomings.

There are, however, some patterns of emotional difficulties that hit the couple out of the blue. In a few marriages a spouse may walk out after a few weeks or months. A detailed examination will show that the loss of freedom is intolerable. With this loss of freedom goes, second, a distaste for emotional intimacy. Such a man or woman finds becoming close unbearable despite the closeness of courtship. The third factor is dominance. A spouse, usually the husband, dominates the wife by insisting on always having his way. He must be obeyed and not contradicted. He will not let his wife out of his sight. A dominant partner usually marries a passive, dependent wife, who accepts his will, but we shall see that with the passage of time she may change. However, there are wives who rebel quickly and, if they cannot persuade their husband to change, leave. The last unexpected emotional feature may be that of immaturity. The husband or the wife, but it is usually the former, shows himself to be unable to handle money, drink or decision-making. The wife soon recognises in him a child who lives by her kind permission. She may find that intolerable.

All these situations may lead to arguments and quarrels which, if not handled properly, escalate and lead to violence and the departure of one partner. The other feature that may take a partner by surprise is the withdrawal of affection. A spouse may have been affectionate enough in courtship but, come marriage, withdraw into themselves.

Sexual

In the chapter on sexuality it was disclosed that sexual difficulties expressed either physiological dysfunction or a deterioration in the relationship. In these early years, the sexual dysfunction is non-consummation, when a couple cannot consummate their marriage. This is a rare problem. More commonly in these early years the wife has to recognise her husband's instinctual sexual drive, which is translated into frequency of intercourse. The man is concerned with quantity of sex. On the other hand, he has to appreciate that a large factor in his wife's sexuality is the link between sex and affection. He has to learn that, for her, sex has to be anticipated by affection, and has to modify his drive for immediate satisfaction with his capacity to show her that he loves her. A wife has to learn that it is sexual drive that governs her husband's needs. These patterns have to be adapted after the arrival of the first child, when for a while the wife's libido may be reduced for reasons that are largely unknown, but may be connected to hormonal changes. (Indeed, many couples say that their sexual difficulties start after the birth of any of the children.)

Intellectual

Couples who marry after a brief courtship may find that when they settle down together they have very little in common. They will find that sex by itself is not sufficient.

Spiritual

Traditionally, couples who share the same active faith have lower divorce rates. Spiritual difficulties used to be more prominent when denominations such as the Roman Catholics had strict rules for marriage and bringing up children. These difficulties have become markedly less. Once again a fair amount of time spent together in courtship allows a sharing of faith or values so that when marriage comes along the couple are not surprised by each other's beliefs.

Phase II From 30–50

The problems of the first phase may spill over into the second phase. But in the second phase the couple, particularly the wife, become conscious that all is not well. Women realise earlier than men that a difficulty exists, are anxious to do something about this, often before their husbands, and are more willing to talk to a counsellor. How do women apprehend the difficulties? Firstly, they experience a contrast between what they have been brought up to believe is appropriate and the reality of their life. Secondly, they may feel intuitively uncomfortable. Thirdly, they may sense that what is happening is beyond the level of adaptation they are expected to accept. Finally, they compare their life with that of their friends and neighbours and what they read and see in the media.

Change

So whilst the second phase may present with problems which belong to the first phase, what is specific about the second phase is the impact of change.

Social

One of the first features of change in these years is the arrival of success at work, with its financial and social advantages. Success may come to either spouse, but traditionally comes to the husband and may express itself in a new house, material affluence, a new set of social acquaintances, further ambition, and a new outlook of prominence and inflated ego. The wife may adapt to all this or she may be left behind, unable to cope, or she may rebel against values that clash with her orientation of life. Often success means more time outside the home and less with the family. The wife finds herself having less of her husband, being expected to entertain, socialise and sometimes give up her own long-term friendships. In these circumstances she may feel that she is gradually losing her husband to a world whose priorities she does not trust. Many men who are successful providers are baffled with the disappointment of their wives, who would like more time with them and better communication, even at the price of a lower standard of living.

The opposite of upward social mobility is downward movement, which is of course a more common cause of problems. Persistent illness, unemployment, alcoholism and gambling are the commonest reasons for loss of status. The presence of such adversity leads to frequent arguments and a rise in irritability, and a spouse may leave the marriage because he or she cannot tolerate the stress.

Emotional

a) Unconscious–conscious. In this phase a good deal of behaviour and attitudes that have been influenced by unconscious factors become conscious. In particular, what we expect from our spouse may have been influenced by what we experienced in our family of origin. Gradually we lose our projections and see our partner as they really are, which may be to our liking or not. Gradually, conscious awareness deepens and the relationship is seen in a new light; this may disclose the depths of discontent, or distress may be hidden by depression.

b) Dependence–independence. It has already been shown that getting married in a dependent relationship dominated by fear, anxiety and lack of confidence and self-esteem is a danger for the marriage. As a result of personal growth, through having children, working, and encouragement from friends and the social network, such a spouse finds their confidence and becomes a person in their own right. They start to feel that they possess themselves and are in charge of their own life, and no longer belong to parents or their substitutes, namely their spouse. A wife said, 'All my life I have done what others want me to do. First it was my parents and then my husband. Now I want to do what I want'.

As a result of these changes, for example, a wife begins to take command of her life. She may want to learn how to drive a car, seek her own friends, do things for herself, go to work, take the initiative with holidays, or even demand separate ones, argue with her husband and refuse to behave in the way she has done for several years. The husband cannot believe what he is witnessing. He protests and tries to block the change. Quarrels increase in frequency and severity, and physical violence may occur. The husband cannot understand what is happening and the change in his wife's behaviour simply raises his anxiety to panic proportions. Tension is very high and the ensuing anger of the wife may make her withdraw sexually, aggravating an already fraught situation. At this point, which may be reached only after years, the wife simply walks out and never returns.

c) Dominance. The commonest pattern of breakdown stems from the growth of independence. Occasionally, however, a dominant person tires of supporting the dependent partner and decides to leave.

d) Self-esteem and lovability. Sometimes men and women start their marriage with a poor image of themselves, feelings of inadequacy, a sense of badness and a high degree of guilt. Gradually they find that their rejection of themselves is not justified. Often they have married a spouse who is overcritical of them and with their changed image of themselves they find the criticism unacceptable. They become aware that if they want love they are not selfish and demanding. They realise for the first time that they are lovable. This may happen as a result of an affair. If they cannot persuade their spouse to be more positive towards them, they too may depart.

Sexual

The commonest sexual problems, namely the lack of affection experienced by the wife and the lack of opportunity to express his sexual drive felt by the husband, may continue in this phase. The specific sexual problems may be those of premature ejaculation and impotence in the male, and painful intercourse or lack of orgasm in the wife. Depressive illnesses, which may impair libido, may effect both partners. More specifically these two decades are the time when extramarital affairs occur and a great deal of restoration work is needed after such an occurrence.

Intellectual

Part of the growth of confidence in a husband or wife, but particularly the latter, is to discover that neither her new approach to her life nor her ideas are silly. There is an increasing trust in one's own judgement, which leads to challenging the spouse with enhanced tenacity. If the husband refuses to take cognisance of the change, the wife may get fed up and seek recognition elsewhere.

Spiritual

Sometimes a couple start with a common faith, which is practised, and later one of them gives it up. This may be a source of acute pain to the other, but is rarely a cause of marital breakdown. Much more insidiously, the values of the couple may change. Husbands may look with horror at their emancipating wives, accusing them of rampant feminism. Other conflicts may ensue when the husband is keen on material possessions and his wife wants simplicity, time for each other and the children. The approach to the children, especially when they become adolescents, may cause a great deal of conflict. Parents may differ on matters of discipline, sexual mores, expressions of freedom and money allowances. When one parent takes an attitude which is not backed up by the other, they may feel betrayed and unsupported.

Phase III From 50 to the death of one partner

Social

The single most common social problem at this stage is the unemployment of the husband. When the husband is ready to stop work, no problem exists, but if he is unprepared or unwilling to stop, the stress in his life is unloaded on to the wife, who may not be able to cope with it. Occasionally the opposite happens and a man may be promoted beyond his capabilities with the result that stress overwhelms him.

At about this time the parents of the couple may become ill or one of them dies. This may lead to the other parent coming to reside in the matrimonial home, with ensuing difficulties for the couple. At this time also, the children leave home and may get married. But their departure may leave the couple looking at each other and seeing a stranger. They may have lived through their children and their work, and when the children depart the emptiness of the relationship is exposed.

Emotional

Most of the emotional difficulties of this phase have a long history behind them and can be traced to an earlier period. The specific pattern is of late development of one of the partners, usually the husband, who often gives a history of a very disciplined and controlled adolescence, marrying early and remaining faithful, with hard work as the only feature of his life. Then suddenly at this stage he breaks loose, has one or more affairs and may even leave his wife for a younger woman. He is in fact living his adolescence at this stage.

Sexual

During the early period of this phase, the wife has her menopause. Normally this is a biological event with no adverse consequences in her sexual life, but when the latter has been poor for some time the menopause may be used as an excuse for discontinuing further sex. However, women do not lose their sexual drive after the menopause and, indeed, freed from the anxieties of reproduction, may gain a renewed vigour for sexual intercourse, which may continue into the sixties, seventies and even later. The problem here is often with the husband, who may increasingly experience impotence with progressive ageing.

Intellectual and Spiritual

This is a phase of life when intellect and spirit flower into wisdom and faith, which is usually enjoyed. However, when there has been little contact at a deep personal level, these years are marked by separate activities, separate bedrooms and a mutual silence.

CLINICAL STUDIES

In addition to the author's model described above, there have been interviews of those divorced, who gave their accounts of why they divorced. These are largely American studies and they do not go into as much detail as the author but they give a flavour of some of the broad reasons.

Goode interviewed 425 divorced women in the metropolitan district of Detroit.[27] The primary reasons for the marriage ending were given as the husband's non-support, excessive authoritarianism, a combination of drinking, gambling and infidelity, personal problems and personal incompatibility.

In his study of 600 couples who had applied for divorce in Cleveland, Ohio,[28] Levinger found social-class differences. Lower-class respondents mentioned inadequate financial resources, excessive drinking and physical abuse. Middle-class respondents complained of lack of love, infidelity and excessive demands. Wives had twice as many complaints as husbands.

Kitson and Sussman investigated the marital complaints of 209 persons who had also filed for divorce in Cleveland, Ohio.[29] They also found that women had more complaints than men, and these were: their husband's personality, authoritarianism, drinking, sexual problems, non-support and infidelity. Men more often complained about their wife's infidelity and problems with relatives. In another study, Kitson found that men were more unsure than women as to what caused the break-up of the marriage.[30]

Thurnher et al. investigated 199 women and 134 men in the

San Francisco area.[31] Women were more likely to mention violence, infidelity and drinking, whereas men mentioned more their wife's desire for freedom.

By and large, these findings are compatible with the author's and describe the greater frequency of dissatisfaction by women, their much longer list of complaints and emphasis on interpersonal nurturance and individual gratification, which are felt to be inadequate. Individuals are now more concerned with the emotional aspects of marriage and this applies particularly to women who, as has already been seen, much more often take the initiative in getting a divorce.

THE LOSS OF ATTACHMENT

Couples start their marriage with an intense affectionate bond and shortly or after many years want to leave their partner. What happens to their love? We have no way to measure the loss of affection, but we can understand it in terms of the models of love expressed in this book. Here it is only possible to speculate. If, however, at the centre of love is an affectionate attachment between two people, then the intensity of this attachment may fluctuate, being stronger at some times than others, which explains the various fluctuations of ordinary married life. The events described in this chapter may over time attenuate the affectionate attachment, and the spouse becomes less and less important to the partner. It is possible that, as the attachment becomes diluted under the influence of adverse factors, the spouse falls 'out of love'.

Placing affectionate attachment at the centre of marriage explains why some couples may split up on a friendly basis, remaining in an affectionate relationship but realising they cannot live together, through to the other extreme when love turns to hate and they will remain bitter about each other for years to come.

I conclude this chapter, then, with an understanding of marital love based on affectional bonds (see Chapter 2), which either remain intact even though they fluctuate or are gradually diluted under the impact of adversity to the point where the partner is no longer someone who elicits an affectionate response. This is likely to have happened in the past but the partners remained together. Indeed, it may still be happening in empty-shell marriages. What has happened in recent times is that the factors that erode the affectional bonds have multiplied as the expectations of marriage have risen dramatically.

CHAPTER 32

The Impact of Divorce and Separation on Children

At current rates, one in four children in England and Wales will experience parental divorce before the age of sixteen.[1] In the United States 40 per cent of children will witness the break-up of their parents' marriage before they reach the age of eighteen.[2] What is the impact of divorce on these children?

In Britain there have been three major national longitudinal studies which have been the source of information about the effects of divorce on children. These studies consist of:

I. Medical Research Council, *National Survey of Health and Development (1946)*. A study of 5362 children born in Great Britain in the week 3–9 March 1946. Information was collected on these children during childhood and adulthood, the latest at thirty-six years.
II. *National Child Development Study (1958)*. A survey of 17,414 children born in Great Britain in the week 3–9 March 1958. Information was collected at birth and ages 7, 11, 16, 23 and 33 years of age.
III. *The 1970 British Cohort Study*. This is a longitudinal cohort study of 17,198 babies born in the United Kingdom in the week 5–11 April 1970.

The advantages of these longitudinal studies are that they can compare the behaviour of children from broken homes with the behaviour of those whose homes have remained intact. In a most comprehensive study,[3] Emery gives information about American studies. But good as these longitudinal studies are they have their drawbacks, fully discussed in a publication by the Family Policy Studies Centre.[4]

THE IMPACT ON BEHAVIOUR OF AGE AT THE TIME OF DIVORCE

The opening words of the conclusion of a study by Richards and Dyson,[5] on behalf of the Department of Health and Social Security, are quoted here to set the scene: 'We may conclude from the studies we have reviewed that marital separation is a process with profound consequences for the children.'

Among children under five, the very young tend to regress; in their toilet training, they return to wetting and possibly soiling themselves, and their sleep may become disturbed. Those slightly older become irritable, whiny, tearful and aggressive. They cling to mother, afraid that if one parent goes the other might go too.

Older children – that is, aged 5–6 – also express anxiety and aggression and a wish that the family can be reunited. Older children aged 7–8 also wanted their family to be put together again. These children show sadness and insecurity about family relations.

At 9–12 years, anxieties and insecurities continued, although the children appeared more externally assured. Now they tended to cease to feel guilty about the breakdown; they did not blame themselves but they were angry, especially at the parent who they thought caused it. Very often this partner is the father, who leaves home, but of course it may be the mother, who wanted him to leave.

Older children who are adolescents have a greater grasp of what is going on but they are no less upset. The pressures on them are considerable because some of them lose the stability of the home from which to develop into adulthood. Many mature too quickly and may be involved in early sexual liaisons.

The *National Child Development Study* found that boys and girls whose parents had divorced when the children were aged 7–11 showed more behaviour problems at age 11, as rated by parents and teachers, and scored lower than other children on reading and mathematics achievements at age 11, even after controlling for predictors such as social class and race.[6] This paper contends that disturbance had started well before the separation occurred. Thus, the impact of divorce adversely affects a situation that had begun to deteriorate before. The implications are that there are two damaging influences for children. The first is the deteriorating relationship of the parents; the second is the divorce itself.

Continuing the short-term findings about the impact of divorce on children, Douglas found that children whose parents had either separated or divorced by the time they were six years old were twice as likely at fifteen years old to be bedwetting as those whose parents stayed together.[7]

SCHOOL AND UNIVERSITY

All studies that have examined the effect of parental divorce have found that children's performance in school is adversely affected.[8, 9, 10, 11, 12, 13, 14]

Specifically, children of divorced parents were more likely to be placed in special reading classes, to be doing less well educationally and socially, and were more likely to have been referred to an educational psychologist.

McClean and Wadsworth found that those who experienced parental divorce during their school years were significantly more likely to have lower educational attainment, whatever the social class of their family of origin.[8] They also found that, following parental divorce, the chances of attending university are considerably reduced. For those from a non-manual background, the chances of a university education are twice as great if the individual comes from an intact family than one affected by divorce (19 per cent versus 11 per cent).

EMPLOYMENT AND INCOME

McClean and Wadsworth make the point 'In view of the reduced chances of educational attainment amongst children from divorced families, relative occupational disadvantage was to be expected'.[8] This was the case. Their analysis of the 1946 cohort found that unemployment was higher for men at eighteen years if their parents had separated or divorced when they were children than if they had remained together. Similar findings were made at thirty-six years.

The income of those whose parents had separated or divorced was significantly lower at both age twenty-six and thirty-six.

Kuh and McClean,[15] using the 1946 cohort, found similar findings for women. Women whose parents had separated or divorced had a greater likelihood of being in a lower achieved social class, being unemployed or having a manual occupation. They too suggest that the difference in social status was explained by earlier educational underachievement.

INTERGENERATIONAL TRANSMISSION AND INSTABILITY IN RELATIONSHIPS

Wallerstein,[16] one of the pioneer writers on the effects of divorce on children, has recently completed a ten-year follow-up. It was found that a significant number of young men and women from divorced backgrounds appeared to be troubled, drifting and underachieving. Almost all confronted issues of love, commitment and marriage with apprehension. Often there was great concern about betrayal, abandonment and not being loved. Almost half of the young men and women in the study threw themselves into short-lived sexual relationships, and compulsive marriages that ended in divorce.

Boys are more likely to leave school by the age of sixteen if they come from a disrupted home than if they came from an intact one. Girls were more likely to leave home early if their family had experienced disruption.

It was also found that young women whose parents' marriage had broken down were more likely to have formed *de facto* or *de jure* partnerships in their teens, to have had a child by the age of twenty or to have had an extramarital birth. Children of both sexes from disrupted families are also more likely to experience the break-up of their own marriage.[17, 18]

DELINQUENCY

There is undisputed evidence of increased behavioural problems and delinquency among both boys and girls whose parents have divorced. Analysis from the data from the second *National Health Interview Survey on Child Health* in the USA has shown that children who experienced the disruption of their parents' marriage were two or three times more likely to have been suspended or expelled from their school and three times more likely to be in need of treatment for emotional or behavioural problems.[14] Delinquent behaviour increased particularly among those whose parents divorced before they were five years old.

IMPACT OF DEATH OF A PARENT

One of the best-attested findings of the specific disruption of marital breakdown is that disruption by death does not on the whole have anything like the adverse effect on the children that divorce or separation has.

IMPACT OF POVERTY

There are those who for a variety of reasons want to play down the adverse effects of marital breakdown on children. They do not deny the findings but seek to explain them on the grounds of the subsequent effect of poverty on the single-parent family. Although poverty does indeed play a part in the adversity of the post-divorce family, there is little doubt that there are adverse psychological effects from the disruption itself. For example, only 57 per cent of former partners of lone parents still maintain contact with their children. Thus the loss of a parent, usually the father, proves a particular source of external deprivation for children.

Wallerstein, whose studies have already been referred to, suggests that children from divorced families may face psychological burdens in addition to the normative tasks of growing up.

GOING OR STAYING?

At the heart of the debate about the interests of the child lies the division of opinion as to whether it is better for the child to stay in a home where the parents are unhappy, or for the parents to separate. The emerging evidence suggests that children want their parents to stay together even if the parents are unhappy but that they are damaged if parental behaviour is overtly aggressive.

STATISTICS

One of the problems with all these findings is that they are statistical; that is to say, they cannot predict how an individual child will fare, and thus there are always individuals who emerge unhurt. However, taken as a whole, the evidence points clearly to severe adverse effects on children.

CHAPTER 33

The Impact of Divorce and Separation on Adults

We have seen in the last chapter the manifold adverse consequences on children. These are not well known. Even less known are the negative effects on adults.

STRESS

Separation and divorce are accompanied by a good deal of stress. Stress in turn compromises immune function, leading to increased susceptibility to disease. In a study by Kennedy,[1] a group of women who were divorced or separated were compared with a matched group of the still-married. Psychological measures of the level of distress and a range of immunological and nutritional assays were performed on both groups. The divorced and separated had significantly lowered cellular immune response, with those separated within one year of the study showing the most profound differences.

A similar study by Kiecolt-Glaser et al.,[2] on a matched sample of men, found that the divorced and separated were significantly more distressed and lonely than their married counterparts. They also reported more recent illness and had significantly poorer immunological function.

Cooper et al.,[3] in a study of 1596 patients at breast-screening clinics, found a significant association between life crisis, particularly involving the loss of a significant relationship, through death or divorce, and breast disease and its severity.

Stress which is clearly associated with separation and

divorce is something that the person can recognise and adapt to, or negate and deny with a flight to overreacting, sexual promiscuity, overwork, or increased smoking and drinking.

Smoking is such a serious cause of ill health that anything that encourages it is of importance. Evidence from the *General Household Survey* shows that at all ages, for both men and women, the divorced and separated are more likely to smoke than their married or never-married counterparts.[4]

Heavy drinking is also a dangerous trait. Information from the *General Household Survey* shows that those who are divorced and separated have the highest rates of heavy drinking from the age of twenty-five.[4, 5]

HEART DISEASE AND STROKE

Deaths from disease of the circulatory system account for 25 per cent of premature mortality in men and 15 per cent in women. In one of the earliest studies in the USA,[6] Carter and Glick found that divorced men aged 16–54 run twice the risk of death from heart disease as married men and were 2.4 times more likely to die from a stroke. Divorced women also ran a high risk, but less than men. A more recent study discovered similar results in Finland over a three-year period, with divorced men experiencing 1.8 times the risk, and divorced women, 1.6.[7]

Following myocardial infarction, there are increased survival rates in the married in comparison with other groups.

CANCER

Cancer is the leading cause of premature death, responsible for 21 per cent of premature deaths amongst men and 39 per cent amongst women. Several studies have been conducted showing an association between marital status and cancer registration,[8,9] cancer mortality,[6, 10] and cancer survival.[11] All these studies show that the divorced population has higher rates of cancer than the married population.

The study of Carter and Glick,[6] based on cancer mortality throughout the USA for 1959–61, suggests that, in addition to raised rates of lung and breast cancer, the divorced population is also more prone to a wide range of cancers of the buccal cavity and pharynx, the digestive organs, the respiratory system, the urinary organs and, in men, the prostate.

PREMATURE DEATH

Since the 1930s, when mortality rates have been analysed by marital status, virtually every study of mortality and marital status shows that the unmarried have higher death rates.[6, 12, 13] Divorced men are particularly vulnerable to premature death, with those aged 35–45 bearing twice the risk of their married counterparts.

Not only deaths but also morbidity (tendency to illness) is higher in the divorced. Morbidity statistics from general practice found that the divorced and widowed are more likely to consult their doctor for almost all categories of illness.[14]

Finally, those who are divorced and separated are more prone to death from accidents, be they at work or in the home, from road traffic, a fall, through fire or drowning.[7]

REASONS FOR ILL HEALTH

Why are the divorced more prone to premature death and ill health? There are essentially three hypotheses.

1. *Protection–Support*. In this hypothesis the argument is that marriage is protective against physical and mental ill health because it acts as a buffer against the effects of anxiety and stress. This view is consistent with the widespread finding that marriage is particularly beneficial for men – the evidence suggests that wives provide a greater degree of emotional support for their husbands than the other way round.
2. *Selection*. This hypothesis suggests that the difference in

vitality and morbidity between marital-status groupings is due to the healthy being selected into marriage, leaving those more likely to be unhealthy unmarried. Thus the unhealthy are selected out of marriage.

3. *Dissolution*. The third hypothesis follows the line adopted in this book that marriage is a special case of affectionate attachment and when the bond is severed it is a source of great stress, leading either directly to illness or making the subject more vulnerable to it.

There is a strong case to be made that all three hypotheses are operating.

MEN AND WOMEN

The reader might have already observed that marital breakdown has a more profound and damaging effect on men than on women and all the evidence supports this view.

MENTAL HEALTH

As described many times already, at the heart of marital love is to be found an affectionate bond which, when threatened or severed, leads to anxiety and depression. Depression is closely associated with divorce and is one of the commonest responses to marital stress. It may occur in the acute phase of marital difficulties, or during the period of separation or divorce. This relationship of depression to divorce has been studied extensively.[15, 16, 17, 18, 19, 20, 21]

Depression is intimately linked with attempted suicide and suicide. Many attempted suicides (parasuicides) are the result of a blind reaction to loss in which immediate relief is sought.[22] Another motive is seeking comfort when other methods have failed. Both these patterns are characteristic of married people whose spouses have left them. These men and women seek an impulse relief to the profound sense of loss.

Early work by Kessel in a study of self-poisoning of 68 married men and 147 married women, showed that marital disharmony was a major precipitating factor for 68 per cent of men and 60 per cent of women.[23] In another study,[24] a sample of 577 cases, 68 per cent of the women complained of marital problems. A third study of parasuicide, this time from Scotland,[25] showed that for both sexes the rates were highest for the divorced.

Although parasuicide may be an isolated event, it can be repeated and it can be a prelude to suicide.[26, 27] Suicide is the ultimate expression of self-destruction. Each year 4–5000 individuals in England and Wales take their own lives. Relationship breakdown is one of the major causes of suicide worldwide. The divorced are around four times as likely to kill themselves as the married.

Psychiatric morbidity consists of the persistent presence of anxiety, irritability, tension, mood swings, tiredness, insomnia, lack of concentration and inability to function. It is a very common syndrome and forms the majority of known mental illness in the community. Men and women, particularly the latter, consult their general practitioners for these conditions. The more severe are referred to a psychiatrist and a few are hospitalised. Both Shepherd,[28] in Britain, and Renne,[29] in the United States, found a greater incidence of neuroticism in the divorced.

Referrals to out-patients show a much higher incidence of the divorced and separated than that represented in the general population.[30, 31] This finding is confirmed in the United States, where the use of these services is five times as high for the divorced as compared to married individuals.[32]

Finally, there comes the point at which the patient needs to be hospitalised. There is clear evidence that the divorced have much higher rates of hospital admission. In 1973 the rates of admission to mental hospitals for England and Wales were 257 per 100,000 of the population for married men and 959 per 100,000 for divorced men; the respective numbers for women were 433 and 1596.

As with children, the adverse effects on the physical and mental health of adults who experience divorce are hidden but nevertheless real and severe.

CHAPTER 34

Counselling

The last three chapters show the massive extent of divorce and the extensive damage it inflicts on the couple and their children. We have become so habituated to divorce that we hardly realise that it is one of the leading social problems of our day.

It is not difficult to realise that contemporary marriage makes heavy demands on any couple and that alienation is something that can happen in any marriage. Indeed for some spouses, particularly women, divorce can be a relief from an intolerable situation and it should be available. Having said all this, there remains the indubitable fact that divorce is highly damaging to society and particularly to the children involved, and everything must be done to curb it as a social phenomenon. We certainly should not develop an attitude that we can get married and if it does not work we can get divorced. We must look at divorce as a sad loss and we must try to do all we can to prevent it.

The challenge is to combine high expectations with an approach of preparation and support that allows these expectations to be met, at least marginally.

Two approaches have arisen in response to the problem of broken marriages; one has been counselling and the other, more recently, cohabitation. This chapter deals with counselling and the next with cohabitation.

In the *Denning Report* of 1947 it was said: 'We have throughout our enquiry had in mind the principle that the marriage tie is of the highest importance in the interests of society. The unity of the family is so important that, when partners are estranged, reconciliation should be attempted in every case where there is a prospect of success.' They recommended that 'It should be recognised as a function of the State to give any encouragement and, where appropriate, financial assistance to marriage guidance as a form of social service'.

And so it was. The Home Office gave grants to the then National Marriage Guidance Council, now called Relate, the Catholic Marriage Advisory Council, the Institute of Marital Studies and the Jewish Marriage Council. These grants have continued to the present day and collectively are around two million pounds a year.

The question that has to be asked is whether this counselling has had any serious impact on divorce. In a sense we shall never know since we do not know how things would have been without the presence of these marriage-counselling bodies. But we are greatly handicapped by the absence of research into who comes to marriage counselling and what benefit they receive from it.

What we do know is not encouraging. Many people are unwilling to go to marriage counselling. A study in British social attitudes found that only 1.7 per cent of people would go to marriage counselling when their marriage was in difficulties.[1] One can only speculate at this reluctance. It is possible that marriage counselling is associated with marital failure and couples are unwilling to acknowledge that their marriage is in such a plight.

Even more important is the study of the Marriage Research Centre, *Marriages in Trouble*,[2] where it was found that men in particular were very negatively orientated towards disclosing their problems.

A Mr Hull (aged 41; a father) said, 'I've never sought help at any time in my life. If I can't solve a problem, then I can't see that anybody else can do anything for me. Now, that is my attitude.'

A Mr Mold (age 53: a self-employed plumber) said, 'I

would go for advice if I wanted some mathematical problem worked out or if there was something I wanted in my car repaired or something like that ... but I can't see really how – unless somebody is a genius – they can sort somebody's marriage out in two or three easy lessons.'

These expressions are typical of many men who find the emotional side of their relationships difficult enough and the idea of dealing with events in counselling almost impossible.

Thus, right from the very beginning there are problems between the sexes about disclosing their private-life situation. When they finally arrive for help many people have reached the point of no return and they simply come to counselling to have their opinion confirmed that the marriage is at an end. After thirty years of counselling I have come to the conclusion that the following rules about counselling apply.

When only one spouse comes for help, very little can be done except to assist that person to understand their partner; but understanding does not mean that they can tolerate their partner's behaviour more easily. When both spouses come but one is committed to leaving the partnership, once again there is very little that can be done for the marriage; but the break-up can be eased. It is only when there are difficulties but the couple are both committed to the marriage that help can be given. Thus, by and large, marriage counselling at present is not very productive of reconciliation of the couple.

What can we say about marriage counselling from the figures that we have? At present there are between 150,000 and 160,000 divorces each year in Great Britain, and the number who are in difficulties must be several hundred thousands more. If we had an effective service, we should be seeing several hundred thousand couples every year. In their report (1992–3), Relate, the largest marriage-counselling organisation, state that the number of cases they saw was 76,000, involving more than 400,000 interviews. Clearly, in their own right these figures are impressive, but in the context of what is needed they are a drop in the ocean.

We must reluctantly come to the conclusion that in its present form marriage counselling is meeting only a tiny proportion of the real need for help. Clearly, more money spent on marriage counselling would help, but it is not the major or long-term answer.

Do we then give up in despair? Not at all. There is evidence, good evidence presented already, that people seek help from those they trust and to whom they are willing to disclose their problems. The first such person is often the family doctor. People find it difficult to go to marriage counselling but they may talk to their doctor, who has their confidence. Shepherd et al.[3] and Mitchell[4] found in their sample of divorces that 34 per cent had sought help from a doctor and only 5 per cent from a marriage counsellor. In fact, people turn first to their relatives and friends, and doctors. In addition they also turn to teachers, managers and colleagues. We simply have to train family doctors, teachers and managers to be sensitive and responsive to these problems at the earlier and therefore preventive stage. At the Marriage Research Centre, now called One Plus One, we have started an approach which has come to be called Brief Encounters in which we are beginning to train these groups of people to assist at the early stages.

We need a vision for the future. The present arrangements are not working out as the early visionaries expected after the end of the war. The size of the problem has greatly increased, the response to counselling is poor and we need much more work and support for marriage.

In outline we need a programme where there is a comprehensive preparation for personal relationship at home and school, followed by a preparation course for every couple getting married and thereafter support for marriage. One of the pointers for the future is the small-scale preparation for marriage that is happening, particularly in religious circles, in Britain and also in the United States. At its best it involves the couples to be married having a weekend or a series of 6–8 weekly evening meetings in which their hopes and expectations, the course of modern marriage, marital satisfaction, love, sexuality and children are discussed with them, and they are given an idea of what they might expect in the future. In America pre-marriage counselling has been researched. Guerney and Maxson,[5] studying the work of the 1980s have this to say: 'There is no doubt that, on the whole, enrichment programmes work and the field is an entirely legitimate one'. In Britain this preparation has to be researched and widened.

Supporting couples in the above way and in the following years means the giving of information to couples at every stage of their marriage so that they can negotiate their difficulties in an informed manner. After this, there is a need for training family doctors, the primary healthcare team, leaders and managers in elementary support for marriage; and finally, as is done in medicine, those cases that need specialised help can receive traditional counselling.

COST OF MARITAL BREAKDOWN

Evidence has been given in the previous two chapters of the human cost of marital breakdown. There is no way of measuring it. It is personal and hidden but it is extensive. The financial cost is also difficult to measure. It includes legal aid and court costs; the largest amount is social security: tax allowances for one-parent families, and children in care; health-service costs, which are virtually impossible to measure; and other costs, such as the expense to the police, courts and people dealing with the sundry effects of broken marriages, the cost of lost production, absenteeism, housing, juvenile care, and so on. An estimate for all this cost is between £2.8 and £3.4 billion![6] The real cost is much more than this.

Against this cost the amount given to the voluntary marriage organisations is of the order of £2 million a year. The discrepancy is monumental. When the voluntary organisations ask for more money, they are asked to show how such a rise will produce better counselling results and, given the inadequacy of research to date, they have not been able to produce such figures.

But the issue is much larger than cost-effectiveness. Marital break-up is one of the major social problems of our age and it deserves much better financial backing for research and services that aim at prevention, both from the government and the private sector. Marital breakdown is more than a private matter affecting the individual couple. Collectively it impinges on the health, social, emotional and moral dimensions of the future of the nation. The family of today is responsible for the citizen of tomorrow and it deserves much more support than it is receiving today. A mere doubling of the government resource, coupled with an equivalent investment from the private sector, would allow real preventive measures to be taken.

CHAPTER 35

Cohabitation

In the last chapter we looked at counselling and its limitations in response to marital breakdown. In the light of the massive increase of divorce in the late sixties, seventies and eighties, there arose amongst young people a second major response, namely cohabitation. The rationale behind cohabitation was the belief that if they lived together before marriage a couple could find out whether they were suited to each other and avoid the pain of marital breakdown. So let us look at this second main experiment at prevention. I am of course perfectly aware that cohabitation is a complex phenomenon and has several reasons beyond prevention of marital breakdown.

The increase in cohabitation is marked. In 1979, when the *General Household Survey* first collected information, only 3 per cent of single women under the age of fifty were cohabiting whereas ten years later, in 1989, 26 per cent were.[1]

Whilst some form of cohabitation always existed, a new form of cohabitation came into operation in the 1980s whereby young people in their twenties and thirties lived together before marriage or as an alternative to marriage. Of women marrying during 1985–8 nearly 58 per cent had cohabited with their future husband. These cohabiting unions tend to be of short duration (around about two years on average) and either proceed to marriage or they dissolve.

The public is equally divided between cohabitation and marrying directly. In the *British Social Attitudes Survey*,[2] the public were asked what advice they would give to a young woman and a young man about forming partnerships with the opposite sex. Just over 4 out of 10 advised a period of pre-marital cohabitation, and 4 out of 10 advised marriage directly. The views of the public reflected their age groups. Nearly 60 per cent of those in the 18–24-year bracket advised cohabitation before marriage and the same applied to the 25–34 age group. But only 20 per cent advised this in the 65+ age group. So the young really believe that cohabitation before marriage is the right thing to do.

This reveals an optimism by young people that cohabitation is a wise precaution before marriage. Of those who cohabit, 63 per cent of both men and women are coming to cohabitation as never-married whereas 28 per cent have been married before. This shows that there are two groups of cohabitees: those who are approaching marriage for the first time and those who have been previously married, usually the divorced.

Thus there is a strong belief that cohabitation has something to contribute to the ensuing marriage. There are three broad categories of cohabitation; that to be found in Sweden, Denmark and Iceland, where cohabitation is the commonest living arrangement amongst young women (20–24); that in countries like Austria, Belgium, England and Wales, Finland, France, Luxembourg, the Netherlands, Norway, Switzerland and West Germany, where cohabitation is emerging as a significant pre-marriage phenomenon; and that in countries like Ireland, Scotland, the Mediterranean countries and the countries of Eastern Europe, where pre-marital cohabitation is negligible.

Cohabitation is currently seen as a temporary prelude to marriage and is largely childless. It rests on the assumption that it serves to screen out potentially incompatible mates more effectively than traditional courtship. So cohabitation has been invested with the belief that it is a good vetting measure for marital stability.

Unfortunately, those who cohabit before marriage have been shown to have significantly higher risks of marital dissolution at any given period.[3, 4, 5, 6, 7, 8] In Britain, Haskey showed that couples who married early in the 1980s who had premaritally cohabited were 50 per cent more likely to have divorced after five years of marriage and 60 per cent more likely after eight years of marriage, than couples who had not.[9]

The reason for this association between premarital cohabitation and subsequent increase in divorce is not clear. Discussion has centred on the possibility that there is a direct link between premarital cohabitation and higher divorce rates. So far, the explanation offered is that such cohabitation is a non-traditional life style. It has attracted individuals who from the outset may be more prone to having unstable marriages. There is no certainty that this is the explanation or, indeed that there is a *causal* link between cohabitation and increased risk of divorce. What is certain is that cohabitation does not contain any magic formula whereby marital problems are avoided or better handled.

So this second preventive measure has not so far offered a way out of the present predicament of large-scale marital dissolution. Clearly we need to look afresh at the measures we can take to prevent marital breakdown. An outline of these has been given in the previous chapter.

PART VIII

The Future

CHAPTER 36

Research

I entered the field of marriage counselling early in 1959 and I soon became aware that the voluntary organisations that received money from the Home Office did not receive funds for research except on special occasions. It is true that the Tavistock Institute of Marital Studies did carry out research, but this was limited by its exclusive psychoanalytical flavour which, while important, appealed to those who approached marriage from the dynamic point of view. There was no broad centre which directed its efforts continuously at psychosocial research on marriage.

In 1971, I set up the Marriage Research Centre, which in 1990 was renamed One Plus One, the Marriage and Partnership Research Charity; it exists to build through research a framework for understanding and supporting contemporary marriage and partnerships. Most people aspire to committed, supportive partnerships. The research of the unit highlights what makes these partnerships difficult to achieve in practice and how people cope when things go wrong. In a tribute paid to the Centre,[1] David Morgan says, 'In the handful of sociological studies of marriage produced in Britain during the past twenty years, three have come from One Plus One.'

In this chapter, I want to give a summary of the main research findings from the three books published by the unit so far.

In the first book, *Who Divorces?*[2] a sample of divorced men and women were compared with another sample of the still-married. The following facts were found to be important. The study showed that divorce rates for social classes V and III non-manual were the highest. Marriages in which the husband is highly educated and especially those in which the partners are church-goers were especially stable.

Marriages preceded by short courtships or without any informal engagement or honeymoon and towards which there was strong parental opposition all had an increased risk of ending in divorce.

The study found two further high-risk factors. One was teenage marriage and the other was premarital pregnancy. Disadvantaged housing, especially in the early years, also appeared to be more typical of those who divorce.

Those who divorced were more likely to have been dissatisfied with the sexual side of marriage, either initially or through experiencing a later deterioration. Furthermore those who divorced adopted a more blaming attitude towards the partner for the sexual difficulties.

The second study, *Marriages in Trouble*, by Julian Brannen and Jean Collard,[3] was a study of the characteristics of those seeking help for their marriage. This study was one of the very few that entered the closed world of marriage counselling and looked at what happens when people seek help. The need for extensive research in this area is imperative.

This study found that both men and women, but particularly the former, experience constraints against the disclosure of marital and personal problems. Instead of facing marital problems, couples could accommodate to them. A partner could deny the existence of difficulties or would turn a blind eye, thus avoiding the definition of a problem altogether. Alternatively one spouse would project blame on to the other. Yet another strategy is to take the blame on to oneself. For both spouses, there is the practice of attributing their problems to events or situations extraneous to the marital relationship.

If couples avoided facing the fact that they had a marital problem, what precipitated seeking help? There were two main marriage-threatening events that prompted such help-seeking. The first was one partner either leaving the home or threatening to do so. The second was the revelation of a close, though not always sexual, relationship with a person of the opposite sex. When they did seek help, men found it much more difficult to talk about their problems than women.

The third study is *The Beginning of the Rest of Your Life*, a portrait of newly wedded marriage by Penny Mansfield and Jean Collard.[4] (It may have been noticed that Jean Collard is co-editor of all three publications and I want to pay tribute to her stalwart efforts in assisting the publishing of the three books.) This book studied sixty-five couples, with a taped interview of the spouses, and the analysis was based on full transcripts of these.

This study examined the readiness for marriage from something that is inevitable to having a place of one's own, becoming an individual in one's own right, being ready to settle down, different gender approaches to courtship, and finding an identity through marriage.

The book examined in detail the preparation for marriage and the wedding itself. It then moved to look at the couple setting up a home and the sharing of work at home, behaving as husbands and wives, creating a domestic life style with different approaches from the traditional wife-orientated to the more egalitarian sharing of responsibilities. It then examined the home where both husbands and wives work, the issues of intimacy and the balance between togetherness and separateness.

These couples were interviewed five years on in their marriages and the impact of the child on their relationship will be the next publication of the centre. As already stated, this study will also show an entirely new conceptualisation of married life in terms of the partnership of the couple. In addition to these books, the centre has published several other publications, and it has two main conferences each year through which information is disseminated nationally. Since its inception, the centre has become nationally and internationally known for its research-focused work on marriage. The centre receives a grant of £60,000 annually from the Home Office and for the rest of its resources relies on charity. In his conclusions,[1] Morgan states, 'It is one of the strengths of the studies from One Plus One that they demonstrate the ways in which everyday concerns, hopes, fears and anxieties may be the legitimate concern of sociological enquiry.'

Clearly the only way to understand marital difficulties is to appreciate the nature of contemporary marriage, and for this research, which has been singularly limited in Britain, is essential.

CHAPTER 37

The Value of Love

In this book I have outlined the contemporary seeking of marriage as a pursuit of love. We have seen that this love starts in a romantic manner but continues as a way of loving with its own form of sustaining, healing and growth. This form of love is not widely understood. Indeed, the only criterion that is widely appreciated is the romantic falling-in-love experience, and the cause of a great deal of the grief that accompanies modern marriage is that, after the initial flourish, couples do not know what to expect.

In this book we have seen that the initial flourish subsides soon after marriage and particularly after the arrival of children, but the expectations remain high. It is a question of educating couples that their personal love will take a different turn from the heights of ecstasy with which they experienced each other at the beginning of their relationship.

Today it is the quality of the relationship that keeps the marriage going, and that in turn means that the couple have to respond accurately to each other's needs. As I mentioned in earlier chapters, these needs mean availability, communication, demonstration of affection, affirmation and resolution of conflict. It is imperative that, in preparation and support for marriage, these characteristics be highlighted and that couples are trained and educated for these experiences. The trouble is that couples are conditioned to believe that their lives will be a continuous high, and get disappointed and depressed when they return to the ordinary experiences of everyday life. But these experiences are the infrastructure of loving and they need skill, discipline and effort.

Beyond the routine of sustaining one another, couples need healing and growth. These are the more long-term aspects of loving that have to be identified and attended to. Couples are so busy with the business of living, the everyday food, housing, and leisure experiences, that they are not always aware of their deeper needs at the personal level of interaction. There they find their wounded selves, who are crying out for attention. It is there also that they find their quest for fulfilment, which has become such an urgent matter, especially for women seeking the realisation of their potential.

This approach to loving produces tensions in the marriage. There are tensions between the heights of expectation with which the relationship starts and the ordinary levels it reaches after a short time. There are the tensions of discovering that the person you married is not the ideal you imagined. You need love to forgive their shortcomings, but after you have adapted to their personality, there is the challenge of the mutual understanding of responding to each other's wounds and the needs of their personality. In this book I have described in detail the development of the personality from dependence to independence, from insecurity to security, from confusion to certainty, and the need for the partner to match the distinctive needs in this journey.

All this is happening whilst the couple are having to take up the challenge of raising their children. The tension between their own needs and the needs of the children looms large in modern marriage. In the past, society and individuals considered the needs of the children as the primary purpose of marriage, and sacrifices were made for them. Now there is also a priority for the needs of the couple and it is very easy to be superficial and condemn the couple for attending to their needs before those of the children. This is a crucial crossroad of modern marriage.

By and large, what has happened is that modern marital expectations have risen rapidly in the last thirty years without adequate preparation and support for these expectations.

There are those who say that these expectations are unrealistic. I do not believe this to be the case. What we need to do is to appreciate the natural history of the unfolding of marriage and inform couples of what they can expect in the ordinary development of their life; that their love story and the peaks of personal sustaining, healing and growth are real achievements of Western civilisation. The quest for such heights is good but we need much greater research to discern how relationships unfold, and here I repeat the plea for financial support to do this. Having done this, we can offer couples an understanding in depth of what their love quest is all about and give them realistic means to achieve it. This book is dedicated to the gaining of this information.

In the meantime, love as a basis of understanding marriage has universal approval. In the Judeo-Christian tradition, love is the central quality for marriage and this can be seen in the teaching that has emerged from the main denominational churches.

In the Second Vatican Council,[1] the Roman Catholic Church emphasises marriage in terms of love. 'The well-being of the individual person and of human and Christian society is intimately linked with the healthy condition of that community produced by marriage and family. Hence Christians and all men who hold this community in high esteem sincerely rejoice in the various ways which men today find help in fostering this community of love.'

The Church of England in its second report on marriage, *Marriage and the Church's Task*,[2] speaks of marriage:

> Marriage is a relationship of shared commitment and love. It is a commitment in which nothing is deliberately withheld. As such it is a profound sharing of present experience. As such it also anticipates the sharing of future experiences. It is a commitment through time. It embraces the future as well as the present. It intends and promises permanence. The logic of such intention and promise is as follows. Love in marriage not only unites two persons as

they are, it also recreates them as they shall become. It is person-making.

These two quotes from Christian background do not mean that marriage for love is only a Christian concept. It applies to all religions and to those without religion. It applies to all, for love unites all human beings.

The limitations of all these faith declarations is that they speak loudly of love but they are desperately short of the practicalities of the actual living experience. The churches and all organisations that are concerned with marriage should be far more familiar with the contents of this book. They have no business marrying people without equipping them with the knowledge of what to expect in their marriage.

On the other hand, the universal religions have traditionally insisted that there are no short cuts to love; that love needs commitment, effort, discipline and sacrifice.

What is needed for the future of marriage as a commitment of love is a combination of the social and psychological characteristics of the relationship as outlined in this book, given as information to couples, coupled with the discipline that traditional religions of all denominations have sustained. In this way the quest of love can be sustained. The value of love is of the highest quality and should be encouraged but *it needs to be supported* by information and effort.

CHAPTER 38

The Future of Marriage

With the high incidence of divorce, an increase in cohabitation and extramarital childbearing, and a reduction in actual marriages, people are asking whether there is any future for marriage. The incidence of divorce and the increase in cohabitation have been recorded extensively in Part VII. It is time to record the fact that in the 1980s nearly one in three children were born outside marriage. The number of marriages in England and Wales were 308,000 in 1961 but were down to 224,000 in 1992. This is a dramatic drop of nearly 80,000.

How is this drop to be accounted for? As has been shown, large numbers of young people cohabit nowadays. This cohabitation may be a prelude to marriage or it may be a permanent feature. The demise of religion means that less of the population have a religiously based commitment to marriage, even though more first marriages take place in church than in registry offices.

This is a challenge for the churches and the community to try to discover what has been taken as implicit in the past. For example, a distinction has to be made between a religious ceremony and the religious commitment of the couple. It has been established that a religious commitment is a barrier to divorce,[1] but we do not know the significance of a public ceremony. We need to find out. Indeed, we need to find out what are the advantages of any ceremony, religious or secular. Does the fact that a couple make a commitment in a public situation mean that it helps them to overcome the tension of marriage? Does it give them extra strength or is there an implicit strength in a committed relationship that has public approval. Only research can reveal these things.

Turning now to what we do know about the positive features of marriage, there is long-established scientific evidence that the mental health of the currently married enjoys a more favourable position compared to the divorced and the widowed, with the never-married in an intermediate position. Experts argue as to whether this favourable position is due to selection of the healthy into marriage or whether marriage generates well-being in itself. This well-being of personal and mental health is noted more in men than in women and may be due to the husband having been looked after by his wife. Experts feel that both selection and implicit well-being are operating in marriage, and that is an advantage that is not going to go away. This advantage compares with the disadvantage of the divorced and widowed, particularly the divorced.

In a recent unpublished paper by Russell and Wells of predictors of happiness in married couples, it was found that the strongest predictor of happiness was the quality of the marriage.[1] It was the strongest predictor for both husbands and wives. So there is research evidence to support the fact that stable marriages are associated not only with mental health but also with happiness for the participants. We have yet to establish whether the alternatives to marriage that are being tried out hold the same sense of well-being for the participants.

In the absence of a public commitment, are these alternative relationships able to cope with the stresses and strains of the everyday relationship? Are children in these relationships looked after as well as they are in traditional marriages? Are the couples able to give security to each other when there are no structures external to them to sustain them? These questions are vital and we have to research them.

In the meantime we must remember what marriage has to offer to a couple. We have seen in this book that from birth we are psychologically primed to attachment behaviour forming a bond. As primates we are born into a one-to-one relationship and the pursuit of all alternatives has to take account of our need for affection and bond formation. It is a small minority who find it difficult and undesirable to form a bond and may desire transient relationships. But even if the adult may find solace in transient relationships the children conceived need the stability and security of a stable parental unit. We have already seen what havoc marital breakdown creates for children; we may yet find out that unstable relationships are not good for children.

Beyond the attachment-bond formation link, men and women need stability and security in their lives. Marriage provides this, and it may be very influential for their physical and psychological health. It may well be that the less committed relationships do not provide such a safe background for couples to remain healthy.

The security of relationship is expressed sexually, and both men and women need to feel safe in their sexual relationship, otherwise jealousy and infidelity erode the sexual links, to the disadvantage of both.

Sexual union leads to procreation, and marriage has been particularly structured for the well-being of children. It takes time to see the adverse consequences of various types of upbringing on children. The welfare of children is one of the primary concerns of society and we have seen how twenty years of research have shown the adverse consequences of marital breakdown. We have yet to see how children fare with alternative parental arrangements. Children need continuous security and the present alternatives do not necessarily give this security.

Thus it may be concluded that the need for bonding, security, love and sexual intimacy will always prompt couples to form relationships, but these relationships have to be secure and continuous, particularly if there are children.

At the centre of the present upheaval of marriage is the fact that expectations of love have risen so enormously and there has not been concomitant education and support for them. Young people – indeed, people of all ages – are exploring in the dark to find the appropriate answer for themselves.

Neither the church nor society has taken seriously the historic changes taking place in the inner world of marriage, described in this book, and the result has been that we have employed alternative solutions, which are currently being tried out. Take any newspaper and see what it emphasises in this area. The emphasis is on dissolutions of marriage, births outside marriage, and so on. There is no attempt to show a consistent inner change in the nature of marriage and what we need to do to support it.

The fact is that the need for marriage remains as clear today as it has ever done. Men and women are formed from bonding and procreation, and marriage is the answer that society has evolved for them. But the inner world of marriage is changing and we need a different preparation and support to achieve the goals of marriage as a love relationship.

This book has been written to show that the inner world of marriage is changing rapidly, but it needs the traditional stability, aided and abetted by large-scale education and support for these new goals, with the particular help of research. Every couple needs to be able to anticipate the unfolding of their relationship with sufficient information to cope with the tensions that arise in the various stages of relationships.

With such a development the amount of marital breakdown will be reduced and there will be a gradual return to stability, the greatest need for couples and children in marriage.

Notes

INTRODUCTION

1. Haskey, J. 'Current prospects for the proportion of marriages ending in divorce', *Population Trends*, No. 55, O.P.C.S., Spring 1989.
2. Martin, T. C. and Bumpass, L. L. 'Recent trends in marital disruption', *Demography*, 26, 37, 1989.

CHAPTER 1

1. Shorter, E. *The Making of the Modern Family*, Collins, Glasgow, 1976.
2. Stone, L. *The Family, Sex and Marriage in England 1500–1800*, Weidenfeld and Nicolson, London, 1977.
3. Gillis, J. R. *For Better, For Worse: British Marriages 1600 to the Present*, Oxford University Press, Oxford, 1985.
4. Fitzpatrick, M. A. *Between Husbands and Wives*, Sage Publications, London, 1988.

CHAPTER 2

1. Bowlby, J. *Attachment and Loss*: Vol I. Attachment, Hogarth Press, London, 1969.
2. Bowlby, J. *Attachment and Loss*: Vol II, Separation, Anxiety and Anger, Hogarth Press, London, 1973.
3. Bowlby, J. *Attachment and Loss*: Vol III, Loss, Sadness and Depression, Hogarth Press, London, 1980.
4. Bowlby, J. 'The Making and Breaking of Affective

Bonds', *British Journal of Psychiatry*, 130,201, 1977.

5. Shaver, P., Hazan, C. and Bradshaw, D. 'Love as Attachment', *The Psychology of Love* (eds. Sternberg, R. J. and Barnes, M. L.) Yale University Press, New Haven, 1988.
6. Ainsworth, M. D. S., Blehar, M. C., Waters, E. and Walls, S. *Patterns of Attachment: A psychological study of the Strange Situation*, Lawrence Erlbaum, Hillsdale N.J., 1978.
7. Cassidy, J. 'Child, Mother, Attachment and the Self in six-year-olds', *Child Development*, 59,121, 1988.
8. Bartholomew, K. 'Avoidance of Intimacy: An attachment perspective', *Journal of Social and Personal Relationships*, 7,147, 1990.
9. Hazan, C. and Hutt, M. J. 'From parents to peers: transitions in attachment', Unpublished manuscript, Cornell University, Dept of Human Development, Ithaca N.Y., 1991.
10. Bartholomew, K. 'From Childhood to Adult Relationships: Attachment Theory and Research', *Learning about Relationships*, (ed. S. Duck) Sage, London, 1993.
11. Hazan, C. and Shaver, P. R. 'Conceptualising romantic love as an attachment process', *Journal of Personality and Social Psychology*, 52,511, 1987.
12. Collins, N. L. and Read, S. J. 'Adult attachment, working models, and relationship quality in dating couples', *Journal of Personality and Social Psychology*, 58,644, 1990.
13. Feeney, J. A. and Noller, P. 'Attachment style as a predictor of adult romantic relationships.' *Journal of Personality and Social Psychology*, 58,281, 1990.

CHAPTER 3

1. Lee, J. A. *The Colors of Love: An exploration of the ways of loving*, New Press, Donn Mills, Ontario, 1973.

2. Hendrick, S. S. and Hendrick, C. *Romantic Love*, Sage, London, 1992.
3. Hazan, C. and Shaver, P. R.'Conceptualising love as an attachment process', *Journal of Personality and Social Psychology*, 52, 50, 1987.
4. Contreras, R., Hendrick, S. S. and Hendrick, C. 'A cross cultural perspective on marital love and satisfaction', Manuscript submitted for publication, 1992.
5. Fehr, B. 'How I do love thee? Let me consult my prototype,' in *Individuals in Relationship*, (ed. S. Duck), Sage, London, 1993.
6. Fehr, B. 'Prototype analysis of the concept of love and commitment', *Journal of Personality and Social Psychology*, 55,557, 1988.
7. Fitness, J. And Fletcher, G. J. O. 'Love, hate, anger and jealousy in close relationships', *Journal of Personality and Social Psychology*, 1991.
8. Tennov, D. *Love and Limerence: The experience of being in love*, Stein and Day, New York, 1979.
9. Beach, S. R. H. and Tesser, A. 'Love in Marriage'. A cognitive account in *Psychology of Love*, (eds. Sternberg, R. J. and Barnes, M. L.) Yale University Press, New Haven, 1988.

CHAPTER 4

1. Sternberg, R. J. 'Triangulating love' in *The Psychology of Love*, (eds Sternberg, R. J. and Barnes, M. L.) Yale University Press, London, 1988.
2. Sternberg, R. J. and Grajck, S. 'The nature of love', *Journal of Personality and Social Psychology*, 47,312, 1984.

CHAPTER 5

1. Buss, D. M. 'Love Acts, the evolutionary biology of love' in *The Psychology of Love*, (eds Sternberg, R. J. and Barnes, M.L.) Yale University Press, Newhaven and London, 1988.

CHAPTER 6

1. Hatfield, E. 'Passionate and companionate love' in *The Psychology of Love*, (eds Sternberg, R. J. and Barnes, M. L.), Yale University Press, London, 1988.
2. Hatfield, E. and Walster, G. W. *A New Look at Love*, University Press of America, Hamilton, MA., 1978.
3. Liebowitz, M. R. *The Chemistry of Love*, Little Brown, Boston, 1983.
4. Kaplan, H. S. *Disorders of Sexual Desire*, Simon and Schuster, New York, 1979.
5. Hatfield, E. 'The dangers of intimacy', in *Communication, Intimacy and Close Relationships*, (ed. Derlega, V.), Academic Press, New York, 1984.
6. Altman, I. and Taylor, D. A. *Social Penetration: the Development of Interpersonal Relationships*, Holt, New York, 1973.
7. Huesman, L. R. and Levinger, G. 'Incremental exchange theory: a formal model for progression in dyadic social interaction', in *Equity Theory; towards a general theory of social interaction*, (eds Berkwitz, L. and Hatfield, E.), Academic Press, New York, 1976.
8. Jourard, S. M. *The Transparent Self*, Van Nostrand, Princeton, 1964.
9. Argyle, M. *The Psychology of Interpersonal Behaviour*, Penguin, Baltimore, 1967.
10. Hatfield, E., Roberts, D. and Schmidt, L. 'The impact of sex and physical attractiveness on an initial social encounter', *Recherche de Psychologie Sociale*, 2,27, 1980.
11. Allgeier, A. R. and Byrne, D. 'Attraction towards the opposite sex as a determinant of physical proximity', *Journal of Social Psychology*, 90,213, 1973.

CHAPTER 7

1. O.P.C.S., *Population Trends 70*, Winter 1992.
2. Surra, C. A. 'Research and theory on mate selection and premarital relationships in the 1980s', *Journal of*

Marriage and the Family, 52,844, 1990.
3. Mansfield, P. and Collard, J. *The Beginning of the Rest of Your Life*, Macmillan, London, 1988.
4. Busfield, J. and Paddon, M. *Thinking about Children: Sociology and Fertility in Post-war England*, Cambridge University Press, Cambridge, 1977.
5. Pincus, L. (ed.) *Marriage: Studies in Emotional Conflict and Growth*, Institute of Marital Studies, London, 1973.
6. Bailey, B. L. *From Front Porch to Back Seat: Courtship in Twentieth-century America*, The John Hopkins University Press, Baltimore, 1988.
7. Burgess, E. W. and Wallin, P. W. *Courtship, Engagement and Marriage*, Lippencote, New York, 1954.
8. Lynd, R. S. and Lynd, H. M. *Middletown: A study in contemporary American Culture*, Harcourt, Brace & Co, New York, 1929.
9. Murstein, B. I. *Love, Sex and Marriage through the ages*, Springler, New York, 1974.
10. Waller, W. *The family, a dynamic interpretation*, Dryden, New York, 1951.
11. Cate, R. M. and Lloyd, S. A. *Courtship*, Sage, London, 1992.
12. Winch, R. F. 'The theory of complementarity needs in mate selection. A test of one kind of complementarities', *American Sociological Review*, 20,52, 1955.
13. Murstein, B. I. *Who will marry when?*, Springler, New York, 1976.
14. Seyfried, B. A. 'Complementarity in interpersonal attraction', in *Theory and Practice in Interpersonal Attraction*, (ed. Duck, S. W.), pp 165–184, 1977.
15. Tharp, R. G. 'Psychological patterning in Marriage', *Psychological Bulletin*, 60,97, 1963.
16. Burgess, E. W. and Wallin, P. W. *Engagement and Marriage*, Lippencote, New York, 1953.
17. Schellenberg, J. A. 'Homogamy in personal values and the field of eligibles', *Social Forces*, 39,157, 1960.
18. Antill, J. K. 'Sex role complementarity versus similarity

in married couples' *Journal of Personality and Social Psychology*, 45,145, 1983.

19. Price, R. A. and Vanderberg, S. S. 'Matching for physical attractiveness', *Personality & Social Psychology Bulletin*, 5,398, 1979.
20. Hendrick, S. S. 'Self disclosure and marital satisfaction', *Journal of Personality and Social Psychology*, 40,1150, 1981.
21. Hill, C. T., Rubin, Z. and Peplau, L. A. 'Break ups before marriage. The end of 103 affairs', *Journal of Social Issues*, 32(1),147, 1976.
22. Reiss, I. L. 'Towards a sociology of the heterosexual love relationship', *Marriage and Family Living*, 22,139, 1960; Reiss, I. L. *Family Systems in America* (3rd Edition), Holte, Reinhart and Winston, 1980.
23. Kirckhoff, A. C. and Davis, K. E. 'Value consensus and need complementarity in mate selection', *American Sociological Review*, 27,295, 1962.
24. Murstein, B. I. 'Stimulus-value-role: A theory of marital choice', *Journal of Marriage and the Family*, 32,465, 1970.
25. Berschied, E. and Walster, E. 'Physical attractiveness', *Advances in Experimental Social Psychology*, 7,158, 1974.
26. Walster, E., Aronson, V., Abrahams, D. and Rottman, L. 'The importance of physical atttractiveness in dating behaviour', *Journal of Personal and Social Psychology*, 4,508, 1966.
27. Lewis, R. A. 'A developmental framework for the analysis of premarital dyadic formation', *Family Process*, 11,17, 1972.
28. Bolton, C. D. 'Mate selection as the development of a relationship', *Marriage and Family Living*, 7,421, 1961.
29. Johnson, M. P. 'Commitment cohesion, investment barriers, alternatives constraint. Why do people stay together when they really don't want to?' Paper presented at the Theory Construction and Research Methodology Workshop. National Council on Family Relations Annual Meeting Dallas, TX, 1985.

30. Rusbult C. E., 'A longitudinal test of the investment model: The development and deterioration of satisfaction and commitment in heterosexual involvement', *Journal of Personality and Social Psychology*, 45,101, 1983.
31. Fernlee, D. et al. 'The dissolution of intimate relationships: a hazard model', *Social Psychology Quarterly*, 53,13, 1990.
32. Surra, C. A. and Longstreth, M. 'Similarity of outcomes, interdependence and conflict in dating relationships', *Journal of Personality and Social Psychology*, 59,1, 1990.
33. Cate, R. M. and Lloyd, S. A. 'Courtship' in *Handbook of Personal Relationships*, (ed. Duck, S.) (409–427), Wiley, New York, 1988.
34. Lloyd, S. A. 'The dark side of courtship', *Family Relations*, 40,14, 1991.
35. Booth, A., 'Divorce and marital instability over the life course', *Journal of Family Issues*, 7,421, 1987.
36. Thornes, B. and Collard, J. *Who Divorces?*, Routledge, Kegan Paul, London, 1979.
37. Kitson, G. C., 'Who divorces and Why?' *American Journal of Family Issues*, 6,255, 1985.
38. Burgess, E. W. and Cottrell, L. S. *Predicting success or failure in marriage*, Prentice Hall, New York, 1939.
39. Burr, W. R. *Theory, Construction and the Sociology of the Family*, Wiley, New York, 1973.
40. Lewis, R. A. and Spanier, G. 'Theorising about the quality and stability of marriage', in *Contemporary Theories about the Family*, (eds Burr, W. R. et al.), Vol 1, (268–294), Free Press, New York, 1979.
41. Norton, A. J. and Glick, P. C. 'Marital Instability in America Past, Present and Future' in *Divorce and Separation. Context, Causes and Consequences*, (eds Levinger, G. & Moles, G.), (6–19), Basic Books, New York, 1979.
42. Adams, C. R. 'The prediction of adjustment in marriage', *Educational and Psychological Measurement*,

6,185, 1946.

43. Kelly, L. E. and Conley, J. J. 'Personality and Compatibility: A prospective analysis of mental stability and marital satisfaction', *Journal of Personality and Social Psychology*, 52,27, 1987.
44. Wambolt, F. S. and Reiss, D. 'Defining a family heritage and a new relationship: Two central themes in the making of a marriage', *Family Process*, 28,317, 1989.
45. Mueller, C. and Pope, H. 'Marital Instability: a study of its transition between generations', *Journal of Marriage and the Family*, 39,83, 1977.
46. White, L. K. 'Determinants of Divorce – A Review of research in the eighties', *Journal of Marriage and the Family*, 52,904, 1990.
47. Vaillant, G. E. 'Natural history of male psychological health: VI correlates of successful marriage and fatherhood', *American Journal of Psychiatry*, 135,653, 1978.
48. Terman, L. M. and Oden, M. H. *The Gifted Child Grows Up*, Stanford University Press, Stanford, 1947.
49. O'Leary, K. D. et al. 'Prevalence and stability of physical aggression between spouses: a longitudinal analysis', *Journal of Consulting and Clinical Psychology*, 57,263, 1989.
50. Aron, A., Dutton, D. C., Aron, F. N., and Iverson, A. 'Experiences of falling in love', *Journal of Social and Personal Relationships*, 6,185, 1989.
51. Shaver, P. R. 'Emotion knowledge: further exploration of a prototype approach', *Journal of Personality and Social Psychology*, 52,1061, 1989.
52. Byrne, D. *The Attraction Paradigm*, Academic Press, New York, 1971.
53. Miller, N. et al. 'Similarity Contrast and Complementarity in Friendship Choice', *Journal of Personality and Social Psychology*, 3,3, 1966.
54. Segal, M. W. 'Alphabet and attraction: an unobtrusive measure of the effect of propinquity in a field setting',

Journal of Personality and Social Psychology, 30,654, 1974.

55. Festinger, L., Schachter, S. and Back, K. *Social Pressures in Information Groups, a Study of Human Factors, in House,* Harper, New York, 1950.
56. Zajinc, R. B. 'Attitudinal effects of more exposure', *Journal of Personality and Social Psychology Monograph,* Suppl. 19,1, 1968.
57. Tesser, A. and Paulhus, D. L. 'Towards a causal model of love', *Journal of Personal and Social Psychology,* 34,1095, 1976.
58. Jones, E. E. and Archer, R. L. 'Are there special effects of personalistic self-disclosure?', *Journal of Experimental Social Psychology,* 8,148, 1976.
59. Aron, A. and Aron, E. N. *Love and the expansion of self: Understanding attraction and satisfaction,* Hemisphere, New York, 1986.

CHAPTER 8

1. Duvall, E. M. *Family Development* Lippencott, Philadelphia, 1957, (rev. ed. 1962).
2. Blood, R. O. and Wolfe, D. N. *Husbands and Wives: The Dynamics of Married Living,* Free Press, Glencoe, Illinois, 1960.
3. Rollins, B. C. and Feldman, H. 'Marital Satisfaction over the Family Lifecyle', *Journal of Marriage and the Family,* 32,20, 1970.
4. Burr, W. R. 'Satisfaction with various aspects of marriage over the life cycle: a random middle class sample', *Journal of Marriage and the Family,* 32,29, 1970.
5. Rollins, B. C. and Cannon, K. L. 'Marital Satisfaction over the Family Lifecycle: A Revaluation', *Journal of Marriage and the Family,* 36,271, 1974.
6. Anderson, S. A. et al. 'Perceived Marital Quality and Family Life Cycle Categories: a further analysis', *Journal of Marriage and the Family,* 45,127, 1983.

7. Menaghan, E. 'Marital Stress and Family Transitions: A panel analysis', *Journal of Marriage and the Family*, 45,371, 1983.
8. Rosenblatt, P. C. 'Behaviour in Public Places: Comparison of couples accompanied and unaccompanied by children', *Journal of Marriage and the Family*, 36,750, 1974.
9. Houseknecht, S. K. 'Childlessness and marital adjustment', *Journal of Marriage and the Family*, 41,259, 1979.
10. Steinberg, L. 'The Impact of Puberty on Family Relations: Effects of Pubertal Status and Pubertal Timing', *Developmental Psychology*, 23,451, 1987.
11. Silverberg, S. B. and Steinberg, L. 'Adolescent Autonomy, Parent-Adolescent Conflict and Parental Well-Being', *Journal of Youth and Adolescence*, 16,293, 1987.
12. Walker, C. 'Some Variations in Marital Satisfaction', in *Equalities and Inequalities of the Family Life* (ed. Chester, R.) Academic Press, London, 1977.
13. Bernard, J. *The Future of Marriage*, World Publishing, New York, 1972.

CHAPTER 9

1. Dominian, J. *Marriage, Faith and Love*, Darton, Longman and Todd, London, 1981.
2. Dominian, J. *Passionate and Compassionate Love*, Darton, Longman and Todd, London, 1991.
3. Murray, H. A. *Exploration in Personality*, Oxford University Press, New York, 1938.
4. Maslow, A. *Towards a Psychology of Being*, Van Nostrand Reinhold, New York, 1968.
5. Jung, C. G. *Memories, Dreams, Reflections*, Vintage, New York, 1961.
6. Rogers, C. R. *On being a Person*, Houghton Mifflin, Boston, 1961.
7. Kelly, G. A. *The Psychology of Personal Constructs*,

Norton, New York, 1955.
8. Bakan, D. *The Duality of Human Existence: Isolation and Communion in Western Man*, Beacon Press, Boston, 1966.

CHAPTER 10

1. Tannen, D. *You Just Don't Understand*, Virago, London, 1991.
2. Altman, I. and Taylor, D. A. *Social Penetration: The Development of Interpersonal Relationships*, Holt, Reinhart and Winston, New York, 1973.
3. Jourard, S. M. *The Transparent Self*, Van Nostrand Reinhold, Princeton, 1964.
4. Berg, J. H. and Derlega, V. J. 'Themes in the Study of Self Disclosure' in *Self Disclosure, Theory, Research and Therapy*, (eds Derlega, W. J. and Berg, J. H.), Plenum, New York, 1987.
5. Ehrlich, H. J. and Graeven, D. B. 'Reciprocal Self Disclosure in a Dyad', *Journal of Experimental Social Psychology*, 7,389, 1971.
6. Morton, T. L. 'Intimacy and Reciprocity of Exchange: A Comparison of spouses and strangers', *Journal of Personality and Social Psychology*, 36,72, 1978.
7. Hendrick, S. S. 'Self Disclosure and Marital Satisfaction', *Journal of Personality and Social Psychology*, 40,1150, 1981.
8. Komarovsky, M. *Blue Collar Marriage*, Vintage Books, New York, 1967.
9. Gilbert, S. 'Self Disclosure, Intimacy and Communication in the Family', *Family Coordinator*, 25,221, 1976.
10. Burke, R. J., Weirr, T. and Harrison 'Disclosure of Problems and Tensions Experienced by Marital Partners', *Psychological Reports*, 38,531, 1976.
11. Levinger, G. and Senn, D. J. 'Disclosure of Feelings in Marriage', *Merrill-Palmer Quarterly*, 13,237, 1967.

12. Altman, I. *The Environment and Social Behaviour, Privacy, Personal Space, Territory and Crowding,* G A Brooks/Cole, Pacific Grove, 1975.
13. Feigenbaum, W. M. 'Reciprocity in Self Disclosure Within the Psychological Interview', *Psychological Reports,* 40,15, 1977.
14. Komarovsky, M. 'Patterns of Self Disclosure of male undergraduates', *Journal of Marriage and the Family,* 36,677, 1974.
15. Jorgensen, S. R. and Gaudy, J. C. 'Self Disclosure and Satisfaction in Marriage', *Family Relations,* 29,281, 1980.
16. Beier, E. G. and Sternberg R. J. 'Marital Communication: Subtle Cues between Newly Weds', *Journal of Communication,* 27,92, 1977.
17. Jones, S. E. and Yarbrough, A. E. 'A Naturalistic Study of the Meanings of Touch', *Communication Monographs,* 52,19, 1985.
18. Rubin, Z. 'Measurement of Romantic Love', *Journal of Personality and Social Psychology,* 16,265, 1970.
19. Fitzpatrick, M. A. *Between Husbands and Wives: Communication in Marriage,* Sage, London, 1988.
20. Markman, H. J. 'The Longitudinal study of couples' interactions: Implications for understanding and predicting the development of marital distress', *Marital Interaction: Analysis and Modification,* (eds Hallveg, K. and Jacobson, N. S.), (253–284), Guildford, New York, 1984.
21. Weiss, R. L. 'The new kid on the block; behavioural systems approach', *Assessing Marriage: New Behavioural Approaches,* (eds Filsinger, E. E. and Lewis, R. A.) (22–37) Sage, Beverley Hills, CA., 1981.
22. Gottman, J. M. *Marital Interaction: Experimental Investigations,* Academic Press, New York, 1979.

CHAPTER 11

1. Homans, G. C. *The Human Group*, Harcourt, Brace, New York, 1950.
2. Burr, W. *Theory Construction and the Sociology of the Family*, Wiley, New York, 1973.
3. Lewis, R. A. and Spanier, G. B. 'Theorising About the Quality and Stability of Marriage', *Contemporary Theories about the Family*, (eds, Burr, W., Hill, R. Nye, F. and Reiss, I.) The Free Press, New York, 1979.
4. Hill, M. S. 'Marital Stability and Spouses' Shared Time'. *Journal of Family Issues*, 9,427, 1988.
5. Orthner, D. K. and Mancini, J. A. 'Leisure Impacts on Family Interaction and Cohesion', *Journal of Leisure Research*, 22,125, 1990.
6. Holman, T. B. and Epperson, A. 'Family Issue: A Review of the Literature with Research Recommendations', *Journal of Leisure Research*, 16,277, 1984.
7. Kingston, P. W. and Nock, S.L. 'Time Together Among Dual-Earner Couples', *American Sociological Review*, 52,31, 1987.
8. Booth, A., Johnson, D. R., White, L. K. and Edwards, J. N. 'Women, Outside Employment and Marital Instability', *American Journal of Sociology*, 90,567, 1984.
9. Galambos, N. N. and Silbereisen, R. K. 'Role Strain in West German Dual Earner Households', *Journal of Marriage and the Family*, 51,385, 1989.
10. Greenstein, T. N. 'Marital Disruption and the Employment of Marital Women', *Journal of Marriage and the Family*, 52,657, 1990.
11. White, L. K. and Keith, B. 'The Effect of Shift Work on the Quality and Stability of Marital Relations', *Journal of Marriage and the Family*, 52,453, 1990.
12. White, L. K. 'Determinants of Spousal Interaction: Marital Structure or Marital Happiness', *Journal of Marriage and the Family*, 45,511, 1983.
13. Zuo, J. 'The Reciprocal Relationship Between Marital

Interaction and Marital Happiness', *Journal of Marriage and the Family*, 54,870, 1992.
14. Gottman, J. M. and Levenson, R. W. 'The Social Psycho-Physiology of Marriage' in *Perspectives on Marital Interaction*, (eds Noller, P. and Fitzpatrick, M. A.) Multilingual Matters, Philadelphia, 1988.
15. Levenson, R. W. and Gottman, J. M. 'Marital Interaction: Physiological Linkage and Affective Exchange', *Journal of Personality and Social Psychology*, 45,587, 1983.

CHAPTER 12

1. Branden, N. 'A vision of romantic love' in *The Psychology of Love*, Yale University, New Haven and London, 1988.

CHAPTER 13

1. Markman, H. 'Application of a behavioural model of marriage in predicting relationship satisfaction of couples planning marriage', *Journal of Consulting and Clinical Psychology*, 47,743, 1979.
2. Fletcher, G. J. O. and Fincham, F. D. 'Attribution in close relationships' in *Cognition in Close Relationships*, (ed. Erlbaum, L.), Hove and London, 1991.
3. Jacobson, N. S. 'A Component Analysis of Behavioural Marital Therapy: The Relative Effectiveness of Behaviour Exchange and Communication/Problem Solving Training', *Journal of Consulting and Clinical Psychology*, 52,295, 1984.
4. Gottman, J. M. *Marital Interaction: Experimental Investigations*, Academic Press, New York, 1979.
5. Jacobson, N. S. and Moore, D. 'Spouses as Observers of Events in their Relationship', *Journal of Consulting and Clinical Psychology*, 49,809, 1981.

CHAPTER 14

1. Peterson, D. R. 'Conflict' in *Close Relationships*, (eds, Berscheid, A., Kelly, H. H., Christensen, A. et al), W. H. Freeman, New York, 1983.
2. Rapoport, A. *Fights, Gains and Debates*, University of Michigan Press, Ann Arbor, 1960.
3. Hendrick, S. S. 'Self Disclosure and Marital Satisfaction', *Journal of Personality and Social Psychology*, 40,115, 1981.
4. Gottman, J. M. and Levenson, R. W. 'The Social Psychophysiology of Marriage' in *Perspective on marital interaction*, (eds, Noller, P. and Fitzpatrick, M. A.) (182–200), Multilingual Matters, Philadelphia, 1988.
5. Fincham, F. D., Beach, S. R. and Baucom, D. H. 'Attribution Processes in Distressed and Non-Distressed Couples: Four Self-Partner Attribution Differences', *Journal of Personality and Social Psychology*, 52,739, 1987.
6. Halford, W. K., Hahlvag, K. and Dunne, M. 'The Cross-Cultural Consistency of Marital Communication Associated with Marital Distress', *Journal of Marriage and the Family*, 52,487, 1990.
7. Billings, A. 'Conflict Resolution in Distressed and Non-Distressed Married Couples', *Journal of Consulting and Clinical Psychology*, 47,368, 1979.
8. Koren, P., Carlton, K. and Shaw, D. 'Marital Conflict: Relations Among Behaviours, Outcomes and Distress', *Journal of Consulting and Clinical Psychology*, 48,460, 1980.
9. Kelly, C., Huston, T. L. and Cate, R. M. 'Premarital Relationship: Correlates of the Erosion of Satisfaction in Marriage', *Journal of Social and Personal Relationships*, 2,167, 1985.
10. Rands, M., Levinger, G., Mellinger, G. D. 'Patterns of Conflict Resolution and Marital Satisfaction', *Journal of Family Issues*, 2,297, 1981.

11. Retzinger, S. M. *Violent Emotions*, Sage, London, 1991.

CHAPTER 15

1. Eysenck, H. J. and Eysenck, M. W. *Personality and Individual Differences*, London, 1985.
2. Eysenck, H. J. *"I Do"*, Century Publishing, London, 1983.
3. Tyrer, P. and Stein, G. *Personality Disorder Reviewed*, Gaskell, London, 1993.

CHAPTER 16

1. Buckley, P. *Essential Papers on Object-Relations*, New York University Press, London, 1986.
2. Freud, A. *The Ego and the Mechanisms of Defence*, Hogarth Press, London, 1966.
3. Erikson, E. H. *Childhood and Society*, Pelican, Harmondsworth, 1965.

CHAPTER 17

1. Dominian, J. *Marital Breakdown*, Penguin, Harmondsworth, 1968.
2. Brown, G. W. and Harris, T. *Social Origins of Depression*, Tavistock, London, 1978.
3. Quinton, D., Rutter, M. and Liddle, C. 'Institutional Rearing, Parenting Difficulties and Marital Support', *Psychological Medicine*, 14,107, 1984.
4. Ruszczynski, S. *Psychotherapy with Couples*, Karnac Books, London, 1993.
5. Clarkson, P. 'Facets of the dance' in *Coupling ... What makes permanence?*, (ed. Brothers, B. J.), Haworth Press, London, 1991.

CHAPTER 18

1. Dominian, J. *Passionate and Compassionate Love*, Darton, Longman and Todd, London 1991.

2. Lyons, A. 'Husbands and Wives: the mysterious choice' in *Psychotherapy with Couples,* (ed. Ruszczynski, S.), Karnac Books, London, 1993.
3. Jung, C. G. 'Psychological types' in *The Collected Works of C. G. Jung,* Routledge and Kegan Paul, London, 1921.

CHAPTER 19

1. Dindia, K. and Baxter, L. A. 'Strategies for Maintaining and Repairing Marital Relationships', *Journal of Social and Personal Relationships,* 4,143, 1987.
2. Mansfield, P. and Collard, J. *The Beginning of the Rest of Your Life,* Macmillan, London, 1988.

CHAPTER 20

1. Burgess, E. W. and Locke, H. J. *The Family: From Institution to Companionship,* (First Edition), American, New York, 1948.
2. Cuber, J. F. and Harroff, P. *The Significant Americans: A Study of Sexual Behaviour Among The Affluent,* Appleton-Century, New York, 1965.
3. Fitzpatrick, M. A. *Between Husbands and Wives,* Sage, London, 1988.
4. Adams, J. S. 'Inequity in Social Exchange' in *Advances in Experimental Social Psychology,* Vol 2. (ed. Barkowitz, L.), Academic Press, New York, 1965.
5. Homans, G. C. *Social Behaviour,* Harcourt Brace and World, New York, 1961.
6. Walster, E. H., Walster, G. W. and Berscheid, E. *Equity, Theory and Research,* Allyn and Bacon, Boston, 1978.

CHAPTER 21

1. Ford, B. *Patterns of Sex,* St Martins, New York, 1980.
2. Blumstein, P. and Schwartz, P. *American Couples,* William Morrow, New York, 1983.

3. Byers, E. S. and Heinlein, L. 'Predicting Initiations and Refusals of Sexual Activities in Married and Cohabiting Heterosexual Couples', *The Journal of Sex Research*, 26,210, 1989.
4. Brown, M. and Auerback, A. 'Communication Patterns in Initiation of Marital Sex', *Medical Aspects of Human Sexuality*, 15,105, 1981.
5. Kinsey, A. C., Pomeroy, W. B. and Martin, C. E. *Sexual Behaviour in the Human Male*, W. B. Saunders, Philadelphia, 1948.
6. Kinsey, A. C., Pomeroy, W. B., Martin, C. E. and Gebhard, P. H. *Sexual Behaviour in the Human Female*, W. B. Saunders, Philadelphia, 1953.
7. Hunt, M. *Sexual Behaviour in the 1970s*, Playboy Press, Chicago, 1974.
8. Wellings, K., Field, J., Johnson, A.M. and Wadsworth, J. *Sexual Behaviour in Britain*, Penguin, London, 1994.
9. Gregersen, E. *Sexual Practices: The Study of Human Sexuality*, Franklin Watts, New York, 1983.
10. Voeller, B. 'Aids and heterosexual anal intercourse,' *Archives of Sexual Behaviour*, 20,233, 1990.
11. Darling, C. A., Davidson, J. K. and Cox, R. P. 'Female Sexual Response and the Timing of Partner Orgasm', *Journal of Sex and Marital Therapy*, 17,3, 1991.
12. Greeley, A. M. 'Faithful Attraction: Discovering Intimacy, Love and Fidelity', in *American Marriage*, Doherty, New York, 1991.
13. James, W. H. 'The Honeymoon Effect on Marital Coitus', *Journal of Sex Research*, 17,114, 1981.
14. Masters, W. H., Johnson, V. E. and Kolodny, R. *Sex and Human Loving*, Little Brown, Boston, 1986.
15. Mosher, D. L. 'Sex Guilt and Sex Myths in College Men and Women', *Journal of Sex Research*, 15,224, 1979.
16. O'Grady, K. E. et al. 'A Multidimensional Scaling Analysis of Sex Guilt', *Multivariate Behavioural Research*, 14,415, 1979.
17. Leary, M. R. and Dobbins, S. E. 'Social Anxiety, Sexual

Behaviour and Contraceptive Use', *Journal of Personality and Social Psychology*, 45,1347, 1983.
18. Eysenck, H. J. *Sex and Personality*, Open Books, London, 1976.
19. Rubin, L. B. *Worlds of Pain: Life in the Working Class Family*, Basic Books, New York, 1976.
20. Wilson, G. 'Personality and Sex' in *Dimensions of Personality. Papers in honour of H. J. Eysenck*, (ed. Lynn, R.), (335–375), Pergamon Press, New York, 1981.

CHAPTER 22

1. Blumstein, P. and Schwartz, P. *American Couples*, New York, William Morrow, 1983.
2. Rubin, L. B. *Worlds of Pain: Life in the Working Class Family*, New York, Basic Books, 1976.
3. Russell, D. E. H. *Rape in Marriage*, New York, Macmillan, 1982.
4. Russell, D. E. H., *Sexual exploitation, Child Sexual Abuse and Workplace Harassment*, Sage, Beverley Hills, CA., 1984.
5. Finkelhor, D. and Yllo, K. *License to Rape*, New York, Holt, Reinhart and Winston, 1985.
6. Frieze, I. H. 'Investigating the Causes and Consequences of Marital Rape Signs', *Journal of Women in Culture and Society*, 8,532, 1983.
7. Koss, M. P. and Dinero, T. E. 'Predictors of Sexual Aggression among a National Sample of Male College Students', in *Human Sexual Aggression: Current Perspectives*, (eds Prentky, R. A. and Quinsey, V. L.), New York, New York Academy of Sciences, 1988.
8. Muehlenhard, C. L. and Falcon, P. L. 'Men's Heterosocial Skill and Attitudes towards Women as Predictors of Verbal, Sexual Coercion and Forceful Rape', *Sex Roles*, 23,241, 1990.
9. Levine, E. M. and Kanin, E. J. 'Sexual Violence among Dates and Acquaintances: Trends and their Implication

for Marriage and the Family', *Journal of Family Violence*, 2,55, 1987.
10. Bidwell, L. and White, P. 'The Family Content of Marital Rape', *Journal of Family Violence*, 1,277, 1986.
11. Bancroft, J. *Human Sexuality and its Problems*, Churchill Livingstone, Edinburgh, 1988 (2nd ed).
12. Kaplan, H. S. *The New Sex Therapy: Active Treatment of Sexual Dysfunctions*, Bailliere Tindall, London, 1974.
13. Kaplan, H. S. *Disorders of Sexual Desire*, Bailliere Tindall, London, 1979.
14. Wellings, K., Field, J., Johnson, A. M. and Wadsworth, J. *Sexual Behaviour in Britain*, Penguin, London, 1994.
15. Bowlby, J. *Attachment and Loss*, Vol I: Attachment, Hogarth Press, London, 1969.

CHAPTER 23

1. Dominian, J. *Passionate and Compassionate Love*, Darton, Longman and Todd, London, 1991.

CHAPTER 24

1. Wellings, K., Field, J., Johnson, A.M. and Wadsworth, J. *Sexual Behaviour in Britain*, Penguin, London, 1994.
2. Lawson, A. *Adultery*, Blackwell, Oxford, 1988.
3. Gorer, G. *Sex and Marriage in England Today*, Nelson, London, 1971.
4. Blumstein, P. and Schwartz, P. *American Couples*, Morrow, New York, 1983.
5. Atwater, L. *The Extramarital Connection*, Irvington, New York, 1982.
6. Buunk, B. 'Extramarital sex in the Netherlands: Motivation in social and marital context', *Alternative Lifestyles*, 3,312, 1980.
7. Edwards, J. N. and Booth, A. 'Sexual Behaviour In and Out of Marriage: An Assessment of Correlates', *Journal of Marriage and the Family*, 38,73, 1976.
8. Spanier, G. B. and Margolies R. L. 'Marital Separation

and Extra Marital Sexual Behaviour', *Journal of Sex Research*, 19,23, 1983.

9. Wiggins, J. D. and Lederer, D. A. 'Differential Antecedents of Infidelity in Marriage', *American Mental Health Counsellors Association Journal*, 6,152, 1984.
10. Buunk, B. 'Conditions that Promote Breakup as a Consequence of Extradyadic Involvement', *Journal of Social and Clinical Psychology*, 5,237, 1987.
11. Swieczkowski, J. B. and Walker, C. E. 'Sexual Behaviour Correlates of Female Orgasm and Marital Happiness', *Journal of Nervous and Mental Disease*, 166,334, 1978.
12. Burns, A. 'Perceived Causes of Marriage Breakdown and Conditions of Life', *Journal of Marriage and the Family*, 46,55, 1984.

CHAPTER 25

1. Aldous, J. *Family Careers, Developmental Change in Families*, Wiley, New York, 1978.
2. Miller, B. C. 'A Multivariate Development Model of Marital Satisfaction', *Journal of Marriage and the Family*, 38,643, 1976.
3. Belsky, J. 'Stability and Change in Marriage Across the Transition to Parenthood', *Journal of Marriage and the Family*, 45,533, 1983.
4. Belsky, J. and Rovine, M. 'Patterns of Marital Change Across the Transition to Parenthood', *Journal of Marriage and the Family*, 52,109, 1990.
5. Feldman, H. 'The Effects of Children on The Family', in *Family Issues of Employed Women in Europe and America*, (ed. Michael, A.), (41–50) E. J. Bill, London, 1971.
6. Feldman, H. and Nash, S. 'The Transition from Expectancy to Parenthood: Impact of the Firstborn on Men and Women', *Sex Roles*, 11,84, 1984.
7. Moss, P., Bolland, G., Foxman, R. and Owen, C. 'Marital Relations during the Transition to Parenthood',

Journal of Reproduction and Infant Psychology, 4,57, 1986.
8. Ruble, D., Flemming, A., Hackel, L. and Stangor, C. 'Changes in the Marital Relationship During the Transition to First-Time Motherhood: Effects of Violated Expectations Concerning Division of Household Labour', *Journal of Personality and Social Psychology*, 55,78, 1988.
9. Cowan, C., Cowan, P., Hemming, G., Garrett, E., Coysh, W., Curtis-Boles, H. and Bowles, A. 'Transition to Parenthood, his, hers and theirs', *Journal of Family Issues*, 6,451, 1985.
10. Belsky, J., Spanier, G. and Rovine, M. 'Stability and Change in Marriage across the Transition to Parenthood: A Second Study', *Journal of Marriage and the Family*, 47,855, 1985.
11. Waldron, H. and Routh, D. 'The Effect of the First Child on the Marital Relationship', *Journal of Marriage and the Family*, 43,785, 1981.
12. Mansfield, P., Collard, J., McAllister, F. *Persons, partners and parents*, Macmillan, London (Forthcoming).
13. Steinberg, L. 'The Impact of Puberty on Family Relations', *Developmental Psychology*, 23,451, 1987.

CHAPTER 26

1. Mansfield, P. and Collard, J. *The Beginning of the Rest of Your Life*, Macmillan, London, 1988.
2. Fitzpatrick, M. A. *Between Husbands and Wives*, Sage, London, 1988.
3. Russell, R. J. H. and Wells, P. A. *Predictors of Happiness in Married Couples* (in press, 1993).
4. Thornes, B. and Collard, J. *Who Divorces?*, Routledge and Kegan Paul, London, 1979.
5. Oakley, A. *The Sociology of Housework*, Martin Robertson, London, 1974.
6. Yogev, S. and Brett, J. 'Perceptions of the Division of Housework and Childcare and Marital Satisfaction',

Journal of Marriage and the Family, 47,609, 1985.
7. Ross, C. E., Mirowsky, J. and Huber, J. 'Dividing Work, Sharing Work and In Between: Marriage Patterns and Depression', *American Sociological Review*, 48,809, 1983.
8. Meissner, M. 'Sexual Division of Labour and Inequality: Labour and Leisure', in *Women in Canada*, (ed. Stephenson, M.), (160–80), Women's Educational Press, Toronto, 1977.
9. Coleman, M. T. 'The Division of Household Labour: Suggestions for Future Empirical Consideration and Theoretical Development', *Journal of Family Issues*, 9,132, 1988.
10. Blair, S. L. and Lichter, D. T. 'Measuring the Division of Household Labour: Gender Segregation of Housework among American Couples', *Journal of Family Issues*, 12,91, 1991.
11. Blair, S. L. and Johnson, N. P. 'Wives' Perception of the Fairness of the Division of Household Labour', *Journal of Marriage and the Family*, 54,570, 1992.
12. Suitor, J. J. 'Marital Quality and Satisfaction with the Division of Household Labour Across the Female Life Cycle', *Journal of Marriage and the Family*, 53,221, 1991.

CHAPTER 27

1. Axelson, L. J. 'The Marital Adjustment and Marital Role Definition of Husbands of Working and Non-Working Wives', *Marriage and Family Living*, 24,189, 1963.
2. Nye, F. I. and Hoffman, L. W. *The Employed Mother in America*, Rand McNally, Chicago, 1963.
3. Orden, S. R. and Bradburn, N. M. 'Working Wives and Marital Happiness', *American Journal of Sociology*, 74,392, 1969.
4. Michael, R. T. 'Why Has the US Divorce Rate Doubled Within the Decade?', Working paper no. 202, National Bureau of Economic Research, 1977.
5. Schoen, R. and Urton, W. L. 'A Theoretical Perspective

on Cohort Marriage and Divorce in Twentieth Century Sweden', *Journal of Marriage and the Family*, 41,409, 1979.

6. Booth, A. 'Wife's Employment and Husband's Stress: A Replication and Refutation', *Journal of Marriage and the Family*, 39,645, 1977.
7. Glenn, N. and Weaver, C. N. 'A multivariate Multistudy of Marital Happiness', *Journal of Marriage and the Family*, 40,269, 1978.
8. Houseknecht, S. K. and Macke, A. S. 'Combining Marriage and Career: The Marital Adjustment of Professional Women', *Journal of Marriage and the Family*, 43,651, 1981.
9. Ladewig, B. H. and White, P. N. 'Dual Earner Marriage: The Family Social Environment and Dyadic Adjustment', *Journal of Family Issues*, 5,343, 1984.
10. Spitze, G. 'Woman's Employment and Family Relations: A Review', *Journal of Marriage and the Family*, 50,595, 1988.
11. Oppenheimer, V. 'The Sociology of Women's Economic Role in The Family', *American Sociological Review*, 42,387, 1977.
12. Huber, J. and Spitze, G. 'Considering Divorce: An Expansion of Becker's Theory of Marital Instability', *American Journal of Sociology*, 86, 75, 1980.
13. Richardson, J. G. 'Wife's Occupational Superiority and Marital Troubles: An Examination of the Hypothesis', *Journal of Marriage and the Family*, 41,63, 1979.
14. Vannoy, D. and Philliber, W. W. 'Wife's Employment and Quality of Marriage', *Journal of Marriage and the Family*, 54,387, 1992.
15. Kelvin, P. and Jarrett, J. E. 'Employment: Its Social/Psychological Effects', Cambridge University Press, London, 1985.
16. Conger, R. D. and Elder, G. H. 'Linking Economic Hardship to Marital Quality and Instability', *Journal of Marriage and the Family*, 52,643, 1990.

17. Liker, J. K. and Elder, G. H. 'Economic Hardship and Marital Relations in the 1930s', *American Sociological Review*, 48, 345, 1983.
18. Mattinson, J. *Work, Love and Marriage*, Duckworth, London, 1988.
19. Leigh, G. K. et al. 'Correlates of Marital Satisfaction Among Men and Women in Intact First Marriages and Remarriages', *Family Perspectives*, 19,139, 1985.
20. Miller, B. C. 'A Multivariate Developmental Model of Marital Satisfaction', *Journal of Marriage and the Family*, 38,643, 1976.
21. Orthner, D. K. 'Leisure Activity Patterns and Marital Satisfaction Over the Marital Career', *Journal of Marriage and the Family*, 37,91, 1975.
22. Holman, T. B. and Jacquart, M. 'Leisure Activity Patterns and Marital Satisfaction', *Journal of Marriage and the Family*, 50,369, 1988.

CHAPTER 28

1. Straus, M. A., Gelles, R. and Steinmetz, S. *Behind Closed Doors: Violence in the American Family*, Doubleday, New York, 1980.
2. Rosenbaum, A. and O'Leary, K. D. 'Marital Violence: Characteristics of Abusive Couples', *Journal of Consulting and Clinical Psychology*, 49,63, 1981.
3. Gelles, R. J. *Family Violence*, C.A. Sage, Newbury Park, 1987.

CHAPTER 29

1. Weissman, M. M., Myers, J. K. and Harding, P. S. 'Psychiatric Disorders in a US Urban Community, 1975–1976', *American Journal of Psychiatry*, 135,259, 1978.
2. Hoover, C. F. and Fitzgerald, R. G. 'Marital Conflict of Manic-Depressive Patients', *Archives of General Psychiatry*, 38,65, 1981.

3. Paykel, E. S. et al. 'Life Events and Depression: A Controlled Study', *Archives of General Psychiatry*, 21,753, 1969.
4. Rounsaville B. J. et al. 'Marital Disputes and Treatment Outcomes in Depressed Women', *Comprehensive Psychiatry*, 20,483, 1979.
5. Brown, G. W. and Harris, T. *Social Origins of Depression: A Study of Psychiatric Disorder in Women*, Tavistock, London, 1978.
6. Hinchliffe, M. D., Hooper, D. and Roberts, F. J. *The Melancholy Marriage*, Wiley, New York, 1978.
7. Arkowitz, H., Holiday, S. and Hutter, M. 'Depressed Women and Their Husbands: A Study of Marital Interaction and Adjustment', Paper presented at the Annual Meeting of the Association for the Advancement of Behaviour Therapy, Los Angeles, 1982.
8. Kahn, J., Coyne, J. C. and Margolin, G. 'Depression and Marital Disagreement: The Social Construct of Despair', *Journal of Social and Personal Relationships*, 2,447, 1985.
9. Robin, A. M. 'Psychological Changes in Normal Parturition', *Psychiatric Quarterly*, 36,129, 1962.
10. Pitt, B. 'Maternity Blues', *British Journal of Psychiatry*, 122,431, 1973.
11. Pitt, B. 'Psychiatric Illness Following Childbirth', *Hospital Medicine*, (815), April 1986.
12. Dominian, J. *Depression*, Fontana, Glasgow, 1990.
13. Kendell, R. E. et al. 'Epidemiology of Puerperal Psychosis', *British Journal of Psychiatry*, 150,662, 1987.
14. Paykel, S. (ed) *Handbook of Affective Disorders*, Churchill Livingstone, Edinburgh, 1992.

CHAPTER 31

1. Cuber, J. F. and Harroff, P. *The Significant Americans: A Study of Sexual Behaviour Among The Affluent*, Appleton-Century, New York, 1965.

2. Phillips, R. *Putting Asunder: A History of Divorce in Western Society*, Cambridge University Press, Cambridge, 1988.
3. Goldthorpe, J. E. *Family Life in Western Society*, Cambridge University Press, Cambridge, 1987.
4. Haskey, J. 'Current Prospects For the Proportion of Marriages Ending in Divorce', *Population Trends*, 55,34, 1989.
5. Martin, T. C. and Bumpass, L. L. 'Recent Trends In Marital Disruption', *Demography*, 26,37, 1989.
6. Dormor, D. J. *The Relationship Revolution*, One Plus One, Marriage and Partnership Research, London, 1992.
7. O.P.C.S. *Population Trends 71*, Spring 1993.
8. Haskey, J. 'Grounds for divorce in England and Wales and demographic survey', *Journal of Biosocial Science*, 18, 1986.
9. Thornes, B. and Collard, J. *Who Divorces?*, Routledge, Kegan Paul, London, 1979.
10. Balakrishnan, T. R. et al. 'A Hazard Model Analysis of the Covariates of Marriage Dissolutions in Canada', *Demography*, 24,395, 1987.
11. South, S. and Spitze, G. 'Determinants of Divorce Over The Marital Life-Course', *American Sociological Review*, 51,583, 1986.
12. Thornton, A. and Rodgers, W. 'The Influence of Individual and Historical Time on Marital Dissolution', *Demography*, 24,1, 1987.
13. Moore, K. and Waite L. 'Marital Dissolution, Early Motherhood and Early Marriage', *Stress Forces*, 60,20, 1981.
14. Landale, B. J. and McLaughlin, S. 'The Effect of Marital Status At First Birth on Marital Dissolution Among Adolescent Mothers', *Demography*, 23,329, 1986.
15. Morgan, S. P. and Rindfuss, R. 'Marital Disruption: Structural and Temporal Dimensions', *American Journal of Sociology*, 90,1055, 1984.
16. Teachman, J. D. 'Early Marriage, Premarital Fertility

and Marital Dissolution', *Journal of Family Issues*, 4,105, 1983.

17. Wineberg, H. 'Duration Between Marriage and First Birth and Marital Stability', *Social Biology*, 35,91, 1988.
18. Lewis, R. A. and Spanier, G. B. 'Theorising About the Quality and Stability of Marriage' in *Contemporary Theories about the Family*, (eds, Burr, W. R. et al.) Free Press, New York, 1979.
19. Becker, G. S., Landes, E. M. and Michael, R. T. 'An Economic Analysis of Marital Instability', *Journal of Political Economy*, 85,141, 1977.
20. Mott, F. L. and Moore, S. F. 'The Course of Marital Disruption Among Young American Women: An Interdisciplinary Perspective', *Journal of Marriage and the Family*, 41,355, 1979.
21. Cutright, P. 'Income Family Events: Marital Stability', *Journal of Marriage and the Family*, 83,291, 1971.
22. White, L. K. 'Determinants of Divorce: A Review of the eighties', *Journal of Marriage and the Family*, 52,904, 1990.
23. Dominian, J. *Marital Pathology*, Darton, Longman and Todd and BMA, London, 1980.
24. Dominian, J. *Marriage, Faith and Love*, Darton, Longman and Todd, London, 1981.
25. Dominian, J. *Make or Break*, SPCK, London, 1984.
26. Dominian, J. *Passionate and Compassionate Love*, Darton, Longman and Todd, London, 1991.
27. Goode, W. J. *After Divorce*, Free Press, New York, 1956.
28. Levinger, G. 'Sources of Marital Dissatisfaction Among Applicants for Divorce', *American Journal of Orthopsychiatry*, 36,803, 1966.
29. Kitson, G. C. and Sussman, M. 'Marital Complaints, Demographic Characteristics and Symptoms of Mental Distress in Divorce.' *Journal of Marriage and the Family*, 44,87, 1982.
30. Kitson, G. C. 'Marital Discord and Marital Separation: A County Survey; *Journal of Marriage and the Family*,

47,693, 1985.

31. Thurnher, M. et al. 'Socio-demographies: Perspectives on Reasons for Divorce', *Journal of Divorce*, 6,25, 1983.

CHAPTER 32

1. Haskey, J. 'Children in Families Broken by Divorce', *Population Trends*, 61,34, 1990.
2. Bumpass, L. L. 'Children and Marital Disruption: A Replication and Update', *Demography*, 21,71, 1984.
3. Emery, R. E. *Marriage, Divorce and Children's Adjustment*, Sage Publications, London, 1988.
4. Burgles, L. 'Lone Parenthood and Family Disruption', *Family Policy Study Centre Occasional Papers*, London, 1994.
5. Richards, M. P. M. and Dyson, M. 'Separation, Divorce and the Development of Children: A Review', *Department of Health and Social Security*, London, 1982.
6. Cherlin, A. J. et al. 'Longitudinal Studies of Effects of Divorce on Children in Great Britain and the United States', *Science*, 252,1386, 1991.
7. Douglas, J. W. B. 'Early Disturbing Events and Later Eneuresis' in *Bladder Control and Eneuresis*, (ed. Kelvin, I. et al.) Spastics International Medical Publications, London, 1973.
8. McClean, M. and Wadsworth, M. E. J. 'The Interests of Children after Parental Divorce: A Long Term Perspective', *International Journal of Law and the Family*, 2,155, 1988.
9. Guidubaldi, J. et al. 'Assessment and Intervention for Children of Divorce' in *Advances on Family Intervention, Assessment and Theory*, Vol IV, JAI Press, Greenwich CT., 1987.
10. Guidubaldi, J. 'Growing up in a Divorced Family', *Annual Review of Applied Social Psychology*, Sage, Beverley Hills, 1987.
11. Guidubaldi, J. 'Differences in Children's Divorce

Adjustment Across Grade Level and Gender' in *Children of Divorce*, (eds Wollick, S., Bordes, P. and Lexington, M. A.), 1988.

12. Furstenberg, F. F. et al. 'Paternal Participation and Children's Well Being After Marital Dissolution', *American Sociological Review*, 52,695, 1987.
13. Allison, P. D. and Furstenberg, F. F. 'How Marital Dissolution Affects Children', *Developmental Psychology*, 25,540, 1989.
14. Dawson, D. A. 'Family Structure and Children's Health', United States 1988 Series, 10:178, *Vital and Health Statistics Public Health Services*, Maryland, 1991.
15. Kuh, D. and McClean, M. 'Women's Childhood Experience of Parental Separation and Their Subsequent Health and Socio-economic Status in Adulthood', *Journal of Biosocial Science*, 22,121, 1990.
16. Wallerstein, J. S. and Blakeslee, S. *Second Chances*, Tichner and Field, New York, 1981.
17. Kiernan, K. E. 'Teenage Marriage and Marital Breakdown, a longitudinal study', *Population Studies*, 40,35, 1986.
18. McLahan, S. and Bumpass, L. 'Intergenerational Consequences of Marital Disruption', *American Journal of Sociology*, 94,130, 1988.

CHAPTER 33

1. Kennedy, S., Kiecolt-Glaser, J. K. and Glaser, R. 'Immunological Consequences of Acute and Chronic Stressors: Mediating Role of Interpersonal Relationships', *British Journal of Medical Psychology*, 61,77, 1988.
2. Kiecolt-Glaser, J. K. et al. 'Marital Discord and Immunity in Males', *Psychosomatic Medicine*, 50,213, 1988.
3. Cooper, G. L. et al. 'Incidence and Perception of Psychosocial Stress: The Relationship with Breast

Cancer', *Psychological Medicine*, 19,415, 1989.

4. Foster, K. A. et al. *General Household Survey 1988*, OPCS, HMSO, London, 1990.
5. Green, H. *General Household Survey 1986*, Supplement A, HMSO, London, 1989.
6. Carter, H. and Glick, P. *Marriage and Divorce: A Social and Economic Study*, Harvard University, Cambridge, MS, 1970.
7. Kosenvuo et al. 'Cause-Specific Mortality by Marital-Status and Social Class in Finland During 1969–1971', *Social Science and Medicine*, 13A,691, 1979.
8. Leon, D. A. 'A Longitudinal Study: Social Distribution of Cancer 1971–75', OPCS, L.S. series no. 3, HMSO, London, 1988.
9. Ernster, V. L. et al. 'Cancer Incidence by Marital Status'. *U.S. Third National Cancer Survey, Journal of National Cancer Institute*, 63,3,567, 1979.
10. Fox, A. J. and Goldblatt, P. O. 'A Longitudinal Study: Socio-Demographic Mortality Differentials 1971–1975', OPCS, L.S. series no. 1, HMSO, London, 1982.
11. Goodwin, J. S. et al. 'The Effect of Marital Status on Stage Treatment and Survival of Cancer Patients'. *Journal of American Medical Association*, 258:21,3125, 1987.
12. Coombs, R. H. 'Marital Status and Personal Well Being: 'A Literature Preview', *Family Relations*, 40,97, 1991.
13. Lynch, J. J. *The Broken Heart*, Harper and Row, Sydney, 1979.
14. McCormick, A. and Rosenbaum, M. 'Morbidity Statistics from General Practice', Third National Study, HMSO, London, 1990.
15. Chester, R. 'Health and Marriage Breakdown: Experience of a Sample of Divorced Women', *British Journal of Preventive Social Medicine*, 25,231, 1971.
16. Paykel, E. S. et al. 'Life Events and Depression: A Controlled Study', *Archives of General Psychiatry*, 21,753, 1969.

17. Briscoe, C. W., et al. 'Divorce and Psychiatric Disease', *Archives of General Psychiatry*, 29,119, 1973.
18. Brown, G. W. and Harris, T. O. *Social Origins of Depression*, Tavistock Publications, London, 1978.
19. Roy, A. 'Vulnerability Factors and Depression in Men', *British Journal of Psychiatry*, 138,75, 1981.
20. Benjaminson, S. 'Stressful Life Events Preceding the Onset of Neurotic Depression', *Psychological Medicine*, 11,369, 1981.
21. Surtees, P. G. et al. 'Psychiatric Disorder in Women from an Edinburgh Community: Association with Demographic Factors', *British Journal of Psychiatry*, 142,238, 1983.
22. Kreitman, N. 'Suicide and Parasuicide' in *Companion to Psychiatric Studies*, (eds Kendell, R. E. and Zeally, A. K.) Churchill Livingstone, Edinburgh, 1988.
23. Kessel, N. 'Self Poisoning', Part I, *British Medical Journal*, 2,1265, 1965.
24. Bancroft, J. et al. 'People Who Deliberately Poison or Injure Themselves, Their Problems and Their Contacts with Helping Agencies'. *Psychological Medicine*, 7,289, 1977.
25. Holding, T. A. et al. 'Parasuicide in Edinburgh: A Seven Year Review, 1968–1974', *British Journal of Psychiatry*, 130,534, 1977.
26. Bagley, C. and Greer, S. 'Clinical and Social Predictors of Repeated Attempted Suicide: A Multivariate Analysis', *British Journal of Psychiatry*, 119,51, 1971.
27. Morgan, H. G. et al. 'Deliberate Self-Harm, A Follow-Up Study of 279 Patients', *British Journal of Psychiatry*, 128,361, 1976.
28. Shepherd, M. et al. *Psychiatric Illness in General Practice*, Oxford University Press, Oxford, 1966.
29. Renne, K. S. 'Health and Marital Experience In An Urban Population', *Journal of Marriage and the Family*, 33,338, 1971.
30. Robertson, N. C. 'Relationship Between Marital Status

and Risk of Psychiatric Reference', *British Journal of Psychiatry*, 124,191, 1974.

31. Innes, G. and Sharp, G. A. 'A Study of Psychiatric Patients in North East Scotland', *Journal of Mental Science*, 108,447, 1962.
32. Sequares, R. T. 'Marital Status and Psychiatric Morbidity', in *Marital Therapy*, (ed. Burnstein, O. J. W.), American Psychiatric Press, Washington D.C., 1985.

CHAPTER 34

1. Jewell, R., Witherspoon, S. and Brook, L. (eds) *British Social Attitudes, Seventh Report*, Dartmouth Publishing, Aldershot, 1990.
2. Brannen, J. and Collard, J. *Marriages in Trouble*, Tavistock Publications, London, 1982.
3. Shepherd, M. et al. *Psychiatric Illness in General Practice*, Oxford University Press, 1966.
4. Mitchell, A. K. *Someone To Turn To*, Aberdeen University Press, Aberdeen, 1981.
5. Guerney, B. and Maxson, P. 'Marriage and Family Enrichment Research: A Decade Review and Look Ahead', *Journal of Marriage and the Family*, 52,1127, 1990.
6. Statistical Section, Research Division, House of Commons Library.

CHAPTER 35

1. Kiernan, K. E. and Estangh, V. *Cohabitation*, Family Policies Study Centre, London, 1993.
2. Jowell, R., Witherspoon, S., and Brook, L. (eds) *British Social Attitudes, Seventh Report*, Dartmouth Publishing, Aldershot, 1990.
3. Balakrishnan, T. R. et al. 'A hazard model analysis of the covariates of marriage dissolution in Canada', *Demography*, 24,395, 1987.

4. Bennett, N. G., et al. 'Commitment and modern union: assessing the link between premarital cohabitation and subsequent marital stability', *American Sociological Review*, 53,127, 1988.
5. Bumpass, L. L. and Sweet, J. A. 'National estimates of cohabitation', *Demography*, 26,615, 1989.
6. Gurak, D. T. et al. 'A comparative examination of the link between premarital cohabitation and subsequent marital stability.' Paper presented at the meeting of the Population Association of America, Baltimore, MD, 1989.
7. Teachman, J. D and Polonko, K. A. 'Cohabitation and marital stability in the United States', *Social Forces*, 69,207, 1990.
8. Trussell, J. et al. 'Union dissolution in Sweden.' Paper presented at the seminar on Event History Analysis, sponsored by the International Union for the Scientific Study of Population, Paris, France.
9. Haskey, J. *Population Trends*, 1992.

CHAPTER 36

1. Morgan, D. 'From "The Problem of Divorce" To "The Problem of Marriage", The Sociological Work of One Plus One, Marriage and Partnership Research 1971–1991', *Journal of Social Work Practice*, 5,2,193, 1991.
2. Thornes, B. and Collard, J. *Who Divorces?*, Routledge Direct Editors, London, 1979.
3. Brannen, J. and Collard, J. *Marriages in Trouble*, Tavistock Publications, London, 1982.
4. Mansfield, P. and Collard, J. *The Beginning of the Rest of Your Life*, Macmillan, London, 1988.

CHAPTER 37

1. Pastoral Constitution on the Church in the Modern World Part II, Chapter 1. *Vatican II documents,*

Chapman, London, 1967.

2. Church Information *Marriage and the Church's Task*, (33), London, 1978.

CHAPTER 38

1. Russell, J. H. and Wells, P. A. 'Predictors of Happiness in Married Couples' (unpublished), 1993.

Index